Teaching on Solid Ground

Robert J. Menges
Maryellen Weimer
and Associates

Teaching on Solid Ground

Using Scholarship to Improve Practice

Jossey-Bass Publishers • San Francisco

This book is a publication of the National Center on Postsecondary
Teaching, Learning, and Assessment.

Substantial discounts on bulk quantities of Jossey-Bass books are
available to corporations, professional associations, and other
organizations. For details and discount information, contact the
special sales department at Jossey-Bass Inc., Publishers (415)
433–1740; Fax (800) 605–2665.

For sales outside the United States, please contact your local
Simon & Schuster International Office.

TCF Manufactured in the United States of America on Lyons Falls
Pathfinder Tradebook. This paper is acid-free and 100 percent
totally chlorine-free.

Library of Congress Cataloging-in-Publication Data

Teaching on solid ground: using scholarship to improve practice/
    [edited by] Robert J. Menges, Maryellen Weimer, and associates.—
    1st ed.
        p. cm.—(The Jossey-Bass higher and adult education series)
    Includes bibliographical references and index.
    ISBN 0-7879-0133-4
    1. College teaching. 2. Learning. I. Menges, Robert J. II. Weimer,
Maryellen, date. III. Series.
LB2331.T418 1996
378.1'7—dc20   95-23211

HB Printing   10 9 8 7 6 5 4 3 2 1
FIRST EDITION

The Jossey-Bass

Higher and Adult Education Series

This book is a publication

of the National Center on Postsecondary

Teaching, Learning, and Assessment

Table of Contents

Part Three: Laying the Groundwork
for Good Teaching

Preface

One of the by-products of the renewed interest in teaching and learning at the postsecondary level is a burgeoning pedagogical literature. The last ten years have seen the advent of newsletters, new periodicals, magazines, and how-to publications known variously as workbooks, handbooks, and sourcebooks. Not a year passes without the publication of new books that look comprehensively at teaching or deal with specific aspects of instruction. This makes asking about the purpose and function of this book a legitimate and justified query—especially when those asking the question are busy faculty who already have more reading obligations than can honestly be met.

The editors of this volume know the pedagogical literature well, have contributed to it, and are concerned about its place in the professional lives of faculty. In this preface, we offer a four-part rationale for this volume. It relates to a need to refocus pedagogical literature and reorient practice and to the dynamic and fluid milieu of circumstances and conditions that now surround our educational work. The book's introductory, bedrock chapter lays a foundation on which the rest of the chapters build. Taken together, those chapters illustrate the kind of solid ground on which we believe the practices of teaching and learning need to rest.

Our Rationale

First, *the scholarship of teaching needs to be defined and illustrated.* The imperative that we reconsider conceptions of scholarship was made most recently by Ernest Boyer (1990), who called for broader, more inclusive definitions. Included in what he proposed was the description of a "scholarship of teaching"—an idea that generated considerable enthusiasm among those at the center of the rekindled interest in undergraduate teaching and learning.

"Scholarship of teaching" has become part of our educational jargon, used most regularly by those interested in upping the ante with respect to teaching. It has become an amorphous term, equated more with a commitment to teaching than with any concrete, substantive sense of definition or consensus as to how this scholarship might be recognized.

We are committed to what the term implies but feel that the cause of better teaching and learning must be served by something more than a trendy phrase. We need clear understanding of why and how notions of scholarship can be applied to teaching. What we offer in this book are the beginnings of a definition—dimensions, aspects, orientations that might be included. We offer illustrations of work that exemplify these characteristics. We submit the book as an example of a "scholarly orientation" to the improvement of instruction, a concept elaborated further in Chapter One.

From our view, a scholarly orientation sees various domains of knowledge as being relevant to teaching and learning and from this orientation argues that teaching and learning gain in explanatory power by virtue of their association with one another. This book fills a gap in the existing literature; it positions itself somewhere between books that report research and those that offer advice on practice. More than just existing in between, this book also tries to join the extremes—to show that research and practice are different arcs of the same circle. When joined, they can stand together rather than in isolation or opposition as they so often are.

In sum, then, we believe that only as we concretely define and illustrate scholarship as related to teaching can we hope to sustain and further its cause. We believe that if we continue to avoid issues of definition, interest in the "scholarship of teaching" will become cliché and then passé. In that case, teaching will continue to rest on ground that is less than solid.

The second need for this book is long-standing: the *practice of instruction* needs to be informed by scholarship. Faculty continue to teach without being prepared to do so. Despite some progress in this area, we are moving forward by inches—and budgetary exigencies put even this recent progress in peril. More serious than the lack of training is the profession's continuing lack of acceptance that teaching skills, just like research skills, need to be developed and adapted. We assert that a faculty member's long-term program for teaching development is just as important and essential as his or her long-range plans for scholarship.

Teaching, aided by this professional compliance, continues to be relatively uninformed, unaware of all sorts of information (such as what follows in this book) that could significantly affect instructional quality. We hope that placing this information before faculty will persuade them individually and collectively that the profession has much to learn about teaching. Until that recognition occurs, efforts to take teaching and learning seriously will remain hollow sounding and less effective.

Closely related is our third justification for this book: *teaching needs to be valued by those who do it*. Uninformed instruction devalues an academic's work. Even faculty who are committed to teaching, who do seek to inform their practice, often hold conceptual orientations to teaching that are largely anti-intellectual. They think of it in terms of techniques, strategies, tips, tricks, sets of never-fail activities. Learning to teach, in such thinking, is like learning to ride a bicycle: you'll take a few spills in the beginning, but once you've got the technique you can ride for the rest of your life. A contrasting orientation holds that teaching (especially good teaching) is a gift—intuitive knowledge, artistry, and unlearnable skills with which some are naturally blessed and the rest get by. Uninformed practice and simplistic orientations to teaching result in teaching being perceived as a low-status endeavor.

To value teaching involves, in part, recognizing its complexity and seeing it as an intellectual phenomenon worth reckoning with. We have chosen for this book work that reflects the richness, complexity, and intellectual muscle that emerge once we begin to grapple with teaching and learning from scholarly viewpoints and perspectives.

Finally, *teaching needs to change, largely in response to a whole new set of realities*. We do not call for change because we believe that teaching is bad. Rather, we are concerned because we see our students changing in terms of who they are and how they learn. We see the landscape of higher education being altered, some of it by our own efforts but much more by what is happening to us. Higher education is under fire: being called to greater accountability, diversity, and efficiency. We call for pedagogical change because we see a different kind of future awaiting our graduates. More and more, the demand will be for lifelong learners, learners able to regulate their own learning and manage mountains of readily available information.

For all these reasons, both the role of the teacher and the mission of higher education (on campus and across campuses) must change, adapting to new conditions and circumstances. This book does not flinch. It addresses those changes head-on. It spells out why and how the practice of teaching and learning must adapt. It is a book that uses current thinking and knowledge to outline the shape of a new future for teachers and students.

Our Goals

Our discussion of the rationale for this book leads logically to what we hope this book will accomplish. We have set for ourselves four goals. If they are met, then we can justifiably claim that this book addresses the needs we have identified.

Our first goal is seen in the book's subtitle: *we aim to improve practice through reflection that results in action*. We restate our belief that teaching can be improved. We take issue with the viewpoint that good teaching is art, a birthright, and therefore impervious to efforts to acquire it. We submit that an infusion and application of what subsequent chapters contain will yield better teaching and learning.

Relevant and useful information can force faculty to face up to the facts of their teaching. But information is not sufficient. Faculty must reflect on the information and then act on it in systematic and planned ways and modify subsequent actions on the basis of feedback. We believe that instructional information that addresses issues of implication concretely in itself encourages application and implementation. We have tried to present information in this book that reflects all the complexity and variability of teaching and yet still offers straightforward and explicit recommendations for instructional policies, practices, and behaviors.

Our second goal is closely tied to the first. *We aim to positively affect the motivation to teach.* Instructional information can be presented in ways that faculty will find motivational. The process works best when faculty are encouraged to think about teaching in more intellectually robust and satisfying ways. We also believe (with a host of others) that process is enhanced when faculty are put at the center of efforts to improve—in charge of them and responsible for them. This explains why our book puts faculty in the driver's seat and offers direction but lets them make their own decisions and implement changes themselves.

Despite difficulties with students (we don't hide our belief that today's students are more challenging to teach), despite financial and other external pressures on our colleges, this is an exciting and rewarding time to be college and university teachers. It is a time when higher education can really and truly make a difference, for our students and for our society.

Third, *we aim to make teaching more student-centered and learning-oriented.* We believe that the focus of pedagogical literature has been too much on the teacher. In the last twenty years, almost every book published has focused largely on what teachers should do. The literature makes much of the aspects of effective instruction, style, delivery, relations with students (from the faculty perspective), the policies and practices of testing and grading, how the teacher manages disruptions, how the teacher prevents cheating, and on and on. We'd like to let students be the heavyweights for a while.

We justify this change in emphasis for several reasons. What is known about effective teaching has been laid out often and completely. Now it is time to make clear what is known about students and how they learn. Much of what has been written about teaching presumes the presence of students *unlike* most of those currently enrolled in our colleges. Also, focusing on students makes an agenda of improvement less threatening. The question to faculty is no longer, Do you want to improve your teaching? with all the defensiveness the question engenders but, Would you like your students to learn more?

Finally, *we aim to further a more interconnected view of teaching and learning.* What happens in the classroom stands not in splendid isolation. It happens in conjunction with lots of other activities in which faculty and students are engaged. Faculty must better understand and respond to the fact that college learning is just one part of lives cluttered with work, family obligations, financial stresses, and sometimes serious personal problems. What happens in class is not always the focal experience, as it was when many of today's faculty attended college.

Not only are teaching and learning interconnected with the lives of students; they are also inextricably bound up in the life of the institution itself. If students' lives are more complicated, so are the lives of our institutions. What is happening across the country with respect to funding (with its concomitant effects on class sizes and course loads), to accountability, and to diversity *will* directly affect the daily practice of instruction (if it hasn't already). The time is past when faculty could hunker down and hide out.

Our Scope and Treatment

Beyond describing the needs to which this book responds and articulating our goals and purposes in preparing it, we need to describe something of its scope and treatment to show how the contents respond to the needs and goals.

The book *contains diverse topics illustrating the range of issues confronting today's college teachers*. We don't claim complete coverage. The issues are so many and the information so vast that no longer can a manuscript of reasonable length expect to cover even what is important. We have included a sampling of significant topics and relevant issues.

This diversity of content not only makes for interesting reading, it illustrates how and why definitions for the "scholarship of teaching" need to be broad. The range of topics also proves how much there is to learn about teaching and learning and how much practice suffers when it is uninformed. The links, relationships, complementarity, and contrasts between these topics show why books can no longer be just about teaching.

In addition to the wide range of topics now relevant to instructional practice, the volume *illustrates diverse ways of knowing about teaching and learning*. It contains work that is qualitative, quantitative, empirical, ethnographic, theoretical, and experiential. It is written in the voices of those who research, those who teach, and those who manage improvement efforts. This illustrates how definitions of the scholarship of teaching can beneficially be open and inclusive.

We think diversity of topics and ways of knowing positively affects motivation by responding to a range of everyday instructional needs and interests. Diversity of topics and methodologies confirms the value of seeking to build a comprehensive, integrated, and inter-connected knowledge base. Such a base increases its explanatory powers, offering more complete and credible answers to the complex questions that arise from scholarly reflective practice.

In every chapter, there is a *commitment to make knowledge concrete,* even when the understandings are theoretical and conclusions tentative. Knowledge will not inform practice unless it is seen by faculty as useful and applicable. In particular, the knowledge generated by research too often fails to articulate practical implications.

Nevertheless, we note again that this book offers little in the way of absolute answers, things teachers should always do or not do, strategies guaranteed not to fail. We do propose answers, make recommendations, offer advice, and list suggestions, but we do so tentatively, seeking to engage faculty in the process of application. The instructional solutions that we propose need to be adapted, refined, revised, altered, modified, and otherwise changed so that they fit specific situations.

We believe that process improves instruction because as it identifies what needs to be changed, it raises questions about details, contexts, and frameworks. Thus faculty are forced to see complexity, to value the complicated process of affecting how and what students learn, and to think about teaching in more intellectually challenging ways. We see this as connected to issues of motivation in that it results in teaching that is more intriguing, engaging, and satisfying.

Such a process also makes for instruction that is more student- and learning-centered because of the fourth and final aspect of the book we have chosen to highlight. *Students and learning are at the center* of this book. Students have changed; our knowledge of learning has grown. If this book has a theme, it is to explore the implications of those changes. Even though Part Two is a section on teaching, its chapters link what we know about students and learning to how we ought to practice instruction.

This approach will improve instruction because it strengthens and makes more obvious the fact that teachers and students stand

in relationship one to the other. Reasserting this inseparable relationship redresses the imbalance of a focus on teaching. As already
noted, the emphasis on students and learning takes teachers out of
the limelight. Made less vulnerable, they are increasingly motivated
to teach in new and more effective ways.

What we describe as aspects and characteristics of the book
may be illustrated by reviewing its contents. We offer a brief highlight of the book's contents here, while noting the fuller discussion in Weimer's opening chapter and summaries in the
introduction to each part of the book. Before you decide which
chapters to read, we strongly recommend you consult that introductory material.

Part One focuses on issues relating to students and learning. Its
premiere position in the book underscores our belief that better
undergraduate education begins with a more complete and informed understanding of students and learning.

Upcraft (Chapter Two) sets the stage for Part One. He documents how students have changed, from the perspectives of both
demographics and personal characteristics. Inherent in those
changes are significant instructional implications, which Upcraft's
chapter begins to outline, explore, and explain.

What Upcraft establishes in general, Terenzini and colleagues
detail in the particular. Chapter Three focuses on students in transition to college, highlighting key elements of those crucial first
experiences in college. Perry and colleagues follow in Chapter Four
with a summary of an important line of research that relates to
motivation. This chapter shifts the focus from students to learning
by exploring orientations to learning that either facilitate or hinder student success.

Matthews (Chapter Five) also emphasizes a particular kind of
learning experience: collaboration. She highlights a host of strategies that offer ways for students to learn from one another, to
create knowledge from their collective experiences, or both. This
chapter also describes new roles for faculty as designers and facili-
tators of learning experiences.

Froh and Hawkes move us back to a larger arena. The interest here in Chapter Six is in the assessment of student experiences, specifically how to find, in measures of student involvement, formative indicators of how well beginning students are connecting to the institution and the academic opportunities it provides.

Part Two focuses on teachers and teaching. It is based on the premise that the knowledge about students and learning reported in the first part mandates new ways of thinking about and practicing instruction. Thus, teaching is considered principally in terms of its effect on students and learning.

In Chapter Seven, Millar sets the stage for this part. She uses theory and a case study to argue for a transfer of power in the classroom. Although much changes for the teacher and the students when students are given the voice they deserve, the classroom is still about a learning enterprise. Geis (Chapter Eight) underscores what stays the same, even when the focus is on students and learning. Teachers still plan courses and design learning experiences; it is just that these activities are now more central, more crucial when instruction occurs on these terms.

Lowman addresses another "detail" of instruction from this learning paradigm: assignments. Chapter Nine focuses on assignments that promote and integrate learning—not just assignments for the sake of grade generation. Menges and Rando, on the other hand, call for something new (at least to many faculty): a way of seeking and using feedback to improve teaching and learning. They spell out a process in Chapter Ten and then illustrate its use via an extended example.

Svinicki and colleagues round out Part Two with a chapter that moves back to the larger context with which it opened. The aim of Chapter Eleven is to summarize research on the effectiveness of various instructional methods. They then comb the research on learning, looking specifically for instructional implications that are inherently part of that body of knowledge.

The third part lays the groundwork for good teaching. The aim here is to identify and explore a sampling of the issues that demand faculty attention and involvement at both institutional and professional levels. Faculty perspectives on teaching and learning need to be broadened, seen from contexts larger than "what I do in my classroom" or "what we do in this discipline."

In Chapter Twelve, Dinham attempts to identify what every teacher should know in order to teach, and she proposes foundational knowledge in three areas besides the commonly accepted pair of knowledge of content and discipline. Walker and Quinn respond to another area of criticism by proposing some new and alternative theories on which to base an understanding of faculty motivation—how it might be sustained and what contributes to its decline. Issues of faculty morale, attitude, and burnout need to be addressed, and Chapter Thirteen suggests some ways to respond.

Another area of controversy is diversity and multiculturalism. Tierney and Bensimon don't argue a position in Chapter Fourteen. They assume that institutions are committed to diversity and see ways that progress toward those goals can be enhanced. Their chapter makes clear what it means to make diversity an institutional priority not only on paper but in practice.

Finally, in Chapter Fifteen Banta addresses issues of accountability by proposing constructive ways to take stock of what our programs in higher education do in fact accomplish. The motivation to assess, as it is articulated here, comes not from external pressure (though that may be an important impetus) but from our own sense of responsibility. Knowing how effective our programs are only serves to help us make them even more effective.

We conclude with acknowledgments. No book, particularly one with multiple authors, happens exclusively as a result of the editors' work.

We are indebted to Sheila Petrosky for able clerical support in early chapter and manuscript drafts. Bette Erickson and Gale Erlandson provided honest, thoughtful, and helpful reviews that made for a much improved volume.

The idea for this book originated as the National Center on Postsecondary Teaching, Learning, and Assessment began its five-year research agenda exploring the factors that facilitate student learning.[1] Our Center colleagues (who have authored many of the chapters in this volume) contributed much to our plan for and design of the volume. We are especially grateful to all our contributors, who stuck with us when the project took longer than we ever imagined.

And we acknowledge each other, as we worked to keep each other motivated, focused, and persuaded that this was a book worth doing. Throughout it all, we managed to preserve our fondness and respect for each other. We wish to note that we contributed equitably to the volume and would list our names on the same line if that were possible.

Howard, Pennsylvania   Maryellen Weimer
Evanston, Illinois   Robert J. Menges
November 1995

Reference

Boyer, E. (1990). *Scholarship reconsidered: Priorities of the professoriate*. Princeton: The Carnegie Foundation for the Advancement of Teaching.

---

1.   Work reported in several chapters of this book was supported by the National Center on Postsecondary Teaching, Learning, and Assessment (NCTLA) through funding to the Pennsylvania State University (Grant No. R117G10037) from the Office of Educational Research and Improvement, U.S. Department of Education. The findings and opinions expressed do not reflect the positions or policies of the Office of Educational Research and Improvement, or the U.S. Department of Education, or Pennsylvania State University. The NCTLA is a research, development, and dissemination center devoted to studying teaching and learning, the improvement of educational practice, and the advancement of theory and practice in the assessment of student and institutional performance. The only federally funded national research and development center devoted specifically to postsecondary education, NCTLA is a consortium housed at Pennsylvania State University and includes the University of Illinois at Chicago, Syracuse University, Northwestern University, Arizona State University, and the University of Southern California.

The Authors

Robert J. Menges is professor of education and social policy at Northwestern University and senior researcher with the National Center on Postsecondary Teaching, Learning, and Assessment. He has been associated with Northwestern's Center for the Teaching Professions since joining the faculty there in 1972. For the National Center, he has directed studies of the socialization of faculty and investigations into how faculty go about improving their teaching. He received degrees in psychology from Gettysburg College (B.A., 1960), Boston University (M.A., 1963), and Columbia University Teachers College (Ed.D., 1967).

In 1991, Menges received the W. J. McKeachie Career Achievement Award from the American Educational Research Association for his contributions to development and evaluation of faculty in postsecondary education. In 1992, he received the Amoco Foundation Faculty Award from Northwestern University. Most of his research deals with teaching and learning in postsecondary education. An overview of those areas is provided in his 1988 book, *Key Resources on Teaching, Learning, Curriculum, and Faculty Development* (Jossey-Bass). Another edited book is in preparation—*Instructional Consultation in Higher Education: Handbook of Principles and Practices* (New Forums Press). Since 1990, he has served as editor-in-chief of the Jossey-Bass quarterly sourcebooks, *New Directions for Teaching and Learning*.

Maryellen Weimer is a faculty member at the Berks campus of Pennsylvania State University where she teaches beginning students.

Prior to her return to full-time teaching, she was an associate director of the National Center on Postsecondary Teaching, Learning, and Assessment. During the 1980s, she directed Pennsylvania State University's instructional development program.

Weimer received a Ph.D. in speech communications from Pennsylvania State University in 1981, an M.A. in rhetoric and public address from the University of Oregon in 1972, and a B.A. in speech from Seattle Pacific University in 1970. She has published numerous books and articles and edits the *Teaching Professor*, a newsletter on college teaching with 20,000 subscribers. Her most recent book is a 1993 Sage publication, *Improving Your Classroom Teaching*, which is the lead volume in a series of books written for new faculty. She is currently writing a book on teaching large classes. She has also consulted with 150 colleges and universities in the United States and Canada on a variety of instructional issues; she is regularly asked to deliver the keynote address at national conferences of various organizations.

Kevin W. Allison is an assistant professor of psychology at Pennsylvania State University. He received his B.A. in psychology from the University of Notre Dame (1981) and his M.A. (1985) and Ph.D. (1989) in clinical community psychology from DePaul University. A former clinical director of City Lights—a community-based school for troubled and troubling adolescents—his recent publications focus on cultural issues in professional training in psychology and the impact of culture and context on the psychosocial adjustment of adolescents.

Trudy W. Banta is professor of higher education and vice chancellor for planning and institutional improvement at Indiana University–Purdue University, Indianapolis. Prior to 1992, she was professor of education and founding director of the Center for Assessment Research and Development at the University of Tennessee, Knoxville. Banta has written or edited seven books, contributed fifteen chapters to other works, and published more than 130 journal articles, monographs, and research reports. She has addressed meetings on the topic of outcomes assessment in twenty-one states, China, and several European countries; she has visited campuses in thirty states to assist faculty in establishing assessment programs.

Banta has been honored by the American Association for Higher Education for her contributions to the field of assessment in higher education. She earned her baccalaureate degree in education (with majors in biology and history) and master's degree in counseling at the University of Kentucky. Her doctorate in educational psychology was awarded by the University of Tennessee.

Estela Mara Bensimon is professor of higher education in the Center for Higher Education Policy Studies at the University of Southern California and director of the Organizational Structures and Policies Research Area in the National Center on Postsecondary Teaching, Learning, and Assessment. She earned her doctorate in higher education administration from Teachers College, Columbia University, in 1984. She is the author or coauthor of several books and articles on higher education leadership and organizational change.

Sarah M. Dinham is professor of educational psychology at the University of Arizona. Her research interest is in college teachers' knowledge, thinking, and planning. Since 1990, she has been a visiting scholar with the New Faculty Project of the National Center on Postsecondary Teaching, Learning, and Assessment; she has also studied architectural and medical education. She received her B.S. (1961, English) from the University of Minnesota and Ph.D. (1966, research design and educational psychology) from Michigan State University.

Robert C. Froh is associate director of the Center for Instructional Development at Syracuse University where he provides support to the university community in the areas of measurement and bench-marking, program evaluation and assessment, and institutional and academic research. He received his B.A. (1970) and M.A. (1975) from Michigan State University in social sciences and educational psychology, respectively, and his Ph.D. (1988) from the University of Chicago in the Measurement, Evaluation, and Statistical Analysis Program, Division of Social Sciences and Department of Education. His research and publications are in the areas of intrinsic rewards and optimal performance in teaching, learning, and scholarship and the evaluation of teaching and curriculum in higher education.

George L. Geis is a professor of higher education at the Ontario Institute for Studies in Education (University of Toronto). He received his B.A. (1953) from Columbia College and his Ph.D. (1965) in psychology from Columbia University. He was previously a faculty member at the University of Michigan and McGill University where he was director of the Centre for University Teaching and Learning. He is the author of numerous articles on instruction and education and has consulted widely in education and the corporate sector.

Patricia L. Gregg is a Ph.D. candidate in higher education at Pennsylvania State University. She received her B.S. (1979) in education from Boston University and her M.B.A. (1983) from the University of South Florida. Her career has included higher education teaching, counseling, and administration. She has jointly or individually authored articles and conference papers dealing with comparative higher education policy, professional education, and the transition to college. During 1994 and 1995, she has been studying the effect of modularization on undergraduate teaching and learning in the United Kingdom.

Anastasia S. Hagen is a visiting assistant professor in the Department of Educational Studies at the University of Delaware. She received her B.S. (1980) in technical communication from the University of Minnesota and her Ph.D. (1992) in educational psychology (with emphasis on learning, cognition, and instruction) from the University of Texas at Austin. She has published several articles on instructional practices at the college level that promote student motivation and learning.

Mark Hawkes is a research and evaluation associate at the North Central Regional Educational Laboratory in Oak Brook, Illinois. After receiving a B.S. in psychology (1990) and an M.S. in instructional science (1992) from Brigham Young University, he completed his doctorate in instructional design, development, and evaluation (1995) from Syracuse University. His current research interests include the effects of educational telecommunications technologies on student learning and optimal dissemination strategies for educational technologies.

Romero Jalomo, Jr., is a research assistant with the National Center on Postsecondary Teaching, Learning, and Assessment. He received his B.A. (1983) in communication and information systems from California State University, Chico; his M.P.A. (1989) from California State University, Dominguez Hills; and his Ph.D. degree (1995) in educational leadership and policy studies from Arizona State University. His current research examines the in- and out-of-classroom experiences of first-year community college students. He is a coauthor of several articles relating to the transition to college for diverse students and Latino student transfer from community college.

Joseph Lowman is professor of psychology and assistant dean of arts and sciences at the University of North Carolina, Chapel Hill, where he has been on the faculty since 1970. He received his A.B. in psychology from Greensboro College (1966) and his Ph.D. in clinical psychology from the University of North Carolina, Chapel Hill (1971). Notable among his publications are *SuperShrink* (1987,

1990), two computer-simulated case studies for psychology students, and *Mastering the Techniques of Teaching* (1995), an instructional book for college instructors that has been translated into three foreign languages and is now in its second edition. He is a frequent speaker at national symposia on college teaching and campus teaching workshops. His teaching of undergraduates has been recognized by students and colleagues at the University of North Carolina with a Tanner Award (1989) and a Bowman and Gordon Gray Professorship (1995).

Roberta S. Matthews is associate dean for academic affairs at LaGuardia Community College (SUNY). She received her B.A. (1965) in English from Smith College, her M.A. (1966) in eighteenth-century English literature from Columbia University, and her Ph.D. (1973) in English and Irish literature from the State University of New York at Stony Brook. Among her publications are *Learning Communities: Creating Connections Among Students, Faculty, and Disciplines* (1991, with F. Gabelnick, J. MacGregor, B. L. Smith) and *Bridging the Gap Between Cooperative and Collaborative Learning* (1995, with J. Cooper, N. Davidson, and P. Hawkes). She has given workshops on learning communities and collaborative learning at colleges and universities throughout the country.

Verena H. Menec is presently completing her Ph.D. in psychology at the University of Manitoba. She received her B.A. (1989) and M.A. degrees (1991) in psychology from the University of Manitoba.

Debra K. Meyer is an assistant professor of education at Elmhurst College, Elmhurst, Illinois. She received her B.A. (1979) in elementary education and developmental psychology from Purdue University and her Ph.D. (1992) in educational psychology (specializing in learning, cognition, and instruction) from the University of Texas, Austin. While there, she worked as a research associate and teaching assistant for the Center for Teaching Effectiveness. She is an author of two articles and five book chapters on college teaching. She is a classroom researcher who is interested in the relationships among teacher-student interactions, motivation, and learning. She was the recipient of the National Reading Conference Student Research Award (1992).

Susan B. Millar is director of the Learning through Evaluation, Assessment, and Dissemination (LEAD) Center, University of Wisconsin, Madison. The first of its kind in the country, the LEAD Center conducts evaluation research in support of faculty efforts to improve student learning. She received her B.A. degree (1970) in English Literature from William Smith College and her Ph.D. (1981) in anthropology from Cornell University. Among her publications is *A Silent Success: Master's Education in the United States* (1993, with C. F. Conrad and J. G. Haworth).

Raymond P. Perry is a professor of psychology and director of research for the Centre for Higher Education Research and Development at the University of Manitoba. He received his B.A. in psychology (1968) from the University of British Columbia and his M.Sc. (1969) and Ph.D. (1971) in social psychology from the University of Calgary. His research over the past twenty years has focused on teaching and learning in higher education. Dr. Perry has received awards for his research accomplishments from the Max Planck Society and the Alexander Von Humboldt Society in Germany, from the American Educational Research Association, from the Canadian Society for the Study of Higher Education, and from the North Atlantic Treaty Organization (NATO). He has been a visiting scholar at the University of California, Los Angeles, Stanford University, the Max Planck Institute (Munich), and the UNESCO Institute for Education (Hamburg). He serves on the editorial boards of the *Journal of Educational Psychology, Research in Higher Education, Higher Education: Handbook of Theory and Research,* and the *Canadian Journal of Higher Education.*

Jennifer Woods Quinn is assistant director of academic affairs at the Illinois Board of Higher Education. She received her B.A. (1988) in sociology from Lake Forest College and her Ph.D. (1994) in educational processes from Northwestern University. Her responsibilities at the Illinois Board include the review of policies regarding faculty roles and responsibilities. She is a researcher for the Faculty and Instruction Program of the National Center on Postsecondary Teaching, Learning, and Assessment and has presented papers for the American Association for Higher Education's Forum on Faculty Roles and Rewards.

William C. Rando is director of the Academy for the Art of Teaching at Florida International University. He received his B.A. (1983) in English from Boston College, his M.A. (1985) from the School of Speech at Northwestern University, and his Ph.D. from the School of Education and Social Policy at Northwestern University. His writing and research on faculty development includes a recently completed book, *Learning from Students* (1994, with L. Firing Lenze). In addition to his active professional life in faculty development, Rando travels nationally giving talks and workshops on topics related to human relations and the professions.

Laura I. Rendón is a professor in the Division of Educational Leadership and Policy Studies at Arizona State University, where her teaching and research focus on K-16 educational partnerships, higher education, community colleges, and student diversity issues in education. Rendón is also director of evaluation of the National Center for Urban Partnerships, which is funded by the Ford Foundation; she is a senior research scientist with the National Center on Postsecondary Teaching, Learning, and Assessment and is affiliated with the Hispanic Research Center at Arizona State University. She is the author of numerous articles and is associate editor of the *Journal of Women and Minorities in Science and Engineering*. She serves on several editorial boards. She has been a member of the National Board of Directors of the American Association for Higher Education, the National Advisory Boards of the Woodrow Wilson Fellowship Foundation, and the Center for the Freshman Year Experience, as well as the Technical Advisory Board of the Quality Education for Minorities Network.

Rendón earned a Ph.D. (1982) in higher education from the University of Michigan and has taught at the University of South Carolina, North Carolina State University, the University of Michigan, Pennsylvania State University, and Texas A & M International University.

C. *Ward Struthers* is a Social Sciences and Humanities Research Council of Canada (SSHRCC) Postdoctoral Fellow in the Department of Psychology, University of California, Los Angeles. He received his Ph.D. from the University of Manitoba in 1995. While attending the University of Manitoba, he worked for the Centre for International Business Studies, the Centre on Aging, and the Centre for Higher Education Research and Development. His research interest is in social cognition—particularly how thoughts, feelings, and actions relate to negative achievement events and how they can influence subsequent motivation and performance.

Marilla D. Svinicki received her Ph.D. in experimental psychology from the University of Colorado, Boulder, in 1972 after receiving a B.A. and M.A., also in psychology, from Western Michigan University in Kalamazoo. She went from Boulder to Minnesota to teach at Macalester College in St. Paul for two years before moving to the University of Texas. In 1990, she became director of the university's Center for Teaching Effectiveness. She has published three books and many articles translating the principles of psychology into the practical concerns of classroom instruction. She served as the executive director of the Professional and Organizational Development Network in Higher Education and is the immediate past editor of *Teaching Excellence*. She serves as associate

The Authors

editor of *New Directions for Teaching and Learning* and teaches graduate and undergraduate courses in the Department of Educational Psychology at the University of Texas.

Patrick T. Terenzini is professor of higher education and associate director for research in the National Center on Postsecondary Teaching, Learning, and Assessment. Terenzini holds an A.B. in English from Dartmouth College, an M.A.T. in English education from Harvard University, and a Ph.D. in higher education from Syracuse University. Before becoming a faculty member, he served nine years (1978–1986) as director of institutional research (including two years as assistant to the president for planning) at the State University of New York, Albany. He is coauthor (with Ernest T. Pascarella) of *How College Affects Students* (Jossey-Bass, 1991). He has received research awards from the Association for the Study of Higher Education, the Association for Institutional Research, the American College Personnel Association, and the National Association for Student Personnel Administrators.

William G. Tierney is professor and director of the Center for Higher Education Policy Studies in the School of Education at the University of Southern California. He received his B.A. (1975) in English from Tufts University, an M.Ed. in education (1978) from Harvard University, and a Ph.D. (1984) in administration policy and analysis from Stanford University. He is the author of numerous books and articles on higher education and organizational change. His most recent work pertains to promotion and tenure. He is currently vice president of Division J of the American Educational Research Association.

M. Lee Upcraft is a research associate in the Center for the Study of Higher Education, professor emeritus of education, and assistant vice president emeritus for student affairs at Pennsylvania State University. He recently concluded thirty-one years of administrative responsibilities in student affairs. Upcraft received his B.A. (1960) in history and M.A. (1961) in guidance and counseling from the State University of New York, Albany, and his Ph.D. (1967) in student personnel administration from Michigan State University. He is the author and editor of several books, book chapters, and journal articles on topics such as residence halls, orientation, the first-year experience, academic advising, assessment, and teaching and learning. He also serves as the associate editor of the *New Directions for Student Services* sourcebooks published by Jossey-Bass.

Charles J. Walker is a professor of social psychology at St. Bonaventure University and an affiliate scholar at the National Center on Postsecondary Teaching, Learning, and Assessment. He was a co-facilitator of the 1993 and 1994 Berkeley Faculty Development Conference and has served as a consultant for the National Endowment for the Humanities, the Bush Foundation, and the Lilly Foundation. On the subject of teaching, he has published articles, chapters, and texts on the teaching of psychology and technical writing. In social psychology, he has published numerous articles and papers on social cognition, small-group performance, and rumor transmission. He received his B.S. degree from the University of Pittsburgh and his Ph.D. from Adelphi University. Currently, his research deals with optimism and instructor vitality.

Teaching on Solid Ground

Chapter One

Why Scholarship Is the Bedrock of Good Teaching

Maryellen Weimer
Pennsylvania State University—Berks Campus

This chapter establishes the book's foundation. It has as its task to explore, explain, and defend the appearance of yet another book on college teaching and learning, one among a virtual library of tomes (some comparatively well known, most obscure) that are part of higher education's pedagogical literature.

The case for *this* book is best made by addressing three questions that arise inevitably from this chapter's title:

1. Is improved practice needed?
2. What do we mean by scholarship?
3. How does scholarship lead to improved practice?

Is Improved Practice Needed?

The answer is yes, but not for tired reasons about the poor quality of teaching and learning in higher education. Who knows if teaching is bad, worse than it used to be, or broken and in need of repair? If the impetus for change derives from a premise of deficiency and remediation, efforts to enhance instruction are doomed to fail. We need better teaching and learning in college, but *not* because it is bad.

The case for improved practice rests on a different set of premises, those that involve the changing realities of higher education and that offer opportunities as well as contain threats.

1

To begin, we need to improve practice by *better responding to our changing student body*. In the next chapter, Lee Upcraft details the kind and degree of those changes. Suffice it to say here that the students now enrolled in college are not much like those who attended college alongside most of today's faculty members. They are older, are working more, are less well prepared. They are more diverse, less politically inclined, more emotionally dysfunctional, less motivated, and more in debt—to highlight just some of the differences. These changes are no surprise to faculty; we experience the consequences daily in the classroom. Unfortunately, we too often respond to the differences by complaining about them.

As some have pointed out, faculty (even back as far as Socrates) have always been disappointed and dismayed by their students. But the issues with these students are substantive and significant. Many tried-and-true instructional strategies of the past now work with obviously poor effect. In essence we complain, we express our frustration, and we become nostalgic because we don't know how to deal very effectively with these students. For professionals, that's a hard confession to make, especially in public. But if we listen closely to our own complaints, we hear cries for help.

We need to improve practice by better connecting with the learning needs of students enrolled in college today. It's not our fault that students have changed, but it is our responsibility to understand those changes and adjust our instruction accordingly. This does not mean merely fine tuning. As some chapters in this book illustrate (Matthews's and Millar's, for example), what we know about our students calls for paradigm shifts in the methods of instruction and the roles of teachers. To ignore the changes is to risk becoming less and less effective with the very groups who stand to benefit the most from education. But there are opportunities here as well—to revise, refresh, and reinvigorate our instructional work.

Secondly, we need to improve practice by *strengthening the links between teaching and learning*. For too long, our ego involvement in teaching has resulted in benign neglect of learning. It is true that better teaching does frequently produce more and better learning, but a focus on learning is just as likely to make for better teaching. It's not that one is more important than the other. The two are inseparably linked, which we understand in theory but often ignore in practice.

A focus on learning takes the spotlight off teaching, and it is easier for faculty when the real impetus for change is improvement in learning. Ask any self-respecting faculty member, "Are you interested in improving your teaching?" and the answer is almost always defensive. "Why? Did somebody tell you I should?" Or "Why should I? Nobody cares about teaching around here anyway." But ask, "Are you interested in improving learning? Would you like to increase how much and how well your students learn?" and the response is decidedly different.

It is especially encouraging that some of the current research on learning (such as that presented in the chapters by Terenzini and others, and Perry and colleagues) connects directly with some of the most instructionally challenging students we have in college today. The research has implications that can be spelled out and responded to in the classroom. The opportunities are enormous, a chance to succeed with students for whom education really and truly can mean a change of life course.

Third, we need to improve practice by *seeing interconnections among student experiences*. Organizational distinctions between student affairs and academic affairs reinforce the faulty conception that what happens to students in courses and classrooms happens independently of all other influences. In reality, nothing could be farther from the truth. As first documented in research that attempted to plot student decisions to stay or leave, student life is a web of interconnected experiences, influences, and activities, all of which overlap, relate, contradict, and otherwise interact in very complicated ways. To conduct classrooms in ignorance of these multiple spheres of influence is to envision teaching and learning as an island, when in fact they exist as an archipelago of separate-yet-connected land masses.

Finally, we need to improve practice by *seeing teaching and learn-ing issues in larger contexts*. It's not just that the student's world is large and complicated; so is the universe of higher education. When the view is only from the front of the classroom, definitions of relevant issues and notions tend to be narrow and exclusive. Higher education exemplifies difference. It must respond to the push and pull of competing and contradictory constituencies (alumni, trustees, state governing boards, legislators, parents, and employers, to name some). Faculty rarely see their work in this much-bigger and more-dynamic milieu. They live in the worlds of their own classrooms, their labs, their departments, their offices, and the peculiarities of their own institution.

As much as we might want to keep the world at bay, changing realities make that less and less likely. The world (or so it seems) is on our doorstep—on some days actually seeming to beat down the door. Outside realities intrude as forces that every individual fac-ulty member must reckon with. These are demands on the conduct of our daily work. How much money do we need? How many hours do we work? What do we teach? How much do they learn? Yes, the intrusion is a threat, a greater one than higher education has faced in many years; but it is equally an opportunity, a chance to see our work from different, larger, and—one is tempted to say—more important contexts.

This book doesn't answer all the questions we're being asked, at least not directly. But it does give us places and perspectives from which to view higher education in larger contexts than we normally do. Some chapters address issues of accountability, both individu-ally (Menges and Rando, for example) and collectively (Banta). Others explore issues of competence (such as Dinham's chapter, which proposes foundational pedagogical knowledge to be shared by all who teach). Still others (such as Tierney and Bensimon's) tackle our diversity as it should reflect our culture's multiplicity.

To sum up, we believe the practice of instruction can and should be improved. We *can* do better. The realities that confront us put the option of change squarely in front of us. Higher education is up to bat. The pressure's on, but information like that which follows can prepare us to play ball and win.

What Do We Mean by Scholarship?

The focus on scholarship is justified in part because of recent interest in scholarship, particularly as it pertains to teaching. Since publication of Boyer's (1990) *Scholarship Reconsidered*, notions of a "scholarship of teaching" have been bandied about as a means of upping the ante with respect to the intellectual credibility of teaching. Being committed to those ends, we worry that, despite the visibility and quotability of the phrase, few institutions seem to be putting in place policies and practices that reflect a more intellectual orientation to teaching.

We fear that if notions of a scholarship of teaching are not soon made real and substantive in publications, policies, and practices, this nice phrase will be replaced by some trendier term. This may happen even though the practice of instruction will indeed be improved when faculty (and administrators) start thinking and talking about teaching and learning in more intellectually robust and intriguing ways.

To illustrate, we point out that this is not a how-to book for better teaching. You will not find in it the ubiquitous 101 teaching tips. While we value the techniques of teaching, we deplore overemphasizing them. As faculty, we must get past the point of thinking that only a few good strategies are necessary to ensure (for example) student participation. Emphasis on technique trivializes the rich complexity that is the situated knowledge of teaching contexts and circumstances. This book does propose strategies, but it presents them in a "scholarly" context, as coming out of research findings, as being part of our understanding of who our students are and how they learn, and as resulting from notions of teaching that are grounded in philosophy and principle.

Here is what we mean by scholarship. The book includes research using both qualitative and quantitative methodologies, and research reporting results of both descriptive and experimental inquiries. That is not unusual; it is as it should be. Research on higher education (although, much like research in other fields, it is not all uniformly good) remains a vast, untapped, overlooked, too frequently demeaned source of relevant information, ideas, insights, and solutions. Often the way it is written prevents easy access. We think of the research contents of this book as exemplars of how research reports can be transformed for audiences not interested in replication so much as in utilization.

Further, we have included work that dares to propose implications. It is true that researchers often are not in the trenches with today's undergraduates, but they can and do contribute much to our efforts when they come out and say what their work means in terms of concrete actions that teachers should and should not consider. Also included in the book is research work that seeks to integrate, organize, and otherwise make accessible and useful research findings that pertain to a given topic. The chapter by Svinicki and colleagues does this for research on learning, focusing especially on what that research implies for practice.

But this book reports much more than research, at least as research is conventionally defined. It breaks new ground with theoretical explanations, as in the chapter by Walker and Quinn that seeks alternative ways of explaining and enhancing faculty motivation. The book includes case studies, narratives, and careful descriptions of "good" practice: programs, policies, and practices that work when the assessment measure is student learning. By example, this book challenges us to learn from experience; it illustrates how and why we ought to teach and learn from one another.

The book includes in its definition of scholarship the wisdom of practice. That notion is much more than "Oh, here's a good idea; we tried it, it worked, and our students liked it." Meaningful learning rarely results from an isolated occurrence. Instead, we need ways of documenting, describing, and integrating the wisdom of practice that celebrate the collective experiences of countless practitioners. We include several such summaries in this volume (the Matthews and Loman chapters, for example). These chapters model notions of scholarship applied to the wisdom of practice as they present collected experience, what many have learned, and as they show how that learning relates to knowledge based in research. This is informed practice. When it presents an individual program, practice, or experience, it does so against the backdrop of what others have discovered and experienced.

We believe this volume illustrates and exemplifies a scholarship of teaching. Using a broad and inclusive definition, it presents scholarly work illustrating a variety of genres and types. We hope it will give substance to the popular and timely notion of a scholarship of teaching. Equally as important, we believe scholarship as defined and illustrated by the work in this volume unquestionably applies to the phenomena of teaching and learning. They are intellectually rich, intriguing, stimulating areas of study. It is time the profession discovered this side of education.

How Does Scholarship Lead to Improved Practice?

The question is equally one of how: how does it work? Why do we believe that scholarship will improve practice?

The first answer is simple and direct, embodied in the contents of this volume. We have chosen to include information that we believe will make a difference. We do not claim to have covered all the important topics—for instance no chapter is devoted to technology or to ethics in professional practice—but we have chosen to include the kind of information that, if applied, would unquestionably result in better teaching and learning. We turn the question back on our readers: will the information contained in this volume improve your educational practice?

The second reason why we believe scholarship will improve practice resides in our belief that the best approach to improvement efforts is one that builds on notions of scholarship. From this vantage point we aim to answer the question of how, not from a content perspective (the first answer), but from a process point of view. Consider three aspects of process we think combine to form a "scholarly orientation" to the improvement of instruction.

First, to think of teaching and learning as scholarly work *encourages systematic, reflective practice*. Ever since Donald Schön (1987) popularized the idea of reflective practice and called for its application in educational contexts, theorists and practitioners (most notably faculty developers) have been proposing that faculty become more instructionally aware. This call begins with an explicit awareness of the nuts and bolts of instruction, but it then demands more complexity. Faculty need more than awareness just of what they and their students do. They need to assess impacts that will very likely result in challenges leveled against long-standing assumptions and practices. Taken far enough, as it is in the work of Paulo Freire (1985), Ira Shor (Shor and Freire, 1987), and Henry Giroux (1986), the classroom becomes a microcosm of the larger world, complete with power struggles and inherent inequities. This "critical pedagogy" challenges most of the basic tenets of education as we know it and hence, not surprisingly, is much contested. However, these descriptions of faculty as keen observers of the instructional context, with all its subtleties and nuances (most having nothing to do with course content), exemplify a scholarly approach that analyzes, evaluates, and then alters what happens in the daily practice of instruction.

How do we encourage faculty to look more closely and to think more deeply about the practice of teaching and learning? We believe that such a goal is accomplished by presenting teaching and learning as intellectually stimulating, as an idea-rich genre, with issues framed and solutions proposed mindful of dynamic contexts and evolving circumstances. Material like that contained in this book becomes the stimulator, the prod, the means whereby faculty begin to think about their own practice, to question what they do, and to consider alternatives.

Second, taking a scholarly approach to instructional enhancement *encourages active inquiry about teaching and learning*. In recent years, literature has emerged that articulates the characteristics of self-directed (Candy, 1991) and self-regulated (Zimmerman and Schunk, 1989; Pintrich, forthcoming) learning. This literature identifies the processes whereby learners effectively develop, manage, and monitor learning strategies. Such knowledge can apply to faculty as well as to students.

When it comes to learning in the disciplinary context, faculty thrive on the life of the mind. They do exactly what this literature proposes as the ideal: they take charge of their own learning. The key then is how we transfer these already effective learning skills to acquisition of instructional knowledge. Approaching teaching and learning as areas of scholarly intrigue accomplishes that end, and we feel that just how effectively this can work has already been demonstrated.

In recent years, much better teaching and learning has come about as a consequence of the classroom research/assessment movement. Patricia Cross, joined by Tom Angelo (Angelo and Cross, 1993; Angelo, 1991), challenged teachers to systematically collect and then act on feedback from students about their learning experiences in a given course. Faculty across the country have engaged in the activity, generating a plethora of strategies and techniques to acquire the information and an equally sizeable body of responses to what might be discovered.

Classroom assessment closely correlates with the idea of self-regulated, autonomous, self-monitoring learners, and we believe its success confirms that faculty can be persuaded to "learn" about instruction. Classroom assessment also demonstrates a "scholarly" approach to instructional improvement. It depends on the cycle of observation, solicitation and analysis of feedback, generation of alternatives, selection and implementation of changes, and subsequent continuation of the cycle.

Said another way, when faculty move beyond technique, beyond a singular conception that sees teaching and learning problems as things in need of a solution, they come to view teaching and learning as challenging, intriguing, perplexing, and profound. In essence they are persuaded that there is in fact something here to be learned.

Third, a scholarly approach works because it *taps sources of intrinsic motivation*. Can faculty be motivated to address instructional-improvement issues despite the climate currently existing at many of our universities? We believe they can. This approach puts faculty at the center and in control of the improvement process. It recognizes the fundamental instructional prerogative they already have. Instructional improvement is not something that can be done to faculty. If something changes in a course or classroom, it is because the faculty member implemented the alteration.

These three reasons should not be seen as independent or in a linear sequence. They work together to create a set of motivating conditions that we believe can stimulate faculty interest and involvement in this process. Good scholarly material on teaching forces faculty to take a long, hard look at their instructional practice. They now see teaching and learning as areas in which relevant, useful information exists. They set about learning, using strategies that have already served them in good stead as scholars. Because they care about student learning (probably more so than about teaching), they are motivated. As they engage in this process, their motivation and commitment increase. The process of improvement happens at their behest, under their guidance, and with results that belong to them alone. This makes for satisfying learning, which of course increases motivation and involvement.

We are describing an ideal here. The realities of higher education put most ideals in peril. These are not easy times, but when compared with the alternatives—trying to improve instruction via technique, trying to impose better teaching by institutional mandate—we believe this to be a reasonable and sensible approach. It works mostly because it empowers faculty. As with students who discover how to use the learning process to their advantage, it becomes a powerful elixir.

These three processes—self-reflection, self-regulation, and intrinsic motivation—together answer the questions of how and why scholarship improves practice. We end with a caveat, that not any old kind of scholarship achieves the desired result. Scholarship results in improved practice when and only when it *exemplifies quality*.

The positive effects of scholarship do not accrue independently of considerations of quality. It is not scholarship in and of itself, but a particular "kind" of scholarship, that serves to make a difference.

First, the scholarship must address important topics—not irrelevant or trivial details (such as whether students who leave class before the end of an exam period do better than students who stay to the end) but issues of significance, such as the kind of content structures that enhance memory and application. (For this instance, see the chapter by Svinicki and colleagues.)

The "right kind" of scholarship must also use rigorous, systematic inquiries. As this volume demonstrates, it is not a question of one method of study being superior to another. Rather, the issue is the match between method and question, as well as the issue of standards and rigor as they have been established for the particular methodology. We believe that part of the devaluing of teaching has been an ignoring of scholarly standards as they apply to pedagogical literature.

Finally, the kind of scholarship we think makes a difference is scholarship that we would describe as committed to pragmatics. Whether they are empirical, theoretical, or descriptive, rarely do the pedagogical facts speak for themselves. We must assume responsibility for a clear (albeit sometimes tentative) delineation of what others should do about what has been learned.

This volume operationally defines these notions of quality scholarship. We are convinced that when work on teaching and learning is truly scholarly, the knowledge it contains has the power to positively affect the practice of instruction. This kind of pedagogical information does indeed make a difference.

Conclusion

We base the justification for this book on the answers we have offered to three questions: Is improved practice needed? What do we mean by scholarship? And how does scholarship lead to improved practice?

With our answers in mind, we encourage readers to move into the book and judge for themselves.

References

Angelo, T. A. (Ed.). (1991). *Classroom research: Early lessons from success*. New Directions for Teaching and Learning, no. 46. San Francisco: Jossey-Bass.

Angelo, T. A., & Cross, K. P. (1993). *Classroom assessment techniques*. San Francisco: Jossey-Bass.

Boyer, E. (1990). *Scholarship reconsidered: Priorities of the professoriate*. Princeton: Carnegie Foundation for the Advancement of Teaching.

Candy, P. C. (1991). *Self-direction for lifelong learning*. San Francisco: Jossey-Bass.

Freire, P. (1985). *The politics of education: Culture, power, and liberation*. Boston: Bergin & Garvey.

Giroux, H. A. (1986). Radical pedagogy and the politics of student voice. *Interchange, 17*, 48–69.

Pintrich, P. R. (Ed.). (forthcoming). *Self-regulated learning for college students*. New Directions for Teaching and Learning, no. 63. San Francisco: Jossey-Bass.

Schön, D. A. (1987). *Educating the reflective practitioner: Toward a new design for teaching and learning in the professions*. San Francisco: Jossey-Bass.

Shor, I., & Freire, P. (1987). What is the "dialogical method" of teaching? *Journal of Education, 169*, 11–31.

Zimmerman, B. J., & Schunk, D. H. (Eds.). (1989). *Self-regulated learning and academic achievement*. New York: Springer-Verlag.

Part One

Students and Learning

The theme of Part One is our belief that better undergraduate education begins with a more complete and informed understanding of students and learning. For most of this century, interest in education at the postsecondary level has centered on teaching. Even until recently, books on how to teach, on methods of instruction, and on issues of excellence and style were the bulk of what constituted pedagogical literature. Students were mentioned only in passing, and learning hardly at all. This emphasis assumed a simple equation: good teaching on the one side and lots of learning and student satisfaction on the results side.

The equation worked well for a number of years, until our students started changing. Now it has become easy to blame the students as being the part of the equation that has changed. But despite the defensiveness and protestations that many faculty voice, changes in students have precipitated some positive effects. Teachers, scholars, and researchers are all thinking and writing about, as well as studying, students and learning in new, innovative, and tremendously valuable ways. If faculty attend to our more complete understanding of students and learning, teaching will inevitably improve. Our new knowledge makes clear that teaching and learning stand in balance, as they relate one with the other. Both are key terms; neither should be thought of as a constant in the teaching-learning equation.

Chapters in this section, collectively and individually, demonstrate the kind and detail of our knowledge of students. They also illustrate the kind and focus of the research on learning and how what we know about learning inevitably links backward to our knowledge of students and forward to the new ways faculty must think about teaching.

The Theme and Variations: Chapter Summaries

Almost any faculty member will tell you that students have changed. Most of the changes we don't much like, often for reasons other than the ones we state. It's easier, safer, and less personal to complain that these are not the students that higher education is best fit to teach, rather than to admit that many time-tested instructional practices (such as lecturing, and grading on the curve) work in visibly less effective ways with these students. What Lee Upcraft makes clear in his chapter is that the students in college today are also indicative of the college population of tomorrow. It is imperative that we accept and learn to connect effectively with our current students.

Upcraft also specifies the changes in students in terms of national trends and historical benchmarks. This chapter not only establishes that students are different but explains how they have changed. Most difficult, of course, are efforts to explore the implications of those differences. For example, students in college today more often and to a much greater degree combine school and work. What can or should a faculty member do differently in the classroom and in the design of assignments for outside the classroom? The Upcraft chapter begins to explore those implications, which up to this time have not been the focus of much attention. His initial propositions are elaborated, supported, and illustrated by the rest of the chapters in Part One and those in Part Two.

From a national portrait of today's college students, this part moves on to show how, for example, individual groups at particular points in their college careers have become the focus of investigative inquiry. Patrick Terenzini and a group of colleagues report on an interview study of students "in transition" to college. These students are just beginning their college careers. They are attending several different kinds of institutions and represent a number of important groups now attending college.

This intimate look at the feelings and experiences of new college students is important for several key reasons. First, research referred to in a variety of places in this book documents the importance of early college experiences in terms of students' commitment to continue and complete a college program. Second, many of the comments and experiences of the students reported here (often in their own voices) confirm the central role that faculty and course experiences play in forming those early impressions. It is no overstatement to conclude that a college student's first courses are the most important ones taken in college.

Third, Chapter Three illustrates on a microscopic level, compared with the more macroscopic view of the Upcraft chapter, the differences between past and present students. Students today undertake to go to college under conditions unlike those when most faculty completed college. It is important that these dissimilar circumstances be understood and their instructional and institutional implications explored, which is what the chapter does.

In Chapter Four, Raymond Perry and associates illustrate how our knowledge of students links with our growing understanding of learning. Like the Terenzini group, Perry's research team has focused on a particular group of students, those with an orientation toward learning based on a psychological construct of helplessness (as opposed to mastery). Perry's work shows how even the presence of an effective teacher (as measured by dimensions of instruction known to correlate with learning outcomes) does not overcome the depowering effects of these ways of thinking about oneself, one's ability, and one's responsibility for education.

Perry's chapter makes several other important contributions. He and his associates show how the pieces of the motivation puzzle fit together in new and intriguing ways. A more complete understanding of motivation is definitely of value to today's college teacher. Some of the changes in today's college students are easily accepted and remedied, but their seeming lack of intrinsic motivation, their unwillingness to expend more than nominal effort, their loss of all vestiges (or so it seems on some days in the classroom) of intellectual curiosity are among the most difficult and frustrating challenges to today's college teacher. In exploring and explaining how and why motivation does and does not drive the need to learn, the chapter offers valuable insights and opportunities to those willing to rethink some of the basic assumptions and practices of instruction.

Additionally, this chapter, like Terenzini's, illustrates something much less common in the research literature than should be: implications of the findings. In Perry's case, attributional retraining, an effective method of changing the orientation to learning, may be "approximated" in the classroom. Perry and colleagues suggest how. Some commonplace instructional strategies exacerbate the student's sense of loss of control. Perry and colleagues name them.

Also illustrative of the new interest in students and learning is Roberta Matthews's chapter on collaborative learning. Chapter Five could easily fit into the next section on teaching, but we chose to place it here because it demonstrates that when the focus is on students and learning, the concomitant instructional strategies center on them as well.

In vivid and compelling ways, collaborative learning moves the focus from the teacher and teaching to the student and learning. These strategies offer the means for students to learn one from another or to create knowledge from the repositories of their own experiences and perspectives. On these terms, the teacher is now arranger, facilitator, designer of learning activities and experiences. What happens, of course, is that students are empowered and motivated by this more central position in the learning process. They move from the helplessness and loss-of-control paradigms described in Perry's perspective to places of power and mastery. Learning now happens on their terms, enlivened and enlarged through the involvement of their fellow learners.

While Matthews summarizes some of the research that grounds our notions about the effectiveness of this approach to learning, the chapter focuses more on the structure and design that group work needs to have if students are to realize its many benefits. It asks, What must a teacher know and be willing to do in order to maximize the learning potential inherent in group work?

Chapter Five also shows how our knowledge base in the area of students and learning can be advanced by the wisdom of practice. Faculty across the landscape of higher education are experimenting with group work. It is being used in the problem-solving disciplines as well as the humanities, in large classes as well as seminars, at research universities as well as community colleges. Fortunately, a number of faculty are recording and sharing what they have learned. Matthews ably summarizes and distills this important but often devalued base of knowledge.

Among many topics related to collaborative learning, the Matthews chapter discusses the need for new ways of assessing the kind of learning that occurs in groups. The last chapter in the section explores assessment in another context. Robert Froh and Mark Hawkes write about assessment issues as they pertain to student involvement. We know from a solid empirical basis that student involvement, be it in the college classroom or in the campus community, garners many positive results. It enhances learning in a variety of different ways, and it decreases drop-out rates. Students who connect to and with the academic community early on stay put until their course of study is complete.

Froh and Hawkes, in Chapter Six, cast assessment as something much broader than grades and subjective judgments. Student involvement can and should be "measured" in various institutional contexts. Such a broad-based consideration underscores the inter-connectivity of all aspects of the college experience. What happens to students in classrooms relates to their lives outside of the class-room, which relates to the kind of living/learning communities that, say, residential colleges provide. If faculty are to more effec-tively teach today's college students, they can no longer see educational experiences (those that occur in class or the lab) as atomistic. Any given experience is part of a web of experiences that ultimately affect individual students.

The Froh and Hawkes chapter is noteworthy for other reasons as well. In essence, it is a case study based on one institution's attempts to assess how involved its students were in all aspects of their educational lives. Despite the many differences that exist between institutions of higher education, too infrequently do we learn from one another. More often, when we look at each other it is for reasons of comparison—to see how we might be positioned relative to the institutions we aspire to be like. Much like students in a competitive classroom, we diminish our own learning in our anxious attempts to be the best, often at the expense of others.

Like the Banta chapter in Part Three, this chapter demon-strates that assessment efforts can be a powerful force for good when an institution undertakes them as vehicles to enhance self-awareness and as the focus of improvement efforts.

Advancing the Thesis

We believe Part One advances the cause of a more scholarly under-standing of undergraduate education in three ways. First, it attempts to redress the imbalance between teaching and learning. It does not say that teaching is unimportant, irrelevant, and passé. It does say that effective teaching is part and parcel of knowing our students and understanding how they learn. We do not believe faculty can succeed in the college classrooms of today independent of that knowledge.

Second, the chapters in Part One demonstrate especially clearly how all aspects of a student's experiences in college are connected. What happens to students in college relates to their past experiences. What happens is also partly a function of their individual orientations to learning. The kind of experiences they have inside and outside the classroom play a major role. Teachers must see their instructional activities as important but not necessarily central or solitary in their impact on student learning.

Finally, Part One advances our cause by revealing the rich diversity that is a part of scholarship in higher education today. This section reports and explores the implications of survey data, of interview information, and of other quantitative and qualitative findings. It summarizes and extrapolates from the wisdom of practice, and it uses a case study to expose and explain one institution's experiences. Taken together, this scholarship in these varied forms can and will contribute to the improved practice of undergraduate education.

Chapter Two

Teaching and Today's College Students

M. Lee Upcraft
Pennsylvania State University

College students have changed. Most of us associated with higher education recognize that fact, but the magnitude of the changes becomes clear when we compare college students of today with those of twenty-five years ago. A condensed description of one provided by Schoch (1980, p. 1) highlights the extent of those changes.

> Remember Joe College? The young man who, after working hard in high school, arrived at Berkeley, where he set out to sample the rich and varied intellectual feast at the University of California. Joe was independent, self-motivated, and academically well prepared. About his junior year, Joe settled on a major field of study, which he pursued with diligence and increasing confidence in order to graduate in four years after his arrival.

Joe doesn't live here any more, Schoch concludes, and a look at the 1992 entering class confirms his conclusion. That class was 40.5 percent Asian, 30.7 percent white, 14.0 percent Hispanic, 6.1 percent African American, 1.1 percent American Indian, 1.5 percent other, and 6.1 percent who declined to state their ethnic backgrounds. In other words, at least 63.2 percent of the students were nonwhite (T. Cesa, personal communication with M. L. Upcraft, May 4, 1993).

But racial and ethnic diversity is only one indicator of how much students have changed, particularly in the last twenty years. This chapter reviews the many ways in which students have changed, including the challenges faculty must face because of today's students' physical and psychological health as well as their family dynamics.

The chapter concludes by exploring some of the instructional implications of these changes as they relate to our dealings with students both in class and out.

The Changing Demographics of Today's Students

Demographic changes in students are apparent across a number of different categories. Some of these are highlighted next.

Racial/Ethnic Diversity

The number of racial/ethnic groups accessing higher education has grown dramatically. In 1990, minorities constituted 22.2 percent of total enrollments, compared to 18.7 percent in 1980. Put another way, from 1980 to 1990, while overall enrollments in postsecondary education increased by 13.4 percent, American Indian enrollment increased 22.6 percent, Asian Americans by 94 percent, African Americans by 10 percent, Hispanics by 60.5 percent, and international students by 30.1 percent. Compare that with an 8.5 percent increase in white enrollment (*Chronicle of Higher Education Almanac*, 1992). Hodgkinson (1985) predicts that by the year 2000, one in three students will be nonwhite.

To be sure, racial/ethnic group participation is quite uneven by type of institution, as well as across the country. For example, 45.1 percent of American Indians, Hispanics, Asians, and African Americans attend two-year institutions, compared to 36.7 percent for whites. In fact, a majority of American Indians (52.9 percent) and Hispanics (54.6 percent) attend two-year institutions (*Chronicle of Higher Education Almanac*, 1992). States with more than 22 percent minority enrollment include, in rank order, Hawaii, Arizona, California, Texas, Mississippi, Louisiana, Florida, Illinois, New

York, Maryland, Alabama, and Georgia (*Chronicle of Higher Education Almanac*, 1992).

Interestingly, differences within groups may be as great as differences among them. For example, there are four major Hispanic/Latino groups in higher education—Mexican Americans, Puerto Ricans, Cubans, and Central/South Americans—each with different histories, traditions, and cultures (Justiz and Rendón, 1989). This same diversity within groups can be found for Asians, Native Americans, and African Americans.

Gender

The opportunity for higher education first belonged only to men. Not until the mid-nineteenth century were women allowed to go to college. But in this century, by around 1980 more women than men were enrolled in college. Since 1978, women have outnumbered men among first-time freshmen (Astin, Green, and Korn, 1987). In 1990, 54.5 percent of students in postsecondary education were women (*Chronicle of Higher Education Almanac*, 1992).

Enrollment Status

Today more of our students enroll part-time. In 1990, 43.3 percent of students were enrolled part-time, compared with 39 percent in 1976. Part-time students are more likely to be women over twenty-four years of age who are enrolled in two-year institutions. Kuh (1990) estimates that by the year 2000, a majority of students in higher education will be part-time.

As a consequence of their part-time enrollment, fewer students are completing bachelor's degrees in four years. According to a survey by the National Collegiate Athletic Association, only 53 percent of full-time freshmen graduated within six years. By racial/ethnic group, these graduates included 62 percent of Asians,

56 percent of whites, 40 percent of Hispanics, 31 percent of African Americans, and 29 percent of American Indians. (*Chronicle of Higher Education*, July 15, 1992). In addition, Hodgkinson (1985) predicts that students will stop out more often and will attend more than one institution.

Age

Since World War II and the GI Bill, older student enrollments have steadily increased, to the point where they represented 40.2 percent of all students enrolled in 1990 (*Chronicle of Higher Education Almanac*, 1992). Students over twenty-four are more likely to be women, enroll part-time, and attend two-year institutions (Kuh, 1990). However, the adult student population has stabilized over the past five years and is not expected to increase in the next few years (Kuh, 1990).

Residence

Given the fact that students are older and studying part-time, it is not surprising that more of them are commuting and living off campus. Hodgkinson (1985) reports only about one in six students in postsecondary education is (1) studying full-time, (2) eighteen to twenty-two years of age, and (3) living in residence halls.

Students with Disabilities

Students with disabilities had little access to higher education until the passage of the 1973 Rehabilitation Act. Section 504 mandated equal opportunity for qualified handicapped people in the educational programs of institutions that received federal assistance. Since then, enrollments of students with disabilities (impairments of mobility, vision, hearing, speech, or learning) have steadily risen, to the point where it is estimated that 7.3 percent of all students in 1990 had some disability (Hameister, 1989).

Sexual Orientation

Today's students are more open about their sexual orientation. According to some estimates, as many as 10 percent of students are gay, lesbian, or bisexual, although most of them choose to remain "in the closet." Those who are openly gay, lesbian, or bisexual frequently experience violence and discrimination, and those who are closeted live in fear of their sexual orientation being disclosed (Evans and Levine, 1990).

International Students

International student participation in higher education rose 30.1 percent from 1980 to 1990. The countries with the most international students are China, Japan, Taiwan, India, Korea, Canada, Malaysia, Hong Kong, Indonesia, and Pakistan (*Chronicle of Higher Education Almanac*, 1992). Culturally different concepts of time, interpersonal relationships, equality, and pedagogy, just to name a few, can make the adjustment of international students to American colleges difficult (Bulthuis, 1986).

The statistics summarized here establish the fact. Joe College has passed on or away, replaced by a population of students that are so demographically diverse that a proper stereotype to replace dear departed Joe is out of the question. But demographics tell only part of the story of what has changed.

Changing Characteristics of Today's Students

Above and beyond these demographic shifts, other significant changes in college population are occurring. They include changes in student attitudes and values, their family dynamics, their physical and psychological health, levels of academic preparation, and sources of financing for education.

Changing Attitudes and Values

Since 1966, the Cooperative Institutional Research Program (CIRP) at the University of California, Los Angeles, has tracked the attitudes, values, and aspirations of traditional-aged high school students who enter college. Students entering college today, compared to those entering in the mid-1960s, are politically more conservative; less interested in "developing a meaningful philosophy of life"; more interested in making money; more concerned about getting a job after college; more interested in the fields of business, computer science, and engineering; and less interested in the humanities, fine arts, and the social sciences. On the other hand, there has been little change in the percentage of entering students who list "obtain a general education" (about three in five) as a very important reason in deciding to go to college (Astin, Green, and Korn, 1987; *Chronicle of Higher Education Almanac*, 1992).

Depending on their age, today's students have been shaped by events including the Great Depression, World War II, the Korean War, the civil rights movement of the 1960s, the Kennedy and King assassinations, the Vietnam War, Watergate, the Reagan years, the collapse of the Soviet Union, and various economic booms and recessions, among other important events.

Changing Family Dynamics

The American family is undergoing a transformation that is already having a significant impact on today's students. Divorce rates increased sharply during the 1970s, and current estimates predict that one in two marriages will end in divorce (Wallerstein and Blakeslee, 1989). By the year 2000, about one-half of freshmen will have been raised by a single parent sometime during their child-hood. Put another way, only 40 percent of students in the year 2000 will come from families in which their mother and father were together from the time they were born to the time they went away to college (Hodgkinson, 1985). Additionally, students themselves who are divorced or single parents make up a significant part of our adult-learner student population.

But changing family stability is only part of the picture. Families characterized by physical violence, sexual abuse, psychological abuse, drug and alcohol abuse, and other problems are on the rise (Gannon, 1989). Consequently, we are seeing more students today who are affected by family instability and dysfunction. Henton and others (1980) found that students who lack family support have a more difficult time adjusting to college. Likewise, many students from dysfunctional families have relationship problems and low self-esteem, as well as higher suicide-attempt rates, sexual dysfunction, social alienation, physical ailments, and psychological trauma (Hoffman and Weiss, 1987).

Changes in Mental and Physical Health of Students

Twenty years ago, students seeking help from college counseling centers presented problems clearly related to their college experiences, such as roommate problems, career indecision, academic difficulty, or relationship problems—in other words, "normal" students with "normal" problems. Today, students with problems present a very different picture. Witchel (1991) describes a substantial increase in psychological disturbance among college students. Waiting lists for treatment in college counseling centers are a sign of the times. There are more students in college today suffering from serious emotional distress, including self-destructive behavior, violence against others, anxiety, depression, and eating disorders, as well as victims of date and acquaintance rape, courtship violence, family or spouse abuse, and family drug and alcohol abuse (Witchel,

1991). Many of these conditions result not from the collegiate environment but from student experiences prior to or outside the collegiate environment.

Physical health problems are also on the increase and often closely linked to some mental health problems. For example, eating disorders result from psychological problems, but they can very quickly become serious physical problems. Drug and alcohol abuse can also create significant physical and psychological problems, as can various kinds of violence such as date rape.

An even more alarming trend is the increase in sexually transmitted diseases among students, the most serious of which is AIDS. The HIV-positive rate among college students in 1990 is approximately 2.4 per thousand, compared to 1.0 per thousand in 1983 (R. Keeling, personal communication with M. L. Upcraft, September 1990). Much of this increase is attributable to the spread of the disease to heterosexuals, particularly women. Among younger age groups, the proportion of women infected with HIV is approaching that of men (Chronicle of Higher Education, December 12, 1992).

Changing Academic Preparation

Perhaps no trend is more disturbing to faculty in higher education than the lack of academic preparation of today's students. A thirty-year decline in Scholastic Aptitude Test (SAT) scores has been well documented (Forrest, 1987). Few students in higher education thirty years ago required remediation in basic reading, writing, and computational skills. According to Forrest, the percentage of first-year students enrolled in at least one remedial course went from nearly zero in 1955 to 35 percent in 1985. That figure is much higher at some institutions.

Changing Sources of Financing for Education

Before 1955, virtually all students paid for their education with their own or their parents' resources, or with limited academic scholarship aid. (A major exception was veterans who received GI Bill benefits.) In 1989, 56.4 percent of all undergraduate students received some form of financial aid, including 70.4 percent of students at private institutions. Today, only about 20 percent of undergraduates between eighteen and twenty-two are pursuing a parent/student-financed education (*National On-Campus Report*, 1992).

Recent trends continue to put more financial pressure on students and their families. From 1973 to 1988, college costs rose more than 200 percent, a pace well ahead of inflation rates for that same period (*Parade*, March 19, 1989). Even more distressing is the declining availability and sufficiency of federal and state grant and loan programs (Astin, Korn, and Berz, 1990). As a result, more students are relying on their families, their savings, and part-time jobs to finance their educations. For example, in 1990 about four in five students said they were getting financial help from their families, compared to two in three in 1980 (Astin, Korn, and Berz, 1990).

Implications for Teaching and Learning

How do these changes in students affect teaching and learning environments in class and on campus? How should faculty respond? What should they do differently? Those questions do not have concrete, definite, always-successful solutions. The remainder of this chapter and the rest of the book offer possible implications and tentative solutions that are still being explored. We have never had students like this in college. We are indeed sailing through uncharted waters.

We do *not* propose here, nor do we anticipate that research will uncover, any sort of one-to-one correspondence between specific student problems and solutions. Said another way, there is no single concrete thing an instructor could or should do for students with, for example, eating disorders. Any problem is part of a constellation of issues relevant to our students. Obviously, there are specific implications in terms of the kind of counseling services institutions must now be prepared to provide, but for the classroom teacher there is no singular response or solution. Rather, student characteristics should be viewed in a larger context, a more general orientation that acknowledges who students are, what issues they face, and how their circumstances relate to educational experiences.

Perhaps we can better characterize an appropriate response by contrasting it to one that is much less desirable and not particularly effective. Some faculty resist the fact that students are changing. They take the stance that they have little control over who is admitted to the institution, who enrolls in their courses, how well prepared those students are, whether or not they are motivated, and what family background they bring with them. Teachers point out that they are not financial-aid experts, not psychological counselors or family therapists, not cultural-diversity experts, and not nurturing nice-guys. Their job is to teach, not rehabilitate.

Also at issue for these faculty are academic standards and the need not to lower or otherwise compromise them for anybody or any reason. They argue that treating "special" students in "special" ways is inherently unfair to students who are ready, willing, and able to learn and represents the very kind of discrimination they are committed to eradicating. If students are coddled, they leave college unprepared for the real world. It takes time to accommodate differences, time that needs to be spent covering content so that standards and academic integrity can be preserved.

Not all faculty respond to the changes in students this way, but it does color the thinking of most of us to some degree or another. The issues represented by this orientation represent legitimate concerns and are not readily resolved, as the solutions suggested here and in the remainder of this book demonstrate. But the facts of the opening section of this chapter stand in sharp focus against whatever we believe about or wish were true with respect to students. Like it or not, the students we have described are the students enrolled in college today and will be our students for the foreseeable future.

Although many of the implications are still being explored, one conclusion already rests solidly on facts. Most of the changes that characterize students today work against their success in college. The literature on retention identifies a number of trends negatively affecting academic achievement and completion. In general, students are more likely to drop out and less likely to graduate if they:

Are from lower socioeconomic classes

Are persons of color (with the exception of Asian Americans)

Are female

Are academically underprepared

Are disabled

Work more than half-time and live off campus

Have mental or physical health problems

Lack family stability and support

Attend college part-time (Pascarella and Terenzini, 1991)

Individual student abilities do count. Success in college has a lot to do with one's prior academic success (such as achievement in high school). But these students don't come to college academically well prepared. Moreover, such personal factors as self-esteem, maturity, quality of effort, time-management skills, goal orientation, and motivation are known to affect student success (Pascarella and Terenzini, 1991) and are issues with these students. College success is no longer (if it ever was) simply a matter of ability plus effort. The factors involved today are different, more complex, and more interconnected, which is why effective faculty response acknowledges that students are not what they once were and must be taught differently.

Implications for teaching and learning that spring from these documented changes in students can be considered as they relate to student experiences inside the classroom and outside it. As will be noted subsequently, the distinction is a convenient one in that it differentiates between spaces in which student experiences occur, but it is an artificial separation when it comes to explaining how, when, and under what circumstances learning occurs.

Implications for Learning Inside the Classroom

Despite the fact that we cannot propose a precise and specific set of implications, we do have relevant experiences and useful knowledge. They provide a foundation on which to build a pedagogy that does respond to increased diversity among our students. No literature base better illustrates this than our growing knowledge of learning styles.

This work began twenty years ago with Whitkin and Moore (1975), who first distinguished between field-dependent learners (who respond best in collaborative environments that take into account their needs, feelings, and interests) and field-independent learners (who prefer environments that focus on tasks, objectives, analysis, and independence). Since then, a variety of other research has expanded our understanding of the different kinds of cognitive processing that learners use. The widely used Kolb instrument, developed by David Kolb (Kolb and Smith, 1986), identifies four basic approaches to learning derived from learning preferences for that which is abstract or concrete, active or reflective.

- *Converger*: Combines the abstract-conceptualization and active-experimentation learning orientations ("thinkers" and "doers")
- *Diverger*: Combines the concrete-experience and reflective-observation learning orientations ("feelers" and "watchers")
- *Assimilator*: Combines the abstract-conceptualization and reflective-observation learning orientations ("thinkers" and "watchers")
- *Accommodator*: Combines the concrete-experience and active-experimentation learning orientations ("feelers" and "doers")

This research on learning styles is general. It applies to all learners. There is also work that attempts to describe differences

between and among groups. For example, there is consid
dence that men may learn differently from women (F
golda, 1992), that older students may learn differently from those
of traditional student age (Cross, 1981; Pearson, Shavlick, and
Touchton, 1989), and that racial/ethnic minorities may learn differently from majority students (Shade, 1989; Tharp, 1989).

Differences spelled out by this research and the literature that
explores its implications (see, for example, Svinicki and Dixon,
1987) are specific and concrete. In a nutshell, if different students
learn in different ways, then faculty must teach in different ways.
Said in the context of this chapter, our teaching ought to be as
diverse as our students.

Again, the realities of higher education (at least as most of us
experience them) preclude a specific and individual response to
each student. But the common approach of yesteryear, when faculty lectured and gave two objective exams, is much less likely to
succeed with students enrolled in college today.

To illustrate and drive home the point: McCarthy (1980) documents that teachers often teach everyone the same way, most
often using lecture/discussion methods. Or, from Kolb's (1981)
perspective, teaching methodologies tend to cluster according to
fundamental differences in the nature of the discipline taught. That
is, many faculty tend to be field-independent, analytical, verbal,
and observational learners ("assimilators" in the Kolb framework)
who learn best from lectures and discussion (Kolb and Smith,
1986). However, use of the lecture/discussion method with learners whose primary style is relational, field-dependent, visual, and
intuitive may connect with only about 30 percent of the students
(McCarthy, 1980). This mismatch becomes even more of a problem at institutions with high racial/ethnic enrollment because their
styles tend to be more relational, field-dependent, intuitive, and
involving (Cox and Ramirez, 1981).

There is another important reason for diversifying styles of
instruction. As noted earlier, an increasing number of students

don't come to college academically well prepared. We can no longer assume that all students in our classes have the required level of reading, writing, and other basic skills to succeed, and this creates some very difficult instructional challenges.

The first challenge is what to do about students with basic-skills deficiencies. Leaving them alone condemns them to almost certain failure. Most of us are not qualified, nor do we have the time, to teach them basic skills. The only option left is to refer them to campus basic-skills centers, if they exist. Even in those circumstances, referrals take time, and there must be close coordination with academic tutors.

The second challenge comes from the breadth of preparedness in our classes that is an inevitable outcome of seeing more academically underprepared students. In previous times, we could assume a much more normal curve of preparedness, with a few gifted students at the one margin and a few underprepared students at the other. We provided individual help for these students and focused our instructional methodologies on the "mass middle" of the preparedness curve, all of whom were at least minimally prepared to succeed in our classroom. In today's classes, the curve has flattened, or at worst become bimodal. At best, we end up with about the same number of underprepared, prepared, and gifted students; at worst, we have a class with no mass middle at all. If we persist in teaching to the middle of the preparedness curve, we may not be teaching to anyone. In classes with great diversity of preparation, there must be greater diversity of instruction.

To sum up, then, the first implication of changing student demography and characteristics is a call for a more diverse and varied style of instruction. Although it is true that an instructor cannot be all things and do all things for all students, we tend to err on the side of consistency as opposed to diversity. We can and should use more instructional techniques, strategies, and activities in our teaching. The research and literature on learning styles is helpful in cultivating a clearer and more complete understanding of the various approaches to learning, which allows for a more thoughtful and systematic inclusion of alternatives.

But that is not the only implication that arises from changes in student demography and characteristics. We also know from a variety of sources and contexts (see, for example, Erickson and Strommer, 1991) that beginning college students, especially those not as academically well prepared, do better in learning environments that are structured and organized—where expectations are clearly articulated. This structure is relevant and positive whether the referent is a whole course or individual assignments. Good suggestions on course structure appear in the Geis chapter (Chapter Eight) of this volume. In Chapter Eleven, Svinicki and colleagues tie the structure of individual lectures and assignments to important gains in learning.

Most of us who teach college students today are impressed (sometimes distressed) by their lack of confidence in their ability as learners. They seem unable to take control of situations and act much more like victims to whom things not of their choosing happen. Many of today's college students need to be empowered, convinced that learning is something over which they can exercise control. The implication here is a call for a change in faculty role in terms of relationships with students. Faculty who help these students succeed act more like guides and coaches and less like guards and judges. In Chapter Seven, Millar explores some of the philosophical changes this new role implies for teachers and addresses issues of standards that become relevant when faculty leave the podium and move out into the class. Also relevant to this implication is the work of Perry and colleagues (Chapter Four), who explore the role of motivation in learning as well as orientations to learning that either hinder or facilitate success.

Still another potential area of implication rests in the assumption that even though students may be very different from their teachers, they do have much in common with their fellow students. They can and should be encouraged to learn with and from each other. Not only can they better help each other connect knowledge with their own experiences, but having a voice, a say, a role in their own learning can be an empowering experience. Much of the current interest in cooperative and collaborative learning derives from the growing diversity of our students and our culture. Education makes an important contribution when it teaches diverse people how to live and work together in communities of respect. As was already pointed out, teachers cannot be expected to respond to all the differences, but students can be enlisted in the effort. Chapter Five, by Matthews, contains many concrete suggestions for using group work that have grown out of experiences with today's college students.

These implications give us places to start our exploration of the ways to adapt, modify, and change instruction so that it better connects with our students. Existing research and literature lead us to believe that courses charted in these directions will lead to desired destinations, but nothing suggested here or in subsequent chapters is surefire. As noted earlier, we are traversing uncharted waters—which makes what Menges and Rando propose in Chapter Ten so important and relevant. At every step in our efforts to change, we need to solicit and respond to learner feedback. As these authors point out, it is not a question of doing what students want but of understanding how they are experiencing education and then modifying what we do so that learning outcomes improve.

The best way to conclude this section is to lead the way to what follows. One of the most significant implications of changing student demography and characteristics rests on the fact that all student experiences influence whatever learning does or does not occur. Faculty may think of their classrooms as secure castles, protected by moats and thick walls, but students bring all manner of unwanted and counterproductive forces into those chambers of learning. They sit in class worried about the next tuition bill; they wonder about children in day care; they fight fatigue and have eight hours of work still ahead; they don't understand why the professor requires them to attend an evening lecture; they can't believe how long it takes to do the reading; they don't have time to work on the group project; and on and on. What occurs in the classroom, as important as it is, happens as part of something larger. More so than previously, today's college students are forcing faculty to see what happens inside the classroom as a consequence of what happens outside. There are implications in that arena as well.

Implications for Learning Outside the Classroom

Research like that summarized by Pascarella and Terenzini (1991) documents that students' experiences outside the classroom may contribute just as much to their success as their performance inside the classroom. In general, students who get involved in activities, participate in orientation, make use of support services, establish effective interpersonal relations with other students and faculty, live in residence halls, belong to student organizations, and attend cultural events are more likely to graduate than students without such involvement (Upcraft, 1985).

Having someone else, such as a family member, friend, or faculty/staff member take an interest in and care about one's success is also very important (Schlossberg, Lynch, and Chickering, 1989). Contact with faculty, both inside and outside the classroom, plays a positive role in the experiences of beginning students, as reported in Chapter Three by Terenzini and colleagues.

The weight of this research stands somewhat in opposition to what has been described by way of the experiences of college students today. Most of them do not live on campus. They commute. Limited time on campus means fewer opportunities to connect with other students and faculty. It means less chance of getting involved with the academic life of the college. Given the implication that success depends to a large degree on student involvement, the challenge for faculty is how to help students structure their out-of-class experiences to promote learning goals.

Again, this means a change in faculty role—the need to see oneself more as a designer, arranger, facilitator, and manager of learning experiences. Lowman devotes Chapter Nine to an exploration of how assignments can be designed so that they promote learning. Other examples to consider involve assignments tied to out-of-class campus activities. Practica and internships can be used to help students apply what they've learned in the classroom. Volunteer service that relates to academic goals offers another vehicle for involvement. Can part-time work experiences, common to so many college students, be somehow connected to their classroom experiences? Engaging students in faculty scholarship and research gets students involved and provides that invaluable contact with faculty.

There is no question that institutions must work harder to create academic communities that connect with today's college students. With students who commute and work, classrooms are about the only place on campus you can be assured the students will be. This puts faculty at the vanguard of efforts to get students involved in the intellectual life of the campus.

Besides this new and expanded role for faculty with respect to out-of-class learning, changes in students spell out implications in two other areas as well. As diversity among our students increases, the diversity of our faculty and staff must also grow. In Chapter Fourteen, Tierney and Bensimon propose means by which the culture of a campus can come to reflect the changes, both real and anticipated, in its student body.

Finally, to reiterate the theme of what the changes in students mean for teaching and learning, the fact is we don't know. Not only is it absolutely essential that faculty keep fingers on the pulse of classes, but institutions too must understand the impact and effectiveness of programming with respect to students. Froh and Hawkes (Chapter Six) showcase one institution's efforts to ascertain levels of involvement for its students. Banta, in Chapter Fifteen, offers much advice as to how the impact of individual programs can be assessed.

In summary and conclusion, changes in students implicate the out-of-classroom environment. To be successful with these students, higher education must abandon the artificial distinction between student affairs and academic affairs. There is no distinction between them in the realm of learning. Faculty must see their work with students in this broad context. Those responsible for intellectual experiences outside of class must work harder to structure them as course-related experiences.

For faculty, success with students in out-of-class venues depends on a clear understanding of how today's college students have changed, an acceptance of those differences, and a move to adapt teaching so that it better connects with what we know about learning. Life in the classroom needs to be changed, we suspect, in some pretty dramatic and significant ways.

Change is often thrust upon us at what seems like inopportune times—when things are going along just fine, when we'd just as soon not have to change, or when we don't have enough money to change. That is how many people in higher education feel. But there are those among us who have caught a sense of what these changes can mean. We have the opportunity to educate students for whom the college experience can be a life-altering one. We have the opportunity to better meet the serious and significant needs of an increasingly complex and diverse society. It is a time when our work in higher education can really and truly make a difference.

References

Astin, A. W., Green, K. C., & Korn, W. S. (1987). *The American freshman: Twenty-year trends*. Los Angeles: Cooperative Institutional Research Program.

Astin, W. W., Korn, W. S., & Berz, E. R. (1990). *The American freshman: National norms for fall, 1990*. Los Angeles: Cooperative Institutional Research Program.

Baxter Magolda, M. B. (1992). *Knowing and reasoning in college: Gender-related patterns in students' intellectual development*. San Francisco: Jossey-Bass.

Bulthuis, J. D. (1986). The foreign student today: A profile. In K. R. Pyle (Ed.),

New directions for student services: No. 36. *Guiding the development of foreign students* (pp. 19–27). San Francisco: Jossey-Bass.

Chronicle of Higher Education Almanac. (1992, August 26). 39(1).

Chronicle of Higher Education. (1992, July 15). 38, p. A29.

Chronicle of Higher Education. (1992, December 12). 39(17), p. A32.

Cox, B. B., & Ramirez, M., III. (1981). Cognitive styles: Implications for multiethnic education. In J. A. Banks (Ed.), *Education in the '80s,* (pp. 61–71). Washington, DC: National Education Association.

Cross, K. P. (1981). *Adults as learners: Increasing participation and facilitating learning.* San Francisco: Jossey-Bass.

Erickson, B. L., & Strommer, D. (1991). *Teaching college freshmen.* San Francisco: Jossey-Bass.

Evans, N., & Levine, H. (1990). Perspectives on sexual orientation. In L. V. Moore (Ed.), New directions for student services: No. 51. *Evolving theoretical perspectives on students* (pp. 49–58). San Francisco: Jossey-Bass.

Forrest, A. (1987). Managing the flow of students through higher education. *National Forum: Phi Kappa Phi Journal, 68,* 39–42.

Gannon, J. P. (1989). *Soul survivors: A new beginning for adults abused as children.* Englewood Cliffs, NJ: Prentice Hall.

Hameister, B. G. (1989). Disabled students. In M. L. Upcraft & J. N. Gardner (Eds.), *The freshman year experience: Helping students survive and succeed in college* (pp. 340–341). San Francisco: Jossey-Bass.

Henton, J., Hayes, L., Lamke, L., & Murphy, C. (1980). Crisis reaction of college freshmen as a function of family support systems. *Personnel and Guidance Journal, 58,* 508–510.

Hodgkinson, H. L. (1985). *All one system: Demographics of education, kindergarten through graduate school.* Washington, DC: Institute of Educational Leadership.

Hoffman, J., & Weiss, B. (1987). Family problems and presenting problems in college students. *Journal of Counseling Psychology, 2,* 157–163.

Justiz, M. J., & Rendón, L. I. (1989). Hispanic students. In M. L. Upcraft & J. N. Gardner (Eds.), *The freshman year experience: Helping students survive and succeed in college* (pp. 261–276). San Francisco: Jossey-Bass.

Kolb, D. A. (1981). Learning styles and disciplinary differences. In A. W. Chickering (Ed.), *The modern American college* (pp. 232–255). San Francisco: Jossey-Bass.

Kolb, D. A., & Smith, D. M. (1986). *User's guide for the learning style inventory: A manual for teachers and trainers.* Boston: McBer.

Kuh, G. D. (1990). The demographic juggernaut. In M. J. Barr & M. L. Upcraft (Eds.), *New futures for student affairs: Building a vision for professional leadership and practice* (pp. 71–97). San Francisco: Jossey-Bass.

McCarthy, B. (1980). *The 4Mat system: Teaching learning styles with right/left mode techniques.* Chicago: Excel.

National On-Campus Report. (1992, September 15). *20*(18), 5.

Parade. (1989, March 19), p. 17.

Pascarella, E. T., & Terenzini, P. T. (1991). *How college affects students.* San Francisco: Jossey-Bass.

Pearson, C. S., Shavlick, D. L., & Touchton, J. G. (Eds.) (1989). *Educating the majority: Women challenge tradition in higher education.* New York: American Council on Education/MacMillan.

Schlossberg, N. K., Lynch, A. Q., & Chickering, A. W. (1989). *Improving higher education environments for adults: Response programs from entry to departure.* San Francisco: Jossey-Bass.

Schoch, R. (1980). As Cal enters the 80s, there'll be some changes made. *California Monthly, 90*(3), 1–3.

Shade, B.J.R. (Ed.) (1989). *Culture, style, and the educative process.* Springfield, IL: Thomas.

Svinicki, M. D., & Dixon, N. M. (1987). The Kolb model modified for classroom activities. *College Teaching, 35*(4), 141–146.

Tharp, R. G. (1989). Psychocultural variables and constraints: Effects on teaching and learning in schools. *American Psychologist, 44*(2), 349–359.

Upcraft, M. L. (1985). Residence halls and student activities. In L. Noel, R. Levitz, & D. Saluri (Eds.), *Increasing student retention* (pp. 75–104). San Francisco: Jossey-Bass.

Wallerstein, J. S., & Blakeslee, S. (1989). *Second chances: Men, women, and children a decade after divorce.* New York: Ticknor & Fields.

Whitkin, H. A., & Moore, C. A. (1975). *Field-dependent and field-independent cognitive styles and their educational implications.* Princeton, NJ: Educational Testing Service.

Witchel, R. I. (1991). The impact of dysfunctional families on college students' development. In R. I. Witchel (Ed.), New directions for student services: No. 54. *Dealing with students from dysfunctional families* (pp. 5–18). San Francisco: Jossey-Bass.

Chapter Three

Making the Transition to College

Patrick T. Terenzini, Pennsylvania State University
Laura I. Rendón, Arizona State University
Susan B. Millar, University of Wisconsin
M. Lee Upcraft, Pennsylvania State University
Patricia L. Gregg, Pennsylvania State University
Romero Jalomo, Jr., Arizona State University
Kevin W. Allison, Pennsylvania State University

The research on college success clearly indicates that student experiences during the first year of college—both inside and outside the classroom—are crucial to their academic achievement, personal development, and retention (Upcraft and Gardner, 1989). Some experts would argue that the first semester, or even the first six weeks, are critical in determining whether students stay or leave (Noel, Levitz, and Saluri, 1985). Thus the transition to college marks a critical passage. If students don't survive this transition, a wide range of cognitive, psychosocial, occupational, and economic benefits may be lost.

In focusing on this transition, we must look at student experiences both *inside* and *outside* the classroom. Faculty and administrators have long assumed (not without reason) that experiences in the classroom contribute to student learning, and most of this

Note: The research reported in this chapter was funded by the U.S. Department of Education, Office of Educational Research and Improvement (OERI), under Grant No. R117G100037. The opinions expressed herein do not necessarily reflect the position or policies of OERI, and no official endorsement should be inferred.

book is devoted to teaching and learning in formal instructional settings. Less evident, although perhaps just as powerful, are student experiences outside the classroom. Considerable research done in the past twenty years indicates that the quality, quantity, and type of students' out-of-class experiences can directly and indirectly influence cognitive development (such as critical-thinking skills and the ability to synthesize and analyze); psychosocial development; attitudes and values; moral development; and perhaps most importantly, in-class learning, academic achievement, and retention (Pascarella and Terenzini, 1991).

This chapter describes and analyzes students' transition to college, both inside and outside the classroom, with special attention to the people and experiences that facilitate or impede this transition. We suggest ways to help make the transition to college easier and increase the likelihood that students will become more deeply involved in their education, learn more, and persist longer.

Importance of the First Year

Approximately one-third of each year's full-time entering students are not enrolled at the same institution one year later. This fact has not changed much in the last twenty years (Noel, Levitz, and Saluri, 1985). Similarly, research evidence consistently indicates that of all the entering baccalaureate degree students who will drop out over a five-year period, one-half will do so before the start of their second year. Why do so many students fail to make it to their second year? What can be done about this?

We start with four assumptions. First, some students leave for reasons that may be beyond institutional control, such as lack of finances, poor student-institution fit, changing academic or career goals, or unrelated personal circumstances. Second, many more students leave because the institution has failed to create an environment, inside or outside the classroom, conducive to their learning and educational needs. Third, institutions, through their people and policies, can successfully intervene in ways that promote learning and simultaneously reduce attrition. Finally, and most critical to this chapter, these interventions must occur during the transition period, particularly in the first weeks and months of enrollment.

A research project conducted in 1990–1991 and sponsored by the National Center on Postsecondary Teaching, Learning, and Assessment sought to better understand what is really going on in the hearts and minds of first-year students that helps or hinders their success. The project attempted to identify ways that institutions could help.

Members of the research group interviewed first-year students at four very different institutions (all names are fictitious): Reallybig University (RBU), a large, eastern, public, research university; Urban State University (USU), a commuter-oriented, predominantly African American, comprehensive university in a major midwestern city; Bayfield College (BC), a small, private, liberal arts college in a Middle Atlantic state; and Southwest Community College (SCC; note that this is not to be confused with the Southwestern Community College in Iowa or the one in North Carolina), a two-year institution that is approximately one-third Hispanic, one-third African American, and one-fourth American Indian.

We spoke with 133 first-year students late in their first (or early in their second) semester and asked them several questions about their collegiate experiences to that point. The goal was to start with no assumptions and to listen as best we could to what students were saying about their transition to college.

We asked students what went into their decision to go to college and why they attended the institution they chose. We asked them what they expected in college and what they found. We asked what people were currently important in their lives. We asked about getting used to college life and what they would do to help new students make a successful transition to college. We wanted to know what their most important experiences in college were and how they felt connected with the institution, if at all. We asked what, if anything, was significant about their being "different" by gender, race, ethnicity, or age. Finally, we asked whether or not they felt they had changed since entering college.

The transition from high school, work, or homemaking to college is an exceedingly complex phenomenon. The process is a highly interrelated, weblike series of interpersonal, academic, and organizational pushes and pulls that shape student learning (broadly conceived) and persistence in studies. Despite this sometimes bewildering complexity, two themes emerge from our interviews as common across all settings.

The first theme has to do with the place of "going to college" in the life of the student, both as a stage of life and in the value attached to college attendance. For many students (predominantly but not exclusively those who are white and recent high school graduates), college represented a continuation of conditions and processes established much earlier in their lives. For other students, going to college constituted a major disruption or disjunction in their "life's passage." For these students, college attendance carried with it considerable potential for stress and far-reaching change.

The second theme concerns the role of "validating" experiences in a student's successful transition to college. By *validating* we mean those actions and outcomes that communicate to students (either directly or symbolically) that they have the capacity and competence to complete college successfully. Validated students had received encouragement or been formally or informally rewarded for achievement (however small the reward or achievement may have been). They were students whose demonstrated ability to perform had been recognized by someone important to them (teacher, parent, friend). This validation increased interest in continued participation and achievement in college. Self-doubt and anxiety over whether they could "make it" was progressively replaced by self-confidence and even joy in their accomplishments.

Our interviews made clear that these two themes are closely related. To illustrate, for students whose transition to college represents a disjunction in the life trajectory, validating experiences played an even more important role than they did in the lives of students for whom college represented essentially a continuation. Equally clear, however, is that few (if any) new students escaped discontinuous experiences entirely. Moreover, virtually all students appeared to find themselves in need of validating experiences of one sort or another. These two themes—continuation versus disjunction and the need for validation—appeared to be woven intricately throughout the academic and interpersonal lives of all the new students we interviewed. There is other evidence that student involvement in their educational experiences is directly tied to their academic and psychosocial development; the evidence clearly suggests that the way the transition is handled can have a direct bearing on the likelihood of subsequent change, development, and persistence (Pascarella and Terenzini, 1991).

The Place of College in Life's Passage

The place of college in the experience of a student varies, depending mostly on family circumstances. Much more is at risk if college is a new and unfamiliar experience than if the student comes from a college-attending family.

College as Continuation: Traditional Students

The educational portion of the American Dream is a story of uninterrupted study and progressively greater academic accomplishment, beginning in kindergarten and culminating in college, or graduate or professional school. For many Americans (primarily but not exclusively white), this passage is completed as expected. When asked what had gone into their decision to attend college at Really-big University and Bayfield College, virtually all those students were surprised by the question, indicating that they had never considered *not* going to college. Two traditional-aged white students at Reallybig University explained:

> Going to college . . . was never even, like, a question! Um, both my parents went to college and I guess they figured that all their kids would go to college. I mean, . . . it was never even too much a question. Um, both my sister and I did pretty well in school and so college was just like the definite thing to follow high school.

The second student chimed in:

> Yeah, I agree. Uh, going to college was never a, a question. You know, that's never something I thought about, whether I'm gonna go to college or not, that was kind of, a given.

These students (and many others like them) and their parents had assumed all along that going to college was simply the next logical step toward personal and occupational achievement. The notion originated in the educational attainment of parents, older siblings, or close relatives who at least attended, and frequently completed, college, and not infrequently some form of graduate or professional education (Pascarella and Terenzini, 1991). For most of these students, the very fact that they had been admitted to a moderately selective college or university was evidence that academically they "belonged" at their institution.

While these students occasionally expressed some concern about their ability to meet the academic competition, making new friends dominated their conversation. For them, the most threatening disjunction was interpersonal, not academic. A new student at Reallybig University described his experience:

> I hated it. [Another student: "So did I. I cried. . . ."] Like, for the first couple of . . . I, I hated it, 'cause I was like, here I am in a situ-

ation where I know absolutely nobody. I mean, it's like, it's like you're just dropped in, it's like "Here you go!" And you know no one. You know, you had all these close friends and good friends, and you're always having a good time. . . . And I got here and I knew nobody. And it was just like, it was terrifying. And I think you have to learn it eventually, to actually, you know, break out into the world and do it. And know that everything will be OK and you will turn out fine, and you always meet these people, and like now, like when I first got here, I wanted to transfer. I was like, "That's it! Send me to a branch campus! I'll commute from home." [Other student: "Oh, God. . . ."] I was gonna commute, and then I was like, then I started thinking of it, like, "OK. It has to get better." And like, it's great. I love it now.

High school friends appeared to be instrumental in how successfully these new students made the transition to college. When a new student had high school friends who were also new students at the same institution, these precollege friends functioned during the early weeks or months of college as a bridge from one academic and interpersonal environment to the next. Older brothers, sisters, or friends already enrolled also helped the new students prepare for what they encountered during the transition. These individuals "had been there." They offered advice on how to deal with the institution's size, where important or useful offices are located, and so on, generally providing an unstructured, informal, but no less effective orientation for new students.

Old friends performed this bridge function, however, for a limited period of time. New students were limited initially to a friendship network linked to high school acquaintances, others living on the same residence hall floor, or other students enrolled in the same classes. These connections not only served as early interpersonal moorings, but they also provided access to other students as the new student's friendship network expanded and relationships developed with more and more new acquaintances. As this network of new friends expanded, reliance on high school friends slowly faded in importance.

For some commuting students, however, the old friendship network may have constrained a student's interpersonal transition to college by anchoring them in their precollege social networks. One white commuter student at Bayfield College commented:

> I think that, me being as a commuter, I expected that I would be, like, a lot more involved with things at school—like school activities, and I found out that I really wasn't interested in doing much at the school, you know, as far as, like, like clubs and whatnot. I'd rather, you know, associate with my friends from before college. . . . A lot of commuters I've talked to feel that same way. They go home from school and they [pause] and they're with their friends that they've had in high school. And they do the things they did in high school, and don't do . . . [Another commuter chimed in: "Oh, I, I agree with him, totally."]

There can be little doubt about the important role the families of traditional students played in encouraging students to attend college and to persist. With very few exceptions, when asked about the most important people in their lives right now students unhesitatingly named one or more members of their immediate family. While the sense of debt to parents for their support was more apparent among students at Southwest Community College and Urban State University, it was also evident at Bayfield College and Reallybig University. Among students at the latter two institutions, the comparatively muted response seems to reflect more their taking parental support for granted than that they enjoyed any less parental support than their commuting peers. The parents of traditional, especially resident, students seem to have functioned as a safety net during the transition. Parents were still a source of advice and counsel. They reinforced what the students already knew: that they could be successful and that the parents were there for them.

Compared to commuter students, residential students also appeared to be developing greater personal independence and autonomy from family and thereby to be redefining the nature of the relationship they had with parents. The new relationship, one of equality among adults, appeared to have replaced the hierarchical parent-child relationship that characterized their high school years when they lived at home.

Faculty and other institutional staff members at Reallybig University and Bayfield College appeared to play an extremely limited part in students' academic or interpersonal transition. When students at Reallybig were asked to name the most important people in their lives, parents and friends at the university dominated their responses. The only university staff mentioned were teaching assistants or residence hall staff, never faculty members. One young woman, hearing her peers talk about their large classes, commented: "One of my classes has two hundred in it [pauses, shaking her head], but the rest are big."

Such large classes virtually ensure that students will remain anonymous to faculty members. Few students believed any of their instructors knew their names or would recognize them if they passed on the street. Such anonymity, for some, was a positive attraction of large classes: students could sit back, "mellow out," and not have to worry about being called on in class. Indeed, some spoke of being able to skip classes entirely, read the text, get the class notes from a friend, and still make high marks on examinations.

By contrast, such comments were never heard from first-generation students at Urban State or Southwest Community College students. In fact, one SCC student who had transferred from a large state university talked openly about missing the large classes. In SCC's smaller classes, she "was afraid that maybe [the instructors] would catch me daydreaming so I paid attention more and learned more." She acknowledged that she could no longer hide in class, that she had to become involved in what was happening in class. She grudgingly allowed as how she was probably learning more at SCC.

College as Disjunction: First-Generation College Students

The adaptation to college was far more difficult for nontraditional, primarily first-generation, college students. Indeed, for many, going to college constituted a major *disjunction* in their life course. For these students, college going was not part of their family's tradition or expectations. On the contrary, those who were the first in their immediate family to attend college were *breaking*, not continuing, family tradition. For these students, college attendance often involved multiple transitions: academic, social, and cultural. A young American Indian student explained her motivation for attending Southwest Community College:

> Right before [mother] died, she took me out to the reservation, and when we were outside the reservation, she pointed it out to me and said, "Do you want to be like this? Sitting around and doing nothing? Or do you want to go on?" So it was probably the reason why I went to college. Because they really have no life out there. She goes, she goes, "The majority," she told me that the majority of the Indians that, that don't, don't, that don't go to college or don't finish school just move back to the reservation and just sit there.

A young African American student at Urban State described being beaten up in high school by classmates who disapproved of his interest in ideas and his attention to his school work. Later in the interview, when asked what was special about USU, he replied without hesitation: "Well, like I said before. It's very open-minded here. . . . You can read in the hall or on the steps, and nobody will throw a brick at you."

A classmate described related reasons:

> I have a lot of reasons, but I guess, basically, because of where I live, a lot of kids are killed, often, and, you know, I decided to further my education just to get away from it. I, I don't like the fact that people are, you know, constantly shooting at you. It, it's, uh, it's bothersome. You don't want to be bothered with these gang bangers

gettin' you, rising up, so I said, "Either I make a difference or I get out of here." And I said "I'll do both. . . ."

Because of their family and educational backgrounds, for the first-generation students in our study the act of going to college often constituted a significant and intimidating cultural transition. Attending and completing college carried the potential for radical changes in these students and the lives they led. Indeed, for many the decision was a conscious choice to escape occupational dead-ends and hopelessness.

Many of these students found the academic transition the most challenging. When asked what they expected to find in college, most spoke of the anticipated academic rigors of college in comparison with high school. Most came expecting to have to study hard. Most found what they had expected, but others (a relatively small minority) commented that college was not all that much more difficult than high school had been. The majority, however, appeared to be deferring involvement in the nonacademic activities and life of the campus until they felt they had their academic feet under them.

But if the academic transition was of greater concern, making friends was commonly cited as being the key to "feeling connected" or "a part" of their institution. Several students spoke of looking forward to the time when they could devote more time to out-of-class activities and people. For a number of Southwest Community College students, the academic and interpersonal activities often overlapped, easing the transition in both spheres. These students spoke positively of meeting other students in their classes or on the patio at the student union, and of engaging in both social conversation and group discussion of what was going on in their classes. Several identified these sorts of sessions as among the most effective learning experiences they had (along with in-class discussion of course material). These reports are highly consistent with Tinto's (1987) finding that collaborative or cooperative learning approaches produce both social and academic links among students.

Like their traditional college student peers, first-generation students also cite their parents, a grandparent, or aunts and uncles as important people in their lives. In a few instances, students mentioned younger sisters and brothers as important people. In virtually all cases, these important individuals were mentioned for the support and encouragement they gave. For first-generation students, however, these important individuals often played an ambiguous role, sometimes supportive and encouraging, but also sometimes restraining.

For some students, particularly those from African American, Hispanic, or American Indian families, parents tried to maintain a relationship that they recognized might change. Some parents may have recognized that their college-going children—as proud of them as they were—would, metaphorically, never return home. Sensing such fears, the students of these parents found their anxiety levels rising in ways and to degrees unimagined by most middle-class white students, faculty members, and administrators. A Southwest Community College student describes this loving tension. Asked who the most important people in his life were, he replied:

> My grandmother. Even though she is a big inspiration to me, uh, she has this way of clinging. She hates to let go of things. And I can understand. I think that's why she takes in a lot of us, as we're going along. She hates to let go. And my cousin and I have told her that we're going off, goin' to college. She goes, "I can't believe you're gonna leave." You know, "I need you here with me to do this or do that." "Listen, Grandma, life goes on. This may sound cold, but when you're gone, we're still here. And, uh, we need to so some things to prepare for our future." And she's startin' to understand that.

Friends also play a role in the level of success that first-generation students experience in making the transition to college. While high school friends at the same college may have performed the bridging role describe earlier, this particular dynamic was less evident. Attending a commuter institution, as many first-generation students do, can dramatically alter the role high school friends play. As with the commuting students at Bayfield College, new students at Southwest Community College and Urban State often found that high school friends who did *not* go on to college complicated and hindered their transition. A new Urban State student described an encounter with an old high school friend:

> Well, after we graduated, I seen him last week, matter of fact, and, um, he was just hanging on the mailbox, just, just, telling me, "What's up man? What you doin'?" And, you know, he seen the bookbag on my shoulder. "Aw, man! You goin' to school? Aw, man, that ain't nothin', man." You know, I just looked at him and hugged my shoulderbag, and left. You know, cause, um, see, he, he's not going to succeed in life. He's gonna be the one that's on the corner with the wine bottle, or he gonna end up dead. See, me, I'm gonna end up in school, you know, probably with a high-paying job, doin' what I like. [Another students comments: "Or at least a job."]

A young woman at Southwest Community College experienced similar pressures:

> My friend . . . plays basketball. But she, like, goes out partying and things like that. But she's after me. She [says]: "You're getting boring. You just stay home and study." I [say] "No, I'm going [to college]. . . . It's something I'm paying for. And . . . I wanna learn something. . . . I'm gonna be needing [it] . . . in the future."

As noted earlier, the nature of the transition for first-generation students, compared with that of traditional students, is more complex, more threatening, and consequently more stressful. Success in college will mean a major redirection of the life course. But if the benefits are greater, so are the risks and the fear of failure. For many of these students, the college years may not be "the best years," but rather a deadly serious struggle. Ironically, even success in college for these students has its downside: as London (1989) notes, only when we begin to recognize that

> mobility involves not just gain but loss—most of all the loss of a familiar past, including a past self—that we can begin to understand the attendant periods of confusion, conflict, isolation, and even anguish that first-generation students [experience]. . . . Modernity creates the potential for biographical and social dislocation, so that freedom of choice, to whatever extent it exists, can also be the agony of choice (p. 168).

Validating Students

In *Women's Ways of Knowing,* Belenky and others (1986) argue that "for women, confirmation and community are prerequisites rather than consequences of development" (p. 194). In their study, they found that "ordinary" women who were treated as stupid or incompetent and incapable of learning yearned for acceptance and validation. The needs of women students were in stark contrast to what was offered to them in college. Women wanted respect for their ideas and information about how to solve problems. Yet, they found that teachers who viewed themselves as experts or authorities usually tried to dominate the less knowledgeable, either by assaulting them with information or by withholding information.

Like our own research findings discussed above, this study helps us understand the potentially harmful effects the traditional model of teaching and learning may have on different kinds of students. In our study of students in two- and four-year colleges, for example, we learned that:

- While some students (especially those attending universities with stringent entrance requirements) felt comfortable with their academic skills, others (particularly nontraditional students) came to college doubting their potential to succeed.

- Students of all kinds yearned for acceptance and validation. They articulated both a need to feel a part of the learning community and to know that they were capable of being successful college students.

- Both academic and interpersonal validation, like involvement, are critical to the successful transition to college.

- Academic *and* interpersonal validation appeared to be most important for many community-college, first-generation, and nontraditional students.

- Interpersonal validation appeared to be most important for traditional and nontraditional students attending larger, four-year campuses.

- Students who encountered invalidating experiences appeared to be less involved in their education and may have experienced learning setbacks.

Self-Doubt and Invalidation

When we asked students, "What did you expect and what did you find when you got here?" many nontraditional students talked about wanting their doubts about being capable of learning erased. Often they talked about wanting to be part of a community of learners, their desire to "start over," and their personal expectations in regard to college life, course work, and career aspirations. These topics were especially common among community college students, women, Hispanic and African American students, and students who had been out of school for some time.

Some students expressed doubts about becoming successful college students. For example, an SCC student, explaining why she enrolled in a two-year college instead of a university, said:

Personally, I think I was unprepared for classes like English. I took
my assessment test and I thought I was unprepared. I wasn't prepared
in high school at all. . . . The way you do homework is different in
high school. I couldn't have done it in a university.

One returning woman said:

I expected to fail. Two weeks and I was out. I didn't think I could
study. I didn't think I could learn.

Some students described invalidating experiences at the hands
of their instructors. An African American woman who held a General Education Degree (GED) and attended Southwest Community College described such an experience:

I went to secretarial school and I started working on Wall Street for
an investment firm. I went in as a file clerk. . . . And within about
two or three years, I was making my $35,000–40,000 a year. . . . But
when I came to [the campus] I was made to realize that I was a
young black woman with hardly any education. . . . To come [here]
and have someone speak to me as if I had the education of a five-
year-old . . . that was a real bummer.

Other students talked about invalidating classroom experiences. Said one community college student:

My math teacher . . . he has a number [for me]. . . . I was a number,
you know, instead of calling us by name, he would call us by our
social security number. There aren't many people in class for him
to go through all that and it's quicker for him to say my name than
my number.

A Reallybig University student described an encounter in an
elevator with one of her large-class instructors. When she com-

mented that she was in the instructor's class, he replied: "So what?"

Reallybig University students also commented on the chilly interpersonal and academic climate. Several students also felt frustrated about what they perceived as coldness from some faculty, classmates, and other students. They were disappointed, for example, when instructors would offer to meet with them after class but when approached later they were "busy," or they failed to show up during scheduled office hours. Students also complained that some staff could be very short-tempered with students. This chilly climate appeared to have less impact on the Reallybig students, however, because they expected it and felt they just needed to get used to a large university. One student reported:

> When you come here and find that you're one of 800—that's my largest class—but there's no way the teacher can possibly know everybody, and I don't think he really knows anybody's name. . . . That's what we bargained for when we came to a big school.

The Role of Validation

With many students expressing the need to be validated and describing disappointment with invalidating experiences, we wondered how students might be transformed into powerful learners. Certainly, our study showed that those students who became involved in the social and academic fabric of the institution appeared to be more excited about learning. These were students who met with their instructors regularly and who were members of clubs and organizations. We even found students with enough initiative that they expressed little need to be validated by faculty or other students while adjusting to college. A man at Bayfield College exemplified this view:

> My parents have always been very supportive. . . . So I don't think it was a big transition for me because I was already pretty independent.

I always tried to do things on my own. All through high school I never really asked my parents for anything; I always tried to do things for myself—I tried not to depend on my parents, because I knew one day I would be on my own, and my parents wouldn't be there for me. . . . I always tried to get involved in everything—like in high school I was very involved.

But not all students involved themselves in college so easily, particularly those who found the transition to college difficult and who were unaccustomed to active participation in academic and social structures. For these students, traditional institutional expectations and their needs were often mismatched. They needed faculty and staff to help them feel a part of the learning community and help them realize that they could and would be successful college students.

A remark made by an African American student at Southwest Community College exemplifies this point. When asked who had been most or least helpful in college, she said:

I find that . . . freshmen coming to college right out of high school . . . there's no sense of direction . . . when a student sits down and says, "Well, I'm not certain of what curriculum I want, what classes I need to be taking. How should I go about registration? How should I go about getting financial aid?" . . . I find that . . . people have to realize . . . that everyone is not aware.

An academic life is much different than that of life at home or in the business world. So sometimes terms are not familiar to you. People throw things at you right off the top of their heads . . . there's no time to explain. You feel out of place. You feel like one in a basket amongst many. And I find that this . . . is what discouraged me when I tried to enroll at a community college twelve years ago . . . I just felt lost, I was going crazy. . . . I felt like I was just lucky enough to be able to leave and not go back.

Academic Validation

Academic validation can take different forms. For example, students can be academically validated through the materials they produce as part of their coursework (getting good grades on tests, papers, examinations, and so on). At Reallybig University, students were validated both by being admitted to what is a moderately selective university and by receipt of good grades during their courses. It is noteworthy, however, that such forms of validation are delayed in that students rarely receive them until a semester is well underway. In some courses, students may receive such formal or product validation on only two occasions: midterm and final examinations.

In contrast to such product-based validation, students may also derive validation through the academic processes, the more subtle indications that others recognize their academic competence (for example, positive oral feedback from instructors and peers in class, being asked for help by another student, casual compliments on their academic knowledge and skills). Academic experiences like these helped students trust their innate capacity to learn and gave them confidence. For example, students reported that they acquired positive attitudes about their academic ability in classes where faculty demonstrated a genuine interest in teaching, were personable and approachable, treated students with respect, structured learning experiences that allowed students to experience themselves as capable of learning, created a caring classroom environment, and provided frequent and meaningful feedback to students. Students at Southwest Community College and Urban State University expressed the greatest need for academic validation.

A returning woman at Southwest, for example, described a transforming experience:

> I was amazed at . . . what I had preconceived that college would be like. I did not believe that the instructors would be so personable with each individual and want to teach you—want to teach you. I

thought it was like what I've heard [the large local university] is like, where you go out there and they don't care whether you come in or out or whatever, you're just a number, and they don't care whether you learn or not, it's up to you to learn. And here people are helping us to get our minds in order to where we can learn. It's a process. It's like a nurturing process.

The kinds of academic experiences in which faculty had students participate served as important mechanisms for validation. A female student at Southwest Community College illustrated by explaining that her most important experience was viewing a videotape of a presentation she had made in front of her classmates:

I don't know quite how to say this, but when you hear yourself talk . . . and you observe this individual that has blossomed into something that I hadn't even been aware. . . . I would sit in awe and say, "That's me! Look at me!" I like me.

Likewise, a Southwest Community College student, an African American student who had not passed his previous college English classes, explained his validating experience with his English teacher:

Most teachers, they consider my failings. They just come to school because they have to get paid. [My English teacher] came to school to teach you. Plus if you had hard times she understood. It was like if you couldn't come to class one day, the only thing you had to do was call her. . . . If something was wrong, she could tell you how she felt. That's what teachers need to do more. Some treat you like you're a statue.

Faculty were not the only people who provided validating, in-class experiences. A young Urban State student recounted the support a classmate gave him:

Recently I got a C on a test in zoology where I was an A student there. And I was [feeling like] "Give up!" You know, I cried a little bit. I was ticked off. But then I had someone constantly behind me saying, "You're going to do this. Sit down and study, and you can do it! Don't worry about it."

In the absence of in-class validating experiences, some students were able to turn for validation to people outside of class. A traditional-aged Urban State student provided an example of this support:

> The single most important person in my life right now is my mother. She's the type of person that does any and everything for her two children. She has sacrificed. She feels that my education and my well-being, as well as my brother's, is the utmost importance. And with that type of parenting, or that type of support, even if you do not finish your goals, you will know that it wasn't because you didn't have any support.

Interpersonal Validation

Validating actions of an interpersonal, as opposed to academic, nature appeared to foster personal adjustment and social integration. Students who expressed the greatest need for interpersonal validation were those who had changed (or wanted to change) their sense of self, needed a sense of belonging, had doubts about their ability to make friends in college, or were attending Reallybig University and felt overwhelmed by the large number of students. Friends and other students played particularly important roles in interpersonal validation.

When asked who were the most important people in her life, a student at Reallybig responded:

> There are seven or eight of us who are friends on the floor [and] who are always [hanging] around [together]. We know that if one of us

has a problem everyone is going to be there to deal with whatever needs to be dealt with. It's your friends at school who you're going to depend on most.

A twenty-six-year-old African American woman at Bayfield noted that "The [younger] girls of color, for some reason, I don't know, they seem to look up to me. They admire me, which makes me feel good."

Several students also recounted the important role parents played as validating agents. One man at RBU commented:

When you are in high school, you think, "My parents are a nui-sance, they kind of just bother me or they leave me alone." Then you don't realize until you're gone what they did for you and how much they are involved.

Toward a Definition of Validation

The "validation" we heard woven through students' discussions of their transition to college differs from the "involvement" described by Astin (1985), Pace (1984), and others (for example, Study Group, 1984). *Involvement* typically describes the level of student effort in the educational process and implies that students have a responsibility to participate actively in that process. *Validation* refers to actions taken by persons *other* than the student. What had transformed these students were incidents where something was done for them or in conjunction with them—when someone else took the initiative to lend a helping hand, to do something that affirmed their capabilities and that supported their academic endeavors and social adjustment. Thus validation appears to have the following dimensions:

- It is an empowering, confirming, and supportive process, initiated by validating agents, that helps move students toward academic and interpersonal development and can ultimately lead to self-empowerment. Thus validation and involvement appear to be at least precursors, perhaps even prerequisites, for student development.

- Validation is a developmental process, not an end. The more students are validated, the richer the academic and interpersonal experience can be.
- Validation is most effective when offered early in the student's college experience, immediately after the student arrives on campus. Validation should continue throughout the college years.
- Validation can occur both in and out of class. In-class validating agents include faculty, classmates, lab instructors, and teaching assistants. Out-of-class validating agents can be significant others (spouse, boyfriend or girlfriend), family members (parents, siblings, relatives, children), friends (classmates and friends attending or not attending college), or college staff (faculty who meet with students out of class, counselors, advisors, coaches, tutors, teaching assistants, or resident advisors).

It is important to keep in mind that holding students accountable for involving themselves with the social and academic infrastructures of an institution is likely to work only for students who possess the skills to gain access to these opportunities or have experience in utilizing these means. The students who get involved on their own are likely to be those who have *already* been validated.

Many students, particularly nontraditional and first-generation students, expect to find the campus climate rather alienating and intimidating. Perhaps the most important implication of our findings is that students who get no validation in class appear to rely on out-of-class validation to carry them through. The compensatory relationship between high levels of academic integration and low levels of social integration, and vice versa, has been observed in other students and shown to be related to retention (Pascarella and Terenzini, 1991). In the absence of both in-class and out-of-class validation, however, it is reasonable to expect the student to become disillusioned with college.

To move students toward full academic and interpersonal development, it is necessary to recognize that not only must the students adapt to the system, but the institutional staff, especially faculty, must help students adjust and help their institution become more accommodating to the needs, interests, and learning styles of different kinds of students. Faculty and staff must go beyond expecting students to get involved. Merely being available will not be enough. Faculty and staff must take the initiative. Somebody has to care.

Conclusion

The implications of these dimensions (and variations in them) of the transition process are nontrivial for all students, but especially for nontraditional students. We conclude with some recommendations, suggested by our research and that of others, of ways faculty members and academic administrators might ease students' transitions to college.

Implications for Faculty Members

Faculty members often hold the key to successful experiences for students. These suggestions will help to ensure that early instructional experiences are positive.

Avoid Student Stereotypes. Think about what you consider to be the "typical" college student at your college. The chances are good that in thinking "typically" you may be overlooking a substantial number of the students on your campus. Such reflection is particularly important for faculty and administrators whose backgrounds and college experiences resemble those of "traditional" students: entered a four-year college at eighteen directly from high school; from middle-class, white parents who also went to college; lived on campus. On some campuses (for example, the University of California at Berkeley), such students now constitute a minority of the student body. Faculty and staff must carefully consider the dramatically different character of the transition process for students from disadvantaged socioeconomic and educational backgrounds. These students often must reconcile competing demands relating to work, family, their peer group, culture, and school. *Very* few traditional students will ever confront all five sets of demands simultaneously. Increased awareness of, and sensitivity to, what is happening in nontraditional students' lives is needed, as are policies and programs that recognize and respond to these differences. Our current instructional practices, academic regulations and policies, office hour schedules, and expectations of students all bespeak a view of students that admits few differences among them.

Look for Opportunities to Humanize the Relationships You Have with Students. College faculty and staff are among the most crucial validating agents. Their contact with students in and out of class has a wide range of important, documented influences on student learning (Pascarella and Terenzini, 1991). Exemplary and validating faculty are those who are willing to work one-on-one with students in need of assistance; who give out their home telephone numbers; who design learning activities so that students can see themselves as capable learners; who provide meaningful, immediate, and consistent feedback; and who are personable and approachable. Such activities send subtle but important symbolic messages that students are valued by the faculty member and the institution.

Structure Courses So That Students Become Active, Involved Learners. This suggestion can take a variety of forms. It could include various approaches to individualized instruction (such

as Personalized Systems of Instruction, the Keller Plan, audio-
tutorial classes, computer-assisted instruction, programmed instruction). It could provide for peer teaching and tutoring, create group
assignments, and encourage study groups. It could give students an
opportunity to help design the course and learning activities. It
could use various collaborative learning activities (see Goodsell,
Maher, and Tinto, 1992), and frequent, detailed, and constructive
feedback on oral and written work (don't wait until midterm exams
to let students know how they're doing).

Look for ways to psychologically "downsize" large classes. For
example, in a large religion class, Harvey Cox, an internationally
known religion professor at Harvard, used teaching assistants as
mentors to discussion-group members, each of whom took responsibility for leading the small-group discussion of a week's readings
and lectures (Light, 1990).

**Treat Students as You Would Want to Be Treated, or as You
Would Want Your Child to Be Treated.** As straightforward as this
might seem, we heard numerous stories about faculty members with
short tempers, who failed to keep posted office hours, who spoke
down to students, who denigrated students' classroom contributions,
who wouldn't take the time to learn students' names, and so on.

But this suggestion goes beyond common courtesy. Be sensitive
to the needs of your students, particularly nontraditional students.
Many of them may be among the most highly motivated individuals in your classes. (One student we interviewed worked two
full-time jobs and was successfully carrying twelve credit-hours of
courses; he slept three or four hours per night.) Be available to students outside of class. Treat students equally. In your classes with
fewer than thirty students, learn their names and something about
each person by the third class session.

**With Colleagues, Review Departmental Regulations, Practices,
Policies, and Attitudes That Might Interfere with Student
Learning.** How is it decided who teaches the lower-division intro-

ductory course? Are these assignments viewed as paying one's dues or as an opportunity to make students' first exposure to the discipline exciting and memorable? How well do the rules and regulations accommodate students who may be unable to study full-time, or who cannot proceed in an orderly march of 12–15 hours per semester toward the degree? Do department members keep their office hours? Do students and faculty ever interact socially (departmental clubs, picnics, intramural athletic teams)? Do faculty advisers ever invite advisees to their homes for dinner? A growing body of evidence indicates that the interpersonal climate within a department is more closely related to student learning than are discipline-based differences among departments (Pascarella and Terenzini, 1991).

Get Involved in Your Institution's Student-Orientation Programs. Student-orientation programs serve an important early socialization function. During orientation, new students are first introduced to the attitudinal and behavioral norms of a new academic setting as well as its expectations of them. It is important that new students make contact with faculty members as early as possible in their college careers. If orientation is little more than an early course registration and an introduction to Old Siwash or college survival skills or the services that are available for various kinds of problems, then an important opportunity to help new students make connections with the academic and intellectual life of the institution will have been lost.

Discourage Thinking About this Sort of Activity as Coddling Students. Too many faculty members and administrators believe that faculty contributions to the education of undergraduate students begin and end with the classroom, laboratory, or office and are properly limited to dealing with class-related questions or with academic advising. Some faculty members consider informal, out-of-class contact with students as coddling, or (worse) irrelevant or inappropriate to the role of a faculty member. Such views are at the heart of much that is currently being criticized in undergraduate education in America. Bear in mind that students may spend up to 85 percent of their waking hours outside of class. Extending the faculty's influence on student learning means having students and faculty be more involved with one another in educationally desirable ways outside the classroom. This kind of treatment of students is not coddling. It is sound educational practice. Don't weed out; rake in.

Implications for Academic Administrators

Administrators provide crucial leadership. These recommendations describe roles and actions that set high standards for students, faculty, and other student support providers.

Help Students Find an Academic and Interpersonal Niche in the Institution. Because friends from high school appear to play an important role in the transition to college, where feasible institutions might help new students identify and locate already enrolled students from their high school or community. Where such matching is impossible because of institutional size, peer counselors and "big brother/sister" programs can be instrumental in helping new students during the orientation and transition period. New students at Bayfield College, for example, noted the helpfulness of that school's "POSSEs" (Peers Offering Support Services for Education).

During the Orientation Period, Give Attention to the Emotions New Students Are Experiencing. One theme common to our interviews, regardless of the students involved or the location or type of their institution, was that the transition process generates feelings. Some students feel excitement, exuberance, and exhilaration with their new adventure. Others, however, feel anxiety, stress, apprehension, even fear. These latter emotions can be both powerful and educationally dysfunctional. Ways must be found to ease or productively direct this tension and anxiety. Students might be advised that most of them are experiencing these emotions and that they should not be surprised when they begin to feel this way.

Orient Parents and Spouses, as Well as Students. The evidence strongly indicates that parents and spouses play a key role in the support of new students adjusting to a new environment. Such support is needed most by first-generation students, whose parents or spouses may be least able to provide it because they have not been through the transition experience themselves. Parents or spouses of all students should be helped to understand the nature of the academic demands that will be placed on the students, and how to deal with the stresses parents or spouses and students will be experiencing.

Review Faculty Promotion and Tenure Criteria, Policies, and Practices. Faculty members are keenly aware of what kinds of activities and behaviors are rewarded at their institutions. While many faculty members are committed to teaching undergraduate students, many are not. Those who are not are unlikely to spend much time in activities that are not rewarded in some fashion or other. If the education of undergraduate students is an important part of an institution's mission, then a redefinition of the faculty role and a restructuring of the faculty reward system, particularly at large universities, may be needed to restore undergraduate education to a position of prominence.

Review Faculty Recruiting and Hiring Criteria, Policies, and Practices. Care should be taken in hiring new faculty members. Important messages about what is and is not valued by an institution are given to candidates for faculty positions. Are candidates asked to make a presentation to undergraduate students, as well as to current faculty members and graduate students? Is evidence of teaching competence required as part of a candidate's dossier, and taken as seriously as evidence of scholarly competence and pro-ductivity?

Assign the Department's Best Teachers to the Introductory Courses Most Likely to Be Taken by New Students. This sug-gestion is likely to benefit not only new students but also the de-partment. It is in the introductory courses that future majors and graduate students are recruited. A student whose first exposure to a discipline is a negative one is unlikely to pursue that discipline fur-ther. Too much is at stake for the job to be left to amateurs or drones.

Review Course-placement Processes and Criteria. Success in the early weeks and months of a semester appears to be important in students' continued interest, involvement, and persistence in the academic setting. How seriously taken is the task of finding the best match between new students' interests and abilities and the courses they are required to take?

No doubt there are other steps that faculty members and administrators can take to ease new students' transition to college. In some respects, the matter boils down to individual and institu-tional will to contribute to student learning. In the successful tran-sition experiences that students described to us, success hung on whether someone inside or outside the college cared enough to put students and their education ahead of other things.

References

Astin, A. W. (1985). *Achieving educational excellence*. San Francisco: Jossey-Bass.
Belenky, M. F., Clinchy, B. M., Goldberger, N. R., & Tarule, J. M. (1986). *Women's ways of knowing: The development of self, voice, and mind*. New York: Basic Books.
Goodsell, A., Maher, M., & Tinto, V. (1992). *Collaborative learning in higher edu-cation: A sourcebook*. University Park, PA: Pennsylvania State Uni-versity, National Center on Postsecondary Teaching, Learning, and Assessment.

Light, R. J. (1990). *The Harvard assessment seminars: Explorations with students and faculty about teaching, learning, and student life*. Cambridge, MA: Harvard University, Graduate School of Education and Kennedy School of Government.

London, H. (1989). Breaking away: A study of first-generation college students and their families. *American Journal of Education*, 144–170.

Noel, L., Levitz, R., & Saluri, D. (Eds.). (1985). *Increasing student retention: Effective programs and practices for reducing the dropout rate*. San Francisco: Jossey-Bass.

Pace, C. R. (1984). *Measuring the quality of college student experiences*. Los Angeles: University of California at Los Angeles, Graduate School of Education, Higher Education Research Institute.

Pascarella, E. T., & Terenzini, P. T. (1991). *How college affects students: Findings and insights from 20 years of research*. San Francisco: Jossey-Bass.

Study Group on the Conditions of Excellence in American Higher Education. (1984). *Involvement in learning: Realizing the potential of American higher education*. Washington, DC: U.S. Department of Education, National Institute of Education.

Tinto, V. (1987). *Leaving college: Rethinking the causes and cures of student attrition*. Chicago: University of Chicago Press.

Upcraft, M. L., & Gardner, J. N. (Eds.). (1989). *The freshman year experience: Helping students survive and succeed in college*. San Francisco: Jossey-Bass.

Chapter Four

Student Motivation from the Teacher's Perspective

Raymond P. Perry, Verena H. Menec,
C. Ward Struthers
University of Manitoba

At no time in a student's education is independence and self-initiative more important than during the college years. Whether writing essays, giving oral presentations, or forming social relationships, a student is expected to acquire new skills and apply them effectively during the academic career. However, many college students do not or cannot adjust to the increased demands for autonomy, thereby placing their success in college at risk. Thus alongside the enthusiastic, determined, and responsible students sit apathetic, bored, and failure-prone students, intermingled with others somewhere between the two extremes. For college teachers, the challenge is to respond to this diversity of learning needs by offering learning opportunities responsive to them.

The challenge raises two key questions: What factors explain these differences between students? and, How does teaching relate to the factors? In studying these differences, Britton and Tesser (1991) estimate that precollege aptitude scores predict no more than 20 percent of variability in later college grades. This makes

Note: Support for this chapter was provided by the Social Sciences and Humanities Research Council of Canada (SSHRCC) in the form of a research grant (#410–91–1296) to the senior author and SSHRCC doctoral fellowships to the junior authors. Correspondence regarding the chapter should be addressed to Raymond P. Perry, Centre for Higher Education Research and Development, University of Manitoba, Winnipeg, Manitoba, Canada R3T 2N2.

motivation a prime candidate for explaining some of the remaining 80 percent and an obvious answer to the first question. With motivation that important, the second question should focus on how student motivation relates to various teaching methods. Said succinctly, differences in motivation may cause some students to respond well and others poorly to the same teaching method. A related implication involves the potential of some methods to reduce differences in motivation.

Understanding what student motivation is and how it relates to teaching provides the impetus for this chapter. We begin by considering student motivation in terms of implicit theories of teaching that guide daily instructional practices. Following this is a theoretical and empirical analysis of the cognitive, emotional, and behavioral antecedents of student motivation. Two motivational profiles of students emerge: helplessness and mastery. Finally, two solutions are proposed as solutions to the negative motivation patterns of students: attributional retraining and the modification of specific teaching practices.

The Teaching-Motivation Connection

The connection between teaching and motivation relates directly to what teachers see as their primary role. Weiner (1990) distinguishes between professors who believe their job is to teach their discipline and those who claim it is to teach *students* their discipline. It is this subtle but critical difference in focus—teaching *content* versus teaching *students*—that raises the issue of motivation. To teach students requires not just mastery of the subject matter but also an understanding of students and how they learn.

These philosophical debates about the role of teaching often arise from the models faculty use to guide their teaching practices. Derived from on-the-job experiences and folk wisdom, these experiential models become the basis for much of what faculty purport to do in the classroom. Aptly labeled "implicit theories of teaching" by Gage (1978), these experiential models orient instructors in their approach to classroom dynamics much as other attitudes, beliefs, and expectations do and thereby direct social discourse. It is at this very basic level that student motivation receives a dramatically different emphasis.

Roughly speaking, the difference is revealed in three distinct models of teaching.

The Information Model of Teaching. Professors endorsing an information model see their role as imparting vital information that develops the student's knowledge base. Motivating students is not part of that role, since students are mature adults and "should be there to learn." Voluminous amounts of course material do not permit a preoccupation with issues of motivation. Imparting essential information is the primary objective.

The Motivation Model. In contrast, those who subscribe to a motivation model see themselves as instilling in students a desire to learn. Since the information is already available in the textbook, the library readings, or electronic databases, their role is to motivate the students to *want* to acquire that information. Teaching methods depart markedly from the *information* model. Here, the objective is to excite, to motivate, to "turn on" students. If students go to coffee after class and discuss issues raised during class (rather than the last football game, the weekend party, or their amorous adventures), then the professor has accomplished an important teaching objective.

The Dual-Process Model. A more holistic approach is taken by those espousing a dual-process model of teaching. Simply stated, at its most fundamental level this model proposes that teaching consists of informing and motivating students during the course of a lecture and throughout the semester. "Which students to inform, which to motivate, when, and how much" is the essence of this model. Unlike the previous two, the dual-process model requires a keen sense of timing and balance between informing and motivating. An English grammar course for science students may require considerable effort by the professor both to inform and to motivate, whereas an anatomy course for medical students may entail little of either. Likewise, curriculum and student differences may cause a psychology professor to place less emphasis on motivation and more on information, while a philosophy professor may focus less on information and more on motivation. In all, the real issue is not whether motivation is important to effective teaching but when and how much.

Aside from these anecdotal models, other sources of information about effective teaching inform classroom practice. Though it may be surprising to some faculty, seventy years of research on college teaching (McKeachie, 1990) reveals a critical core of empirical evidence on teaching effectiveness in the college classroom (see, for example, Cohen, 1981; Costin, Greenough, and Menges, 1971; Marsh, 1984; Marsh and Dunkin, 1992; McKeachie, 1963; McKeachie and Kulik, 1975; Murray, 1991). Multiple indicators of scholastic attainment, many of which have an implicit or explicit motivational component, have been examined in relation to specific teaching behaviors; for example, both student achievement and student attrition presuppose a prior level of motivation that can enhance subsequent performance and increase willingness to attend classes. Consequently, this empirical literature is a valuable source of information about college teaching and student motivation, apart from experiential models. More will be said about the empirical approach in subsequent sections of this chapter.

Two of the three experiential models imply that increased motivation has direct, positive consequences on academic achievement and the more intangible benefits associated with a commitment to learning and education. Motivation also mediates student achievement in the empirical approach. But whichever perspective is taken, experiential or empirical, the desirability of motivation is abundantly clear. Any attempt to address motivation in the college classroom must take into account the teaching-motivation connection.

Student Motivation

Motivation has been a major research topic since the inception of psychology as a science over one hundred years ago. In fact, psychologists have long considered motivation to be the driving force behind much of human endeavor. For them, human motivation results from biological, emotional, and social factors that instigate, direct, and maintain behavior. In this chapter, however, we consider only that small part of the motivation literature directly related to academic achievement.

Two issues of interest to educational researchers and classroom practitioners underlie recent models of achievement motivation. First, motivation arises from sources both inside and outside a person. When motivation results from those sources inside the person, the student is seen as an *active*, rather than passive, participant in the learning process (Zimmerman and Schunk, 1989). External factors affecting student motivation include classroom characteristics such as instruction methods, curriculum structure, or peer pressure. Second, motivation tends to be *domain-specific*. The bored and apathetic student enrolled in a history class might be highly committed in a mathematics course or excel in physical education.

Historically characterized in terms of arousal, energy, or persistence, motivation was thought to result from achievement or from time spent on a task (Ames, 1984). However, the limitations of this view have become apparent. Consider two students who study equally hard for an upcoming test. In the traditional view, both would be described as highly motivated and would be expected to do well. Recent research indicates, however, that this is not necessarily the case (Covington, 1993). Let us assume, for example, that the two students have different *reasons* for studying. The first may be concerned only with getting a good grade, whereas the second may study out of interest in the material. These different reasons will have a profound impact on future study efforts. While the latter student is likely to continue learning activities such as reading textbooks and research articles, the former is unlikely to do so.

To better explain these complexities, researchers have started to incorporate constructs such as attributions, affects, expectations, and goals (Ames and Archer, 1988; Dweck and Leggett, 1988; Weiner, 1986). This approach allows them to identify adaptive versus maladaptive motivational patterns and better understand the origins of these motivational patterns. One factor that is increasingly being recognized as important is perceived control (see Figure 4.1 and Table 4.1). As Table 4.1 (left column, 'Helpless Students') shows, a low sense of control can lead to a variety of outcomes that together form a negative motivation profile. In contrast, students with a greater sense of perceived control are apt to see the situation very differently (right column,'Mastery Students')—that attending class, taking notes, and studying for tests and exams lead to academic success. Thus students with a higher sense of perceived control think, feel, and respond differently when faced with academic challenges than students with a lower sense of perceived control. These reactions are discussed in more detail subsequently.

Cognitions: An Attributional Analysis

How students explain their performance on achievement-related tasks has direct implications for student motivation. Several theoretical models, among them learned-helplessness theory (Abramson, Seligman, and Teasdale, 1978), self-efficacy theory (Bandura, 1982; Schunk, 1985), and attribution theory (Weiner, 1986), help to account for and explain the reasons students give for their success or lack of it. Weiner's (1986) attribution theory is especially useful. He points out that people routinely try to explain outcomes, particularly if they are important, negative, or unexpected. The

Figure 4.1.   Perceived Control.

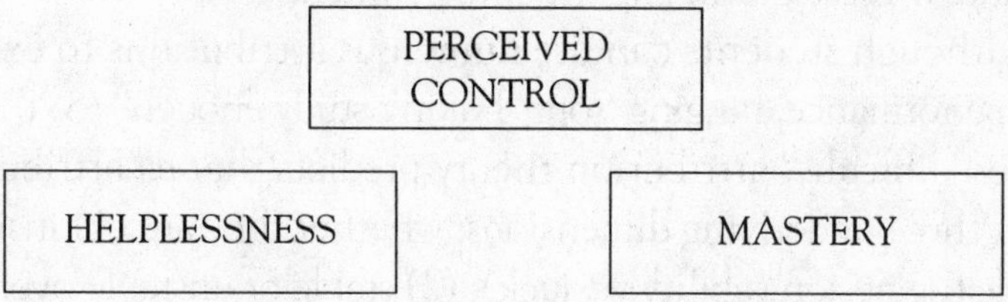

```
            ┌─────────────────┐
            │    PERCEIVED    │
            │    CONTROL      │
            └─────────────────┘

┌─────────────────┐       ┌─────────────────┐
│  HELPLESSNESS   │       │    MASTERY      │
└─────────────────┘       └─────────────────┘
```

- At-risk
  High-risk
  Learning-disabled
  Educationally disadvantaged

- Educationally gifted
  Educationally exceptional

- Related constructs in which motivational deficits comprise a
  significant part of the construct

Table 4.1.   Profiles of Helpless and Mastery Students.

Helpless Students	*Mastery Students*
1. Lack of ability responsible for failure	1. Lack of effort responsible for failure
2. Goal is to get good grades	2. Goal is to increase competence
3. Develops negative emotions toward task	3. Welcomes challenge of task
4. Attempts to withdraw from failure situation physically and psychologically	4. Intensifies efforts when experiencing failure
5. Fails to develop effective problem-solving strategies	5. Develops effective problem-solving strategies to reduce failure and increase success
6. Prior successes forgotten and/or viewed as irrelevant to future success	6. Past successes remembered and considered relevant to future performance
7. Loses concentration and focus for learning tasks	7. Focuses attention and concentration on learning tasks

realities that students may need to explain include such outcomes as grades on tests, term papers, or assignments.

Although students can use numerous attributions to explain their performance, ranging from "I didn't study enough" to "the test was too difficult," attribution theory predicts that *all* attributions reflect three underlying dimensions: whether they are (1) inside or outside the person (ability vs. luck), (2) stable or unstable over time (ability vs. test difficulty), and (3) controllable or uncontrollable by the individual (effort vs. luck). These dimensions of locus, stability, and controllability then influence expectations of future success and individual effectiveness.

The different consequences of ability versus effort following failure lie at the heart of the helpless-and-mastery distinction (Dweck, 1975; Diener and Dweck, 1978). Consider the student who receives a low grade on a test and concludes that it resulted from his or her lack of ability. Such an attribution implies that failure will reoccur no matter what the student does or how hard she or he tries. As a result, self-esteem is lowered and expectations of success in the future are reduced. In effect, the student says, "Why bother trying since I'm going to fail anyway?" Not surprisingly, such a helpless-oriented student is likely to perform poorly on future tests. In contrast, mastery-oriented students tend to attribute failure to lack of effort, thereby maintaining expectations for success. In the future they are more likely to expend the effort success requires.

Emotions: A Self-Worth Analysis

A second aspect of the helpless-and-mastery distinction is related to students' self-esteem or sense of self-worth (Covington, 1993). Covington argues that students attempt to maintain and promote a positive sense of self-worth at all costs. In his research, he has identified a number of coping strategies that enable them to do so, even though these strategies are often self-defeating in the long run. Self-worth theory hinges on the assumption that students' self-worth frequently becomes tied to their ability to perform well in school or college. If they do well, it is because of high ability; if they perform poorly, they don't have the ability. Because of these assumptions, students make it a priority to avoid failure, or to fail without appearing stupid.

This dynamic explains why expending effort can become a double-edged sword (Covington and Omelich, 1979). Trying hard and failing reflects negatively on one's abilities and consequently one's sense of self-worth, which may well be what happens to the student who has put a lot of effort into studying for a test and yet receives a low grade.

One strategy, albeit a questionable one, that students sometimes use to avoid this dilemma involves working as little as possible. If failure results, it can be attributed to lack of effort, rather than lack of ability, thereby protecting their self-esteem. Alternatively, students may *appear* to try less hard, reflected in their frequent comments about how little they have studied for an upcoming test. Of course, this provides an excellent excuse for failure, and in the event of success it contributes to the impression of superior ability. Procrastination may serve a similar purpose (Covington, 1993). Cramming for a test or allowing only a few days for writing a major term paper appears to be self-defeating. However, from a self-worth perspective, procrastination may help to protect the student's sense of self-worth, since a low grade can readily be attributed to lack of studying and preparation.

In addition to these "self-handicapping" (Covington, 1993) strategies, students may alternatively maximize their chances to succeed. Some consistently choose easy courses that are quite below their capabilities. They routinely withdraw upon learning that a course involves difficult tests or assignments.

To conclude, self-worth theory posits that students differ in terms of their *reasons* for learning. These reasons can either interfere with or facilitate motivation and academic achievement. Students concerned only with obtaining good grades often feel threatened by the possibility of failure and as a consequence may study less and avoid challenges. The alternative to this maladaptive approach is a learning orientation based on increasing competence. These students choose challenging courses and put effort into learning the material in order to have positive feelings about academic tasks. Such a motivational profile greatly improves their chances of success in their academic careers.

Behavior: A Learning Strategies Approach

To this point, we have focused on the cognitive and affective factors that are responsible for student motivation (Weiner, 1986). It is equally important, however, to consider students' behavioral responses toward achievement tasks, specifically their learning strategies (Pintrich, 1989). Learning strategies and achievement motivation are frequently treated as separate topics, although they are, of course, interrelated. That is, students with a low sense of control, who believe that their efforts will not contribute to success, are unlikely to make use of effective learning strategies. Alternatively, even though mastery-oriented students may be highly motivated, learning will be difficult if they lack adequate study skills. As a consequence, students' perceived control is thought to mediate use of learning strategies, with mastery orientation being necessary but not sufficient for academic success. In college, students are expected to assume greater responsibility for their education than in high school. However, college teachers rarely teach students how to take notes or read text material. Using effective learning strategies, therefore, becomes essential for their academic success.

The literature on learning strategies is voluminous and describes numerous techniques, ranging from specific skills (for example, note taking and test taking) to cognitive and metacognitive activities, such as selective attention and self-monitoring (Dansereau, 1985; Kiewra, 1987). More basically, however, learning involves a number of information-processing activities, including among others attending to and concentrating on the task at hand, processing course content, and storing relevant information in memory. Whether students effectively engage in these information-processing activities depends in part on their level of motivation. Highly motivated students, such as mastery-oriented students, should be better at concentrating on tasks, processing information, and remembering the material.

Students' learning activities are also influenced by teaching practices that can either hinder or facilitate information processing in students. During a lecture, for example, students are required to attend selectively to the lecture content, a task that involves blocking out both internal distractions (thoughts of partying, romance, or an upcoming exam) and external distractions (noise in the classroom) (Corno, 1989; Kuhl, 1985). Teaching strategies (such as vocal inflection or humor) focus students' attention on the lecture, thereby diminishing the effect of the distractions. Similarly, the instructor who provides examples or analogies can facilitate students' memory of the material. Conversely, of course, instructors can hinder information-processing activities. For example, the teacher who lectures in a monotone and is disorganized makes it more difficult for students to listen and identify critical ideas. Ultimately, however, the success of teaching practices rests on how well an instructor can adapt such methods to the needs of his or her students. This interaction between teaching practices and student characteristics is discussed in more detail in the next section.

In sum, researchers have identified a number of factors critical to student motivation and academic achievement, including attributions, expectations, emotions, and learning strategies. The literature indicates that students' attributions for achievement-related events affect their expectations of future success as well as their emotions. Expectations and emotions, in turn, contribute to students' use of effective learning strategies and, ultimately, their success in college.

We have further argued that these cognitive, emotional, and behavioral responses, resulting from students' perceived control, influence students' motivation and academic development. Helpless students believe that they will fail, regardless of how hard they try or how much they study. They attribute failure to lack of ability and are unlikely to make use of effective learning strategies, with potential consequences ranging from failure on future tests to absenteeism and dropping out. In contrast, mastery-oriented students attribute failure to lack of effort and therefore study to become competent or skilled in a given area, as well as employ effective learning strategies. As a result, they are more likely to succeed in college.

Student Motivation and Instruction

To complicate matters further, helpless students learn little from otherwise effective instruction, in contrast to mastery students (Perry, 1985; 1991). The typical pattern of low motivation, negative affect, and poor performance characteristics of at-risk college students can occur even in the presence of high-quality teaching. An explanation of these findings follows, along with some suggestions about what instructors can do to resolve the dilemma.

Loss of Control and Motivation

Although perceived control is important across all levels of education, it is more important during the college years. In college, students make choices about their courses, instructors, and academic majors. They face personal and academic challenges including exams, pop quizzes, and disorganized instruction, all of which cause them to experience a loss of control.

Sometimes a student's motivation, self-esteem, and personal identity hinge precariously on these capricious experiences; in some cases, the latest test score is the most current measure. Paradoxically, while perceived control is most important to academic development at the college level, it is here that the student's sense of control is subject to greatest threat.

Our research (Perry, 1991) makes clear that classroom factors that cause loss of control have three qualities in common. First, they are likely to be unpredictable events, for example, pop quizzes. Second, they create the impression that the student can do little to change them, as in the case of poor instruction or difficult course content. Third, their occurrence is usually the prelude to a negative outcome, particularly failure on a test or social rejection. Together, these qualities engender loss of control in students and result in helplessness, which erodes a student's overall achievement motivation.

It is also clear that certain psychological qualities within students predispose them to loss of control. The common denominator between these qualities is a set of beliefs that imply that the student has little influence over his or her academic development. In the case of the locus-of-control construct, external-locus students believe that much of what happens in their academic world, good or bad, is the product of external factors, such as the professor, other students, or course content (Perry and Magnusson, 1989). Some students exhibit beliefs that disavow hard-driving, aggressive, goal-oriented behavior and thereby make them more prone to academic failure (Perry and Tunna, 1988).

Attributional style can also cause loss of control in students who attribute academic failure to the difficulty of the test (Perry and Magnusson, 1989). In these cases, the common ingredient is a belief pattern portraying disinterest or inability to personally influence academic developments, coupled with the view that such events are determined by outside forces. These belief patterns can precipitate loss of control, culminating in helplessness and lack of motivation.

In our work, we have found that some college students can enhance their motivation and perform well despite threats to their control. We believe these students possess certain characteristics that shield or *buffer* them from the negative effects of academic failure. Apparently, these students think differently and possess personalitylike qualities, such as an optimistic view of life, an internal locus of control, or a feeling of self-worth, that insulate them from the demotivating effects of failure (Aspinwall and Taylor, 1992; Perry, 1991).

Mastery students who experience test failure attribute poor performance to lack of study effort or inappropriate use of study strategies. Consequently, they are more likely to remain motivated to study for subsequent tests, whereas helpless students who fail a test are more likely to be less motivated because the experience makes them believe they do not have the ability to succeed. Of course, these patterns vary depending on the quality of instruction that students experience. In spite of being in control, many college students who fail a test and face ineffective instruction are motivationally at-risk, indicating that there is only so much of the motivational and achievement burden that we can ask our students to bear.

Effective Instruction and Motivation

Generally, researchers interested in the connection between college instruction and student motivation have examined what instructors do in the classroom and the effect they have on students. In particular, considerable attention has been given to student achievement, an outcome variable that reflects motivation antecedents. To illustrate, in an extensive reanalysis of research on effective instruction, Feldman (1989) reviewed thirty-two meta-analysis studies and found several teaching behaviors to be significantly correlated with student achievement: organization, clarity,

Table 4.2. The Relation Between Teaching Behaviors and Achievement.

Teaching Behavior[a]	Correlation Achievement[b]
Organization/Structure	.55 (30.3%)
• The presentation of the material is well organized.	
• The instructor plans the activities of each class period in detail.	
Clarity/Skill	.51 (26.0%)
• The instructor makes good use of examples and illustrations to get across difficult points.	
• The teacher effectively synthesizes and summarizes the material.	
Interaction	.45 (20.3%)
• Students feel free to ask questions or express opinions.	
• The instructor stimulates class discussion.	
Stimulation	.38 (14.4%)
• The teacher gets students interested in the subject.	
• It is easy to remain attentive.	
Elocution	.35(12.3%)
• The teacher has the ability to speak distinctly and be clearly heard.	
• The instructor changes pitch, volume, or quality of speech.	
Feedback	.29 (8.4%)
• The teacher tells students when they have done a good job.	
• The teacher is prompt in returning tests and assignments.	

Source: Modification of Table 4.3 (Perry, 1991, p. 20).

[a]Teaching behaviors and examples taken from Cohen (1987) and Feldman (1989).

[b]Average correlation coefficients between student ratings of the teaching behavior and student achievement (Cohen, 1987; Feldman, 1989). The numbers in parentheses refer to the percent of variance explained by each dimension.

interaction, stimulation, elocution, and feedback. Table 4.2 summarizes these findings.

The left-hand column lists various teaching behaviors and examples of specific questionnaire items. The right-hand column presents a value for each behavior, obtained by correlating the class-average ratings of the behavior with end-of-term class-average achievement results. Thus, a correlation of +.55 for instructor organization indicates that being well organized and planning class activities in detail are likely to contribute to higher student achievement. The +.35 correlation for instructor elocution suggests that speaking clearly and varying one's speech also may contribute to better achievement, but the relation is not as strong as for instructor organization. Based on this information, instructor organization and instructor elocution would both be considered integral to effective college teaching, but organization would be judged as more important.

Effective Teaching and Those Who Need It Most

Common sense suggests that one sure way to assist students academically is to teach better, a solution especially pertinent to failing students. As expected, findings confirm that mastery students who receive expressive instruction perform better than those who have an unexpressive instructor (see Figure 4.2). Helpless students, on the other hand, perform poorly regardless of the quality of instruction. More importantly, even when they experience optimal learning conditions, such as expressive instruction, their motivation and achievement remain paradoxically lowered. As Perry and Penner (1990) claim, "students who are most in need of effective teaching are least likely to gain from it" (p. 262).

Theoretically, one would expect that effective instruction should overcome the debilitating motivational deficits experienced by helpless students. In practice, however, a different pattern emerges. First, college students who lack control over their academic performance can be deprived of the motivational benefits of

Figure 4.2.   The Teaching–Perceived-Control Interaction.

A perceived control by instruction interaction in which helplessness (noncontingent feedback) students are unable to benefit from effective (high expressive) teaching.

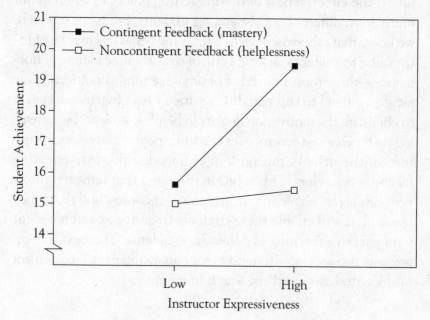

Instructor Expressiveness

Notes: Mastery may result from contingent feedback, internal locus of control, Type A behavior, and so forth.

Helplessness may result from noncontingent feedback, external locus of control, and so forth.

effective instruction because of their belief patterns (for instance, external locus). Second, students who have a sense of mastery can be disadvantaged motivationally when they face an unexpressive instructor. However, it is the helpless students who suffer more, since they do not have the internal qualities to succeed; nor do they benefit from optimal learning conditions.

In sum, empirical results support the motivational effects of perceived control, expressive instruction, and their interaction. As such, student dispositions and instructional quality are not as useful on their own as they are together in explaining student motivation.

Responding to Differences in Student Motivation

As previously noted, one of the most challenging tasks facing faculty is the effectiveness of their teaching practices when major motivation differences exist among students. From our research, we know that otherwise-effective teaching behaviors may be of little value to students lacking control over their academic performance—those most in need of optimal learning conditions. How faculty respond to this paradox is critical. An obvious solution is to eliminate the motivation deficits in helpless students by increasing their perceived control over academic performance. Once eliminated, the deficits can no longer impede otherwise-effective teaching behaviors. This solution presumes that remedial interventions are available to restore perceived control and that, once restored, it will enable these students to derive as much benefit from effective teaching as do mastery students. The next section presents two specific alternatives for enhancing perceived control in students, based on the research literature.

Enhancing Motivation Through Perceived Control

The two techniques described here were selected because they share a common quality: their potential to enhance perceived control in students, to move them from the helpless to the mastery end of the continuum.

The first technique, known as *attributional retraining*, is a remedial intervention derived from attribution theory (Weiner, 1986). It aims to change students' maladaptive thoughts about their successes and failures, thereby elevating their perceived control.

The second technique involves a systematic analysis of common teaching practices in terms of their impact on students' perceived control. Whenever perceived control is jeopardized, changes should be considered expressly to restore control.

Attributional Retraining. Faculty frequently observe that test results affect students differently. Poor performance can demotivate some, energize others, or create hostility in still others. Success seems to have equally variable consequences. As noted previously, students' explanations of their successes and failures can enhance or diminish their perceived control over their academic tasks, leading to corresponding increases or decreases in motivation and performance. Many faculty find themselves trying to assist students who appear destined for self-defeat.

For these professors, attribution theory provides an opportunity to intercede with their students using attributional retraining (Försterling, 1985; Weiner, 1986). The procedure is a highly structured, remedial intervention designed to change faulty thought patterns. Its goal is to alter undesirable attributions of success and failure to ones having positive academic outcomes. Attributing success to luck or attributing failure to lack of ability can have dire consequences for motivation and achievement striving. In each case, attribution creates the impression that achieving the goal is beyond the student's control.

These maladaptive attributions, however, can be changed to desirable ones. A "luck" attribution is replaced with a "high ability" one, "lack of ability" with a "poor strategy" attribution, and desired motivational change results (see Table 4.3). Under normal circumstances, attributional retraining is provided by trained therapists during several therapy sessions. The therapist communicates the desired attributions, while the client is engaged in structured cognitive exercises. Through repeated exchanges and analysis, the client eventually incorporates the desired attributions.

Similar dynamics occur between faculty and students, as students attempt to make sense of their academic performance. During and after class, faculty often hear students claim: "I don't have the smarts to do well," "I was lucky this time," or "This course is too difficult." Hearing these maladaptive attributions, the instructor is

Table 4.3.   Interventions: Attributional Retraining.

Achievement Results	Student Explanation	Perceived Control	Motivation and Achievement-striving
Success	luck[a]	Helplessness	lack of approach toward achievement tasks
Failure	lack of ability	Helplessness	lack of persistence, avoidance of achievement tasks
		Desirable	
Success	high ability	Mastery	approach toward achievement task
Failure	lack of effort	Mastery	persistence, approach toward achievement tasks

Source: Cognitive restructuring of undesirable success-and-failure attributions to desirable ones. Taken from Försterling (1985).

[a]*Note:* There is a distinction between "It was luck" versus "I am a lucky person."

ideally situated to engage in some rudimentary attributional retraining. The instructor can encourage the student to think differently about the test or course by suggesting a more desirable attribution: "If you didn't have the smarts, you wouldn't be here"; "Forget luck; what about your effort?" or "Difficult courses get easier with enough effort." These informal, often spontaneous exchanges provide the opportunity for the instructor to apply some basic elements of attributional retraining.

Obviously, these brief encounters cannot duplicate the structure and precision of formal attributional-retraining sessions. For an analysis of the many critical differences between formal training sessions and the brief exchanges that occur in the college classroom, see Perry and others (1993). In judging the utility of formal training, however, consider the impact of desirable attributions in contrast to comments faculty can and do sometimes make: "Only those who have the 'right stuff' will pass this course"; "The next exam will separate the wheat from the chaff"; "You'll be lucky to get through this course." The impact of such attributional statements on student motivation and self-worth can be devastating.

Likewise, the ethical implications of these admonitions require careful scrutiny. In some instances, they are seemingly well intended though misdirected (to motivate students by challenging them); in others they are inspired by more sinister motives of power or dominance. However, assiduous application of attributional retraining offers the potential to make a difference: for helpless students by increasing their motivation, and for faculty by reducing the motivational complexity of their classrooms.

Analysis of Teaching Practices. It is no surprise to faculty that their teaching practices do not have equally positive, universal effects on all students. It is disquieting, however, when they have serious negative effects, even opposite to those desired. In fact, some teaching practices intended to motivate students actually curtail their achievement striving, as we have seen with some attributional statements made by instructors. Accordingly, teaching practices require careful scrutiny to determine their impact on students' perceived control and subsequent motivation.

An analysis of teaching practices begins by identifying those considered most instrumental to one's model of effective instruction. Specific practices are usually associated with different aspects of a course, involving organization, content, assessment, feedback, and so on. Assessment, for example, generally includes several practices such as pop quizzes, scheduled tests, and homework assignments. Each practice should be examined in terms of its intended objectives and whether they have been achieved. The pop quiz is a teaching practice that will serve to illustrate this point. As Table 4.4 shows, a pop quiz may be intended to motivate students, to focus student attention, to accentuate the importance of the course, or to accustom the student to unexpected demands. Although all

Table 4.4.   Teaching Practices Assumed to Influence Student Academic Development: Pop Quiz.

Intended Objectives	Perceived Control Consequences	Resolutions
• to motivate student through anticipation or anxiety • to focus student's attention on course • to emphasize importance of keeping up in course • to accustom student to unexpected academic demands and challenges	*Positive* • anticipation and excitement about meeting challenge • increased commitment excelling in course *Negative* • uncertainty and loss of control • anxiety, threat, and foreboding directed towards course and professor • problems with assignments and attending classes, perceived control	• determine degree of positive versus negative developments • if largely *positive* then continue. for small minority who have problems, approach directly • if largely *negative* then modify by a) aborting, or b) approaching class directly • if b), then discuss objectives (column 2) • if b), provide interventions for enhancing

positive, these objectives may not all be realized, as suggested in column two of the table. Negative consequences are also possible in the form of uncertainty and loss of control, negative emotions, and course attrition.

Column two of the table indicates that if the consequences are positive, practice should be continued. Negative consequences signal the need to abort the practice or, if continued, to compensate with other practices, such as attributional retraining, as described previously. Such an analysis of teaching practices provides a better fit between intended objectives (column one) and consequences (column two) through specific modifications (column three). The end result is an increased sense of control for more students, leading to a better motivation profile of the entire class.

A Role for Faculty Developers and Administrators

In the previous section, we have described some teaching techniques designed to enhance students' perceived control. Of course, effective use of such methods requires a solid grounding in the notions of perceived control, helplessness, and mastery, and their effects on student motivation and learning. Faculty developers can play an important role in conveying this information to faculty, the goal being to equip them with specific techniques designed to remediate helplessness and optimize mastery orientation in students.

For administrators, an understanding of the teaching-motivation connection can provide the impetus for developing effective instructional policies. Policies designed to improve the quality of teaching would adjust working conditions so that faculty are able to place greater emphasis on the benefits of perceived control for student motivation. Administrators need to support training opportunities for faculty. The potential consequences of such policies include better faculty morale, but perhaps more importantly, enhanced student motivation and learning.

References

Abramson, L. Y., Seligman, M., & Teasdale, J. (1978). Learned helplessness in humans: Critique and reformulation. *Journal of Abnormal Psychology*, 87, 49–74.

Ames, C. (1984). Achievement attributions and self-instructions under competitive and individualistic goal structures. *Journal of Educational Psychology*, 76, 478–487.

Ames, C., & Archer, J. (1988). Achievement goals in the classroom: Students' learning strategies and motivation processes. *Journal of Educational Psychology*, 80, 260–267.

Aspinwall, L. G., & Taylor, S. E. (1992). Modelling cognitive adaptation: A longitudinal investigation of the impact of individual differences and coping on college adjustment and performance. *Journal of Personality and Social Psychology, 63,* 989–1003.

Bandura, A. (1982). Self-efficacy mechanisms in human agency. *American Psychologist, 37,* 122–147.

Britton, B. K., & Tesser, A. (1991). Effects of time-management practices on college grades. *Journal of Educational Psychology, 83,* 405–410.

Cohen, P. A. (1981). Student ratings of instruction and student achievement. *Review of Educational Research, 51,* 281–309.

Cohen, P. A. (1987). A critical analysis and reanalysis of the multisection validity meta-analysis. Paper presented at the 1987 Annual Meeting of the American Educational Research Association, Washington, D.C. (ED 283 876).

Corno, L. (1989). Self-regulated learning: A volitional analysis. In B. Zimmerman & D. Schunk (Eds.), *Self-regulated learning and academic achievement: Theory, research, and practice* (pp. 111–141). Orlando: Academic Press.

Costin, F., Greenough, W. T., & Menges, R. J. (1971). Student ratings of college teaching: Reliability, validity and usefulness. *Review of Educational Research, 41,* 411–435.

Covington, M. V. (1993). A motivational analysis of academic life in college. In J. Smart (Ed.), *Higher education: Handbook of theory and research* (pp. 50–93). San Francisco: Jossey-Bass.

Covington, M. V., & Omelich, C. L. (1979). Effort: The double-edged sword in school achievement. *Journal of Educational Psychology, 71,* 169–182.

Dansereau, D. F. (1985). Learning strategy research. In J. W. Segal, S. F. Chipman, & R. Glaser (Eds.), *Thinking and learning skills: Vol. 1. Relating instruction to research* (pp. 209–239). Hillsdale, NJ: Erlbaum.

Diener, C. I., & Dweck, C. S. (1978). An analysis of learned helplessness: Continuous changes in performance strategy and achievement cognitions following failure. *Journal of Personality and Social Psychology, 36,* 451–462.

Dweck, C. S. (1975). The role of expectations and attributions in the alleviation of learned helplessness. *Journal of Personality and Social Psychology, 31,* 674–695.

Dweck, C. S., & Leggett, E. L. (1988). A social-cognitive approach to motivation and personality. *Psychological Review, 95,* 256–273.

Feldman, K. A. (1989). The association between student ratings of specific instructional dimensions and student achievement: Refining and extending the synthesis of data from multisection validity studies. *Research in Higher Education, 30*(6), 583–645.

Försterling, F. (1985). Attributional retraining: A review. *Psychological Bulletin, 98,* 495–512.

Gage, N. L. (1978). *The scientific basis of the art of teaching.* New York: Teachers College Press.

Kiewra, K. A. (1987). Notetaking and review: The research and its implications. *Instructional Science*, 16, 233–249.

Kuhl, J. (1985). Volitional mediators of cognition-behavior consistency: Self-regulatory processes and action versus state orientation. In J. Kuhl & J. Beckmann (Eds.), *Action control: From cognition to behavior* (pp. 101–128). Berlin: Springer-Verlag.

Marsh, H. (1984). Students' evaluations of university teaching: Dimensionality, reliability, validity, potential biases, and utility. *Journal of Educational Psychology*, 76, 707–754.

Marsh, H. W., & Dunkin, M. J. (1992). Students' evaluations of university teaching: A multidimensional perspective. In J. Smart (Ed.), *Higher education: Handbook of theory and research* (Vol. 8). New York: Agathon Press.

McKeachie, W. J. (1963). Research on teaching at the college and university level. In N. L. Gage (Ed.), *Handbook of research on teaching*. Chicago: Rand McNally.

McKeachie, W. J. (1990). Research on college teaching: The historical background. *Journal of Educational Psychology*, 82, 189–200.

McKeachie, W. J., & Kulik, J. A. (1975). Effectiveness in college teaching. In F. N. Kerlinger (Ed.), *Review of Research in Education* (Vol. 3, pp. 165–209). Itasca, IL: Peacock.

Murray, H. G. (1991). Effective teaching behaviors in the college classroom. In J. Smart (Ed.), *Higher education: Handbook of theory and research* (Vol. 7, pp. 135–172). New York: Agathon Press.

Perry, R. P. (1985). Instructor expressiveness: Implications for improving teaching. In J. Donald & A. Sullivan (Eds.), *Using research to improve teaching* (pp. 35–49). San Francisco: Jossey-Bass.

Perry, R. P. (1991). Perceived control in college students: Implications for instruction in higher education. In J. Smart (Ed.), *Higher Education: Handbook of Theory and Research* (Vol. 7, pp. 1–56). New York: Agathon Press.

Perry, R. P., Hechter, F. J., Menec, V. H., & Weinberg, L. E. (1993). Enhancing achievement motivation and performance in college students: An attributional retraining perspective. *Research in Higher Education*, 34, 687–720.

Perry, R. P., & Magnusson, J.-L. (1989). Causal attributions and perceived performance: Consequences for college students' achievement and perceived control in different instructional conditions. *Journal of Educational Psychology*, 81, 164–172.

Perry, R. P., & Penner, K. S. (1990). Enhancing academic achievement in college students through attributional retraining and instruction. *Journal of Educational Psychology*, 82, 262–271.

Perry, R. P., & Tunna, K. (1988). Perceived control, type A/B behavior, and quality of instruction. *Journal of Educational Psychology*, 80, 102–110.

Pintrich, P. R. (1989). The dynamic interplay of student motivation and cognition in the college classroom. In M. L. Maehr & C. Ames (Eds.), *Advances in motivation and achievement: Motivation enhancing environments* (Vol. 6, pp. 117–160). London: JAI Press.

Schunk, D. (1985). Self-efficacy and school learning. *Psychology in the Schools*, 22, 208–223.

Taylor, S. E. (1991). Asymmetrical effects of positive and negative events: The mobilization-minimization hypothesis. *Psychological Bulletin*, 110, 67–85.

Weiner, B. (1986). *An attributional theory of motivation and emotion*. New York: Springer-Verlag.

Weiner, B. (1990). History of motivational research in education. *Journal of Educational Psychology*, 82, 616–622.

Zimmerman, B., & Schunk, D. (1989). *Self-regulated learning and academic achievement: Theory, research, and practice*. Orlando: Academic Press.

Chapter Five

Collaborative Learning: Creating Knowledge with Students

Roberta S. Matthews
LaGuardia Community College

Collaborative learning occurs when students and faculty work together to create knowledge. The kind of shared inquiry that occurs suggests that knowledge is "continuously evolving . . . through dialogues with the self and others. . . ." (MacGregor, 1990). A class engaged in collaborative learning looks and feels different from a traditional classroom. It is more student-centered, active, and task-oriented. Issues of authority and boundaries are less clearly defined, but at its best the collaborative classroom "provides a social context in which students can experience and practice the kinds of conversation valued by college teachers" (Bruffee, 1984, p. 642). Collaboration asserts that learning is a mutual endeavor undertaken by students and faculty; the process welcomes students into the academic community. The term *collaborative learning* embraces various active learning approaches that value the voice and contributions of all participants.

This article could not have been written without the good conversations about collaborative learning I have had with colleagues and friends all over the country; discussions with participants in the CUNY Faculty Development Seminar on Collaborative Learning that began in 1988; spirited exchanges with the wonderful teachers from CUNY and from alternative and comprehensive public high schools in New York City who work with the American Social History Project; and continuous talk with my talented colleagues at LaGuardia Community College, who are always willing to think about teaching. I have learned from them all. Special thanks to Susan B. Cohen, Bret Eynon, Faith Gabelnick, Jerri Lindblad, Jean MacGregor, and Bob Matthews, whose suggestions improved each draft of this paper.

Faculty often view the practice of collaborative learning as a building block toward the development of a society based on interdependence and cooperation rather than rivalry and confrontation. Others come to collaborative learning believing that students must be empowered as learners. Some are attracted because they wish to experiment with approaches to managing their classrooms and presenting their disciplines. Regardless of the initial pull, however, this starting point leads inevitably to other ways of thinking about the process.

The chapter begins with an introduction and orientation for beginners. Recent and ongoing quantitative and qualitative studies are reviewed and assessed in terms of implications for practice, but the major focus and substance of the chapter is what those of us who use collaborative learning have learned. In addition to concrete guidelines, some of the intellectual and social assumptions behind collaborative learning will be used to explain how and why practice has evolved as it has.

The Idea of Collaborative Learning

The practice of collaborative learning, rooted in the social construction of knowledge, assumes that students bring ideas and experiences to learning situations that advance and enrich understanding for everyone else. An extensive body of literature (see, for example, Belenky and others, 1986; Bruffee, 1986; Dewey, 1966; Freire, 1973; Geertz, 1983; Kuhn, 1970; Vygotsky, 1962) explores and redefines how we acquire knowledge, and in the process it challenges traditional assumptions about how we learn.

The collaborative experience invites students to join the intellectual conversation. "A collaborative learning setting becomes— to one degree or another—what has been called 'a small republic of the intellect'—democratic, participatory, active" (Landa and Tarule, 1992, p. 2). Students engaged in collaborative learning activities work cooperatively with professors and peers to understand and use the conceptual and cognitive foundations of a particular discipline. Often, because collaboration occurs in the interdisciplinary setting of a learning community, students discover the epistemological uniqueness of a field of study—what it shares with other disciplines and how practitioners may work together to address common problems.

In addition, at a time when higher education and society beyond are torn by divisiveness, collaborative learning offers a way into community. It is a pedagogy that has at its center the assumption that people make meaning together and that the process enriches and enlarges them. A recent collection of essays (Murchland, 1991) explores the impact of our failure to "educate citizens for a democratic society" (p. 2). Benjamin Barber, a contributor in the volume, explains:

> The point where democracy and education intersect is the point we call community. . . . Underlying the pathologies of our society and our schools . . . is a sickness of community: its corruption, its rupturing, its fragmentation, its breakdown; finally, its vanishing and its absence. . . . If little learning is taking place in American schools and colleges it may be because there is too much solitude and too little community among the learners (and the teachers, too) (p. 166).

Starting Out

Teaching in collaborative settings is a dynamic process. The initial plunge involves sorting through a myriad of basics: how to introduce collaborative learning to students, how to form and sustain groups, how to design tasks that pose worthy questions and problems, and how to assess learning. Sustained association with collaborative learning underscores its dynamic quality: there is always something more to learn. In fact, exploring and applying collaborative learning helps balance content and process by focusing attention on the practice of the discipline rather than solely on content.

Three caveats about collaborative learning are worth mentioning for those new to the process. First, despite the apprehensions of the uninitiated, a commitment to collaborative learning need not be equivalent to a religious conversion. Those of us who use collaborative learning still assign readings from primary and secondary texts; we still lecture; we continue to use media and take classes on field trips. Second, although much accumulated experience about the practice of collaborative learning now exists, individual faculty need to discover what works for them and what is possible given their local conditions. Finally, the introduction of collaborative techniques takes place over time, during which teachers develop a repertoire of successful approaches.

However, the collaborative classroom is different, from simple differences such as participants' knowing each other's names to the more complicated ones embedded in the assumption that students and faculty can learn from each other. Thus, although the cast of characters might remain the same and familiar practices are still in place, the context changes—and that makes all the difference.

Successful collaborative learning requires that instructors manage a class differently. One faculty member explains:

> As a young teacher I felt I needed to be in complete control. I wouldn't have taught in clusters [three or four courses linked across disciplines] then. I needed to stand up in front of a class with tight control. As I got more confident, I began to loosen up. That's the way it is with most people as they discover collaborative learning (Gabelnick and others, 1990, p. 83).

With its assumptions of socially constructed knowledge, collaborative learning blurs the lines between teacher and learner.

Ironically, the decision to try collaborative learning may isolate some instructors at first. Most faculty have had fairly traditional educational experiences, a mix of lectures (where they took notes) and seminars (where they delivered papers). Too often, they cannot look to their own experience for models and do not find them readily among peers. Instructors who wish to introduce collaborative learning in the classroom might begin by seeking out like-minded colleagues to share experiences and to learn from each other.

Collaborative learning is not easy to introduce and sustain in a class. It requires a lot of planning; there are no guarantees that it will work; and it makes some students and teachers, as well as administrators, uncomfortable. However, the following guidelines help to ensure success.

Forming Groups

Creating groups for collaborative learning is like priming a piece of wood or preparing a room for painting: the quality of the final product depends on the preparation. Fundamental group-process issues pertain and should be addressed before any group work is used (Knowles and Knowles, 1989). For example, Finkel and Monk (1983) contrast approaches to student-teacher interaction, moving from the teacher as Atlas (center-stage and shouldering the entire burden of learning) to a more student-centered approach that welcomes students as partners in the learning process and thoughtfully supplies them with the tools to participate actively.

Students often have little experience or skill in group work. They need to be introduced to the new context, and many instructors begin by creating an environment hospitable to collaborative learning. A variety of exercises are helpful in creating a sense of community in the classroom. For example, students can participate in generating a list of what they are most interested in learning in the course and the background information they bring to it. Or they can be divided into pairs where each partner interviews and then introduces the other to the entire class.

The next challenge is winning a class over to collaborative learning. Too often, students have been socialized to believe that teachers talk and students listen. They believe that teachers have all the right answers. Their peers are generally not worth listening to. Students therefore need help understanding the responsibilities and the dynamics of a collaborative setting. Munns (1990) suggests a number of ways to ensure quality group interactions, including the delineation of various task or process roles and sample "scripts" for students who take on such roles. This accessible pamphlet, written for students and teachers alike, defines basic operating procedures and goals for collaborative work.

Once students have been prepared for collaborative experiences, the groups are formed. Their size is a key issue, driven by such considerations as the physical arrangement of the classroom, the age and experience of the students, how many groups an instructor might want for a particular task, and how many students are available for each group. Some groups function together for a term, while others might exist for one class. The life span of a particular group depends on the task at hand. Whether or not groups are assessed, how their products are assessed, and whether assessment is individual or not all depend on the purpose of the group and its task.

Similarly, how groups are formed varies widely in practice and depends on context and purpose. Some tasks work well with groups formed spontaneously from geography (where they happen to be sitting at the time) or friendship. Others depend heavily on a mix of skills and abilities, while still others exist precisely because the students are at the same level or the same place during a particular task. Indeed, the same instructor in the same class might assign students to groups for some tasks and let students form their own groups for others.

For faculty who use groups, a common thread runs through all the different ways they form groups: they understand the purpose of each group and pay careful attention to the kinds of students best suited to complete a particular task. The choice of how to form groups is always a conscious, thoughtful act based on the task.

Despite even the best planning, some groups do not work well. Like Tolstoy's unhappy families, nonfunctional groups demonstrate a daunting array of dysfunctional behaviors. Sometimes individual students cause problems; on occasion, an entire group cannot work together productively. An understanding of group process, a sense of humor and perspective, and knowledge that students and colleagues can offer helpful solutions can help instructors alleviate problems. Even in the best of circumstances, however, group work can be problematic along with rewarding.

Creating Tasks

The collaborative classroom is suffused with a tremendous amount of freedom, an atmosphere of exploration and discovery that, paradoxically, depends upon considerable planning and structure (as in creating the group tasks). Whether collaborative learning is introduced occasionally in group activities or whether an entire course is structured collaboratively, the guiding principle is the same: the open-ended quality of collaboration depends upon conscious shaping.

Teachers talk less in a collaborative classroom. They decide what elements in a standard lecture are absolutely necessary to communicate in this form and transform the remainder into collaborative tasks that allow students to puzzle things out for themselves in cooperation with their peers. The challenge is to create tasks that involve a variety of levels of learning, from problem solving to concept organization, and that appeal to a variety of learning styles.

The collaborative experience sends students out on unfamiliar seas. In order to find their way, they need navigational instruments and charts. The extent to which students need detailed instructions depends on their familiarity with collaborative learning and the task itself. Those new to the process tend to need more guidance than seasoned students acquainted with collaborative learning. Task formation at the beginning of the semester is more detailed than at the end, when students understand the process and are comfortable with each other.

The Structure of Tasks

The instructor must devote time to careful crafting of the task. Students need clear instructions that lay out the process and suggest directions for discussion. The required outcomes (questions that need to be framed, issues that should be explored, papers or reports that must be submitted) should be explained in detail. Generally, it is a good idea to put the task in writing.

The importance of how much time is spent on task depends principally on two factors: whether or not the class is new to collaborative learning, and whether or not the task is confined to one session or is an ongoing project. The time allotted to the task should be clearly delineated but may be adjusted depending on the discipline and on the time individual groups need. A writing teacher might decide that a brainstorming or peer review session is going so well that more time is well worth it; an accounting instructor whose task simulates a corporate situation might view the timely completion of the task as essential.

The nature of the task itself depends on the particularities of the teaching situation and the demands of individual disciplines. *Practicing Collaborative Learning* (Castelluci and Miller, 1986) provides concrete examples of collaborative tasks for reading, writing, and literature classes. These include detailed instructions for a number of group activities. Other examples suggest the wide range of possibilities for which collaborative tasks may be created, such as understanding metaphor, revising papers, discussing particular poems or stories, brainstorming, or taking a collaborative exam. The generic formats serve as models for tasks that may be adapted to a number of disciplines precisely because the underlying principle is consistent across disciplines. The goal of any collaborative task is to engage students with each other in order to shape a response that represents their understanding of that discipline.

Balancing Content and Process

The issue of covering content—what it means and whether or not it can be done in a collaborative setting—is at the center of the debate about collaborative learning. Since the meaning of the phrase "covering content" is variable, it helps to start by suggesting that context affects coverage. Instructors of sequential courses that lay the foundation for future learning are under different kinds of pressure than those who teach courses that by their very nature are open-ended and exploratory.

However, covering content boils down to a pair of stark questions: If I am not talking, is anybody learning? and When I am talking, is anybody learning? These two questions are not rhetorical; the answers reside in the papers and exams generated by students. If student work consistently reflects an engaged, rich, and robust understanding of course content, there may be little incentive to consider other options. But if student work elicits a Prufrock-like "That's not what I meant at all," then there is probably room to consider alternatives.

We need to stop asking pejoratively, How much content must be sacrificed in order to do collaborative learning? That assumes collaborative learning and content coverage are not compatible. Rather, we need to start asking, How can collaborative learning be used to help students understand what it means to study the essential content of this discipline?

Whether or not a collaborative classroom "covers content" depends on the design of tasks that move learning forward, tasks that either integrate material with prior learning or introduce new themes. B. L. Smith and J. MacGregor (in Goodsell and others, 1992) point out that case studies, learning communities, and peer teaching have been shown to be effective designs for advancing understanding. A worthwhile collaborative activity must be an integral part of the class, not a vacation from learning content or from applying it to relevant problems. For example, consider the practice of having groups report out. Group reports are often time-consuming and boring. The idea of sharing, of harvesting learning, makes sense; but it will not contribute to covering content. Large-group discussions should not merely summarize the deliberations of smaller groups that have all considered the same questions. Rather, small groups emerging from similar conversations should explore where consensus and difference emerge, while groups that have worked on different tasks around the same content learn from each other as each contributes to the creation of a larger context.

When used effectively, the collaborative process supports and enhances content by giving students opportunities:

- To use what they are learning and therefore to integrate it at a deeper level
- To identify for themselves and discuss with their peers the important elements of their learning
- To actively contribute what they already know and to enrich content discussion through the introduction of additional content and dimensions that may be beyond the experience of the instructor
- To feel valued and engaged in learning

When this happens, collaborative learning facilitates and enriches content coverage.

How collaborative learning supports the coverage of content depends on the particular discipline as well. Faculty in technical areas sometimes believe that collaborative learning takes time away from the facts of content. However, these instructors often discover that students retain material better if they are allowed to discuss how factual material can be approached and learned. Cooperative problem solving and brainstorming enrich all ways of knowing and are the basis for contributions to any discipline. Successful practitioners in the areas of mathematics, science, and computers do use collaborative learning to balance content with process and to help students learn and apply the content of their disciplines. To illustrate, a "discipline-specific bibliography" (found in Goodsell and others, 1992, pp. 75–79) provides annotated references to articles about implementing collaborative and cooperative learning in thirteen different fields of study.

The range of collaborative learning modes, which facilitate so many kinds of student and faculty cooperation, suggests the potential of the process as an aid to covering content. The more we examine our assumptions about what constitutes course coverage, the more we can reexamine practice and re-form it to better purpose.

Assessing Individuals and Groups

Initially, it is possible to ignore the mismatch between the kind of learning that occurs in a collaborative classroom and traditional evaluation techniques. Sooner or later, however, it becomes an issue. Students who have learned in the collaborative mode begin to question (sometimes loudly and bitterly) the validity of standard exams with thirty multiple-choice questions and two short essays.

Student perceptions about the mismatch are supported by research. Terence J. Crooks (1988) concludes:

> Classroom evaluation guides [students'] judgment of what is important to learn, affects their motivation and self-perceptions of competence, structures their approaches to and timing of personal study . . . and affects the development of enduring learning strategies and skills (p. 367).

It counts little to wax eloquent about how a course develops analytical abilities and enriches one's experience if the exams value the regurgitation of bits of knowledge.

Because the importance of grades continues to be a driving force, sooner or later faculty must confront the issue of grading group work. Committed students resent "carrying" less energetic peers and demand that their own grades neither influence nor be influenced by those of group members. Faculty responses range widely. Some use groups solely to provide support and context for individual efforts that receive individual grades. Others insist that group efforts receive one group grade and that group members have to work out their own solutions to perceived inequities. Compromises include averaging individual and group grades for group projects; having group members grade each other's efforts; and assigning individual grades but using the group average to determine whether a group may, for example, be excused from the final. The degree to which a course encourages individual effort or interdependence should be reflected in the degree to which individual or group efforts contribute to a final accounting.

One outcome of the FIPSE-funded Lesley College Project on Collaborative Learning (Cohen, 1990) contrasts the kinds of assessment that emerge from collaborative learning with traditional means of evaluation, the latter resulting from the assumption that learning is a product "consisting of discrete segments passed on by a series of transmission activities . . . taking snapshots" (pp. 3–4). Collaborative learning assessments are "cinematic," in order to capture "learning . . . as a dynamic, continuous process in which knowledge is created and transformed in a social context and learners themselves experience change as a result of this process" (p. 5).

Cohen (and other authors) suggest that instructors begin by constructing an "assessment matrix," a chart that cross-references the intentions of a course (aligned across the top of a page) with proposed assessment techniques (listed vertically along the left margin). The matrix provides instructors with the opportunity to articulate their goals, list their assessment tools, and establish the relationships between them.

Cohen also describes a number of these assessment tools, including well-known standards such as journals and portfolios, and some lesser-known ones such as dialogic journals and evaluation interviews. She includes examples of self-assessment statements, specially designed course evaluations, and various instruments that measure intellectual development and critical thinking.

Finally, Cohen includes criteria that can be used to gauge the propriety and effectiveness tools used to assess collaborative learning. Assessment methods should:

- Define and describe the context and the intentions of the course
- Permit and encourage participants to document the learning experience in their own voice and language
- Facilitate self-assessment and meta-cognition
- Capture the social, interactive process that is fundamental to a collaborative learning experience
- Examine content learning in context
- Connect learning to prior knowledge, personal experience, and the real world
- Encourage and support teacher-student collaboration in the assessment process
- Generate a clear, detailed, and comprehensive picture of the learning experience for the purposes of understanding, to the extent possible, "what happened here" (pp. 8–9)

Clearly, the issue of assessing collaborative learning is part of the larger, sometimes acrimonious national debate about appropriate means of assessment and evaluation. No one has yet resolved how best to evaluate the products of learning (whether of individuals or groups) for the purpose of assigning grades and credit, and how best to assess the process of learning and its impact upon how people learn. The relationship between process and product, how to measure their impact upon one another, and the relative merits and purposes of each also have not been explored fully and will continue to be debated as well.

Details and Realities: Issues of Time, Class Size, Noise, and Disbelief

Collaborative learning does not occur in a vacuum. Institutional mores and circumstances affect the individual instructor attempting to change classroom practice. Shrinking budgets, disappearing course sections, and soaring class sizes make for even more impersonal and alienating educational environments. Conditions like these make collaborative learning all the more necessary and all the more difficult.

Collaborative learning takes time. Where does one find the time to prepare collaborative tasks and implement them in class? The answer depends heavily on the other issues surrounding collaborative learning: how important is the development of group skills—in this class and in general? Will student groups work well together and accomplish their goals? Will collaborative tasks help the class master content efficiently and effectively? Will the products of collaborative groups justify the time spent on them? The value of the time spent on collaborative learning depends directly on the quality of the experience. Evaluation of collaborative learning is critical because it becomes a concrete way to assess the value of time spent.

Is it possible to introduce or sustain collaborative learning activities in large classes? It is difficult to form student groups in classrooms packed with chairs, or in large lecture halls with fixed seating. But it has been done. Those teaching large lectures introduce collaborative activities by having students work with peers on either side of them; groups in large classes are sent to lounges or cafeterias; some have students meet together outside of class time.

When thirty people are conversing, the noise level in collaborative classrooms is considerably higher than in classrooms where one individual lectures or orchestrates a typical class discussion. Thin walls may threaten attempts at collaboration by carrying its results as an unwelcome intrusion into adjoining rooms. Faculty need to be prepared to make alternative arrangements and deal with irate colleagues. At one college, the leaders of a learning community arranged with the library to have a special "noise room" set aside for their students to research, study, and work together without disrupting neighboring students.

When outsiders look in at a collaborative classroom, they see a professor sitting at a desk or wandering around, apparently aimlessly, occasionally joining a group, but not doing much. Faculty whose tenure and promotion depend in part on peer review need to understand the hazards of being observed by colleagues who are ignorant of—or hostile to—collaborative learning and take steps to minimize the potential damage. Harvey Wiener (1986) enumerates the features of a collaborative classroom that an outside evaluator should consider:

- The nature and quality of the task statement
- The social setting of the collaborative activity and the behavior of students during the execution of the task
- The teacher's behavior during the execution of the task
- The teacher's role in group composition and management
- The nature and quality of the reports made by each group
- The teacher's performance as synthesizer and as representative of the academic learning community
- The relation of the collaborative activity to the design of the course

- The teacher's knowledge of and commitment to the rationale of collaborative learning (p. 60)

Faculty who are planning to implement collaborative learning are well counseled to anticipate the obvious and figure out how to cope with it before it mushrooms into a major crisis.

Outcomes Assessment and Research

Much research supporting the effectiveness of cooperative learning on the precollegiate level exists. More recently, a number of studies have been undertaken at the college level (Goodsell and others, 1992, pp. 68–74). For example, "Student Involvement in Learning: Cooperative Learning and College Instruction" (in Goodsell and others, 1992) surveys the admittedly limited research about the impact of cooperative learning on college students. Citing studies undertaken in the fields of nursing, geology, and mathematics, Cooper and Mueck (1990, p. 72) point out that students who studied together performed better and achieved higher results on examinations than students who relied on individual efforts. Cooper and Mueck also note that "the most consistent positive findings for cooperative learning [at the college level] . . . have centered on affective or attitudinal change."

Looking at learning communities that involve students in collaborative learning, Tinto, Goodsell-Love, and Russo (1993) examine the impact on students' continuation, retention, and progress toward the degree. The study is based on the experiences of new college students in three learning-community programs at the University of Washington, Seattle Central Community College, and LaGuardia Community College. These colleges serve a representative sample of the students currently in higher education, those who commute to college and often have work and family obligations in addition to their full- or part-time course loads. Learning communities at all three institutions accomplished a number of important goals. They facilitated the building of supportive peer groups during the first term of college and laid the groundwork for a network of associations that would continue beyond the initial learning community as students entered their majors. They bridged the "social-academic divide that typically plagues student life" (p. 6) and led to the creation of academic support mechanisms that eased the transition into the requirements of the academic community. Especially at Seattle Central, where a large block of students were collaboratively taught by a group of faculty, the experience produced students who became actively involved in "deciding what they knew and how they knew it" (p. 8). In a variety of ways, students at all three institutions were more involved in learning and more positive about their engagement in learning than students who were not participating in learning communities.

Learning communities improve both learning and persistence because they provide an opportunity for students to participate in collaborative learning groups and to participate in settings where learning comes from a variety of perspectives, instead of from one faculty member. As revealed by participants at LaGuardia, the collaborative learning experience was as significant for students in developmental and remedial courses as it was for those in regular college courses. In light of these positive results, Tinto and colleagues (1993, pp. 15–16) make a number of suggestions, two of which are especially relevant here:

- Institutions should assist faculty collaboration and their utilization of teaching strategies that actively involve students in classroom learning.

- In considering the direction of educational reform, institutions should focus less on student behaviors and . . . obligations, and more on the character of their own obligations to construct the sorts of educational settings and provide the types of educational pedagogies in which all students, not just some, will want to become involved.

Collaborative Learning and Learning Communities

Studies supporting the use of collaborative learning are often embedded in research conducted about learning communities. Nationally, there is a good deal of agreement among students that participation in collaborative learning situations enriches their education. Experiences in collaboration yield friendships and a sense of belonging (community building as part of the educational experience), growing self-confidence along with a growing appreciation of the perspectives of others, renewed intellectual energy and a growing ability to make intellectual connections, deeper engagement with texts, and an appreciation of complexity (Gabelnick and others, 1990, pp. 67–72). As one student sums it up (p. 68):

> Perhaps the most important thing I am learning about learning . . .
> it is easier, and more logical, not to suffer through it by myself.
> Asking teachers and other students for their ideas or criticism is so
> beneficial.

Studies consistently suggest that collaborative learning has a salutary effect on learning. For example, E. Mould and J. Moore (in MacGregor, 1991, p. 5) compare the performance of 650 biology students, learning in situations that substituted group problem solving, minilectures, and collaborative preparation for tests, with that of students (with the same instructor) who were being taught in a more traditional, lecture-centered approach. Ninety-two percent of the students in the collaborative biology class finished the course, as opposed to a retention rate of 80 percent in the "regular class." More students passed the collaborative course, and grades among these students were consistently higher than in the control group.

An evaluation of "Enterprise," a program at LaGuardia Community College for business and career students, further suggests the potential of collaborative approaches. Enterprise uses collaborative learning strategies in thematically linked learning communities or in sections of high-risk courses that are "enhanced" by student-led study groups. An evaluation of the 1990–1991 cohort revealed that in over 50 percent of Enterprise courses (learning community and study group), 10–50 percent more students received grades of C or higher when compared to equivalent students in traditionally taught sections of the same courses. Overall, Enterprise students earned over 15 percent more of the credits attempted and ended the year with higher cumulative GPAs. Qualitative responses support these findings. Faculty appreciate the exposure to real-life group situations in the business world and the more advanced cognitive connections students make. They also enjoy the extended professional contact with faculty from other disciplines. Students cite increased self-confidence and participation in class and point to the value of exposure to different viewpoints (Sussman, 1991).

Assessing Expectations

Interviews conducted at two large universities, one small state college, and one small private college form the basis of research on how students assess their collaborative learning experience. J. Tarule (1990) describes work she and Whipple are currently doing, which involves a narrative analysis of how the collaborative experience affects cognitive structures. They are especially interested in three aspects of collaborative learning: its context, its support of dialogue, and how context and dialogue interact to revise the participant's understanding of the learning process, especially in relation to the exercise of authority in the classroom. The research distinguishes between two phases of collaborative learning: an introduction to the common vocabulary and to the major paradigms of a particular discipline, and then construction of an inquiry that leads into the heart of the discipline's central issues and questions.

Other research documents how collaborative techniques improve achievement for the "nontraditional" student—who is currently the mainstream student. An impressive array of evidence attests to the effectiveness of essentially collaborative approaches, such as supplemental instruction (*Supplemental Instruction*, 1992), guided design (Wales and Stager, 1978), and learning communities (MacGregor, 1991), as well as discipline-specific techniques (Treisman, 1986; Heller, Keith, and Anderson, 1992).

These studies demonstrate how in collaborative classrooms students become more involved, learn better, and become more conscious of how they are learning. On the other hand, teachers new to collaborative learning need to temper their expectations with a dose of reality. Student performance sometimes may not reach faculty expectations (Matthews, 1989). It takes time for teachers to develop the skills and confidence to facilitate collaborative learning effectively.

The research about collaborative learning suggests that in all its myriad forms, it is an approach that works and we should be using it. To find out how to implement collaborative learning and the implications of committing to such an approach, we need to turn to the wisdom of practice and the literature that is grounded in it.

Implications

If, as Barber (1991) insists, democracy and education indeed "intersect" at "the point we call community," may we look to the collaborative classroom as one way to prepare active citizens? Such questions lead us to the broader, more challenging aspects of collaborative learning. Discussions about how to define consensus and authority in a collaborative setting open areas for discussion with implications beyond pedagogy and the educational process.

To illustrate, John Trimbur (1989) explores the meaning of consensus in collaborative learning and develops a "utopian view of consensus" that does not end at the classroom door (p. 615):

> We need to see consensus . . . not as an agreement that reconciles differences through an ideal conversation, but rather as the desire of humans to live and work together with differences. . . . Students

can learn to agree to disagree, not because "everyone has their own opinion," but because justice demands that we recognize the inexhaustability of difference and that we organize the conditions in which we live and work accordingly.

From another, related perspective, Geertz (1983) claims that the value of interpretive anthropology lies in a "fugitive truth," which, interestingly enough, resembles Trimbur's definition of consensus at its best:

> To see ourselves as others see us can be eye-opening. To see others as sharing a nature with ourselves is the merest decency. But it is from the far more difficult achievement of seeing ourselves among others . . . a world among worlds, that the largeness of mind, without which objectivity is self-congratulation and tolerance a sham, comes (p. 16).

The recent focus on multicultural education acknowledges our diversity and demands that we accept it. In these contexts, the practice of collaborative learning appears especially promising. In Trimbur's view, the collaborative classroom would replace "the expert-novice model of teaching" with one that provides "students with a critical measure to identify the relations of power in the formation of expert judgment" (p. 613).

Like the instructor whose growing self-confidence allowed her to give up tight control, teachers must redefine their power relationships with students. Romer and Whipple (1991) point out that the issue of control is often expressed in terms of authority. They suggest that authority defined as enforcing obedience and influencing action suggests a power that controls, directs, or restrains. This kind of authority runs counter to the collaborative process. Alternatively, Romer and Whipple see authority as the capacity to inspire belief, to "augment or induce growth" (p. 68). The "largeness of mind" Geertz holds as an ideal translates in the classroom into authority based on power that adds to understanding and nurtures growth. It implies, outside the classroom, a need to reexamine the way we define authority and how we wield power.

We teach our students about democracy but too often do not provide the opportunity for them to act democratically through the practice of public discourse in our classes. For those who have absorbed its lessons, collaborative learning aids in transforming the classroom into "small republics of the intellect" (Landa and Tarule, 1992). Beyond the walls of academe, if teachers and students acknowledge the reality of interdependence and experience cooperation then they may very well develop habits of mind that will promote constructive participation in an increasingly interdependent world.

References

Barber, B. R. (1991). The civic mission of the university. In B. Murchland (Ed.), *Higher education and the practice of democratic politics: A political education reader* (pp. 160–169). Dayton, OH: Kettering Foundation.

Belenky, M., Clinchy, B., Goldberger, N., & Tarule, J. (1986). *Women's ways of knowing: The development of self, voice, and mind.* New York: Basic Books.

Brann, E. T. H. (1979). *Paradoxes of education in a republic.* Chicago: University of Chicago Press.

Bruffee, K. (1984). Collaborative Learning and the "Conversation of Mankind." *College English, 46*(7), 635–652.

Bruffee, K. (1986). Social construction, language, and the authority of knowledge: A bibliographical essay. *College English, 48*(8), 773–790.

Castellucci, M. F., & Miller, P., with the Collaborative Learning Study Group. (1986). *Practicing collaborative learning.* City University of New York: College of Staten Island.

Cohen, S. B., in collaboration with Landa, A. M., and Tarule, J. (1990). *The collaborative learning assessment packet.* Cambridge, MA: Lesley College, Collaborative Learning Project.

Cooper, J., & Mueck, R. Student involvement in learning: Cooperative learning and college instruction. *Journal on Excellence in College Teaching,* 1990, 1, 68–76.

Crooks, T. J. (1988). The impact of classroom evaluation practices on students. *Review of Educational Research, 58*(4), 438–481.

Dewey, J. (1966). *Democracy and education: An introduction to the philosophy of education*. New York: Free Press.

Finkel, D. L., & Monk, G. S. (1983). Teachers and learning groups: Dissolution of the atlas complex. In C. Bouton & R. Y. Garth (Eds.), New directions for teaching and learning: No. 14. *Learning in groups* (pp. 81–95).

Freire, P. (1973). *Education for critical consciousness*. New York: Continuum Press.

Gabelnick, F., MacGregor, J., Matthews, R. S., & Smith, B. L. (1990). New directions for teaching and learning: No. 41. *Learning communities: Creating connections among students, faculty, and disciplines*.

Geertz, C. (1983). *Local knowledge: Further essays in interpretive anthropology*. New York: Basic Books.

Goodsell, A., Maher, M., Tinto V., Smith, B. L., & MacGregor, J. (1992). *Collaborative learning: A sourcebook for higher education*. National Center on Postsecondary Teaching, Learning, and Assessment.

Heller, P., Keith, R., & Anderson, S. (1992). Teaching problem solving through cooperative grouping. Part 1: Group versus individual problem solving. *American Journal of Physics, 60*(7), 627–636.

Knowles, M., & Knowles, H. (1989). *Introduction to group dynamics* (rev. ed.). Englewood Cliffs, NJ: Cambridge Books.

Kuhn, T. S. (1970). *The structure of scientific revolutions* (2nd ed.). Chicago: University of Chicago Press.

Landa, A., & Tarule, J. (1992). *Models II: Collaboration in postsecondary education*. Cambridge, MA: Collaborative Learning Project of Lesley College Center for Research, Pedagogical, and Policy Studies.

MacGregor, J. (1990). Collaborative learning: Shared inquiry as a process of reform. In M. D. Svinicki (Ed.), New directions for teaching and learning: No. 42. *The changing face of college teaching* (pp. 19–30).

MacGregor, J. (1991). Assessment and learning communities: Taking stock after six years. *Washington Center News, 6*(1), 5.

Matthews, R. S. (1989). *Using portfolios to evaluate student writing: A feasibility study at the City University of New York*. Written for City University of New York, Office for Academic Affairs.

Munns, W. (1990). *Effective group participation*. Seattle: North Seattle Community College, Title III.

Murchland, B. (Ed.). (1991). *Higher education and the practice of democratic politics: A political education reader*. Dayton, OH: Kettering Foundation.

Romer, K., & Whipple, W. (1991). Collaboration across the power line. *College Teaching, 39*(2), 66–70.

Supplemental instruction (SI): Review of research concerning the effectiveness of SI from the University of Missouri–Kansas City and other institutions from across the United States. (1992). Kansas City, MO: University of Missouri–Kansas City, Center for Academic Development.

Sussman, M. (1991). *Evaluating the experience of students and faculty in enterprise: An analysis of the cohort in the 1990–91 academic year.* Prepared for LaGuardia Community College Office for Academic Affairs.

Tarule, J. (1990). Connected and collaborative learning: Toward a theory of contextual epistemology. Paper delivered at the Colloquium on Human Development, University of Massachusetts at Amherst.

Tinto, V., Goodsell-Love, A., & Russo, P. (1993). *Building Learning Communities for New College Students.* State College, PA: Report: National Center on Postsecondary Teaching, Learning, and Assessment, Penn State University.

Treisman, U. (1986). A study of the mathematics performance of black students at the University of California (Doctoral dissertation, University of California, Berkeley). *Dissertation Abstracts International, 47,* 1641A.

Trimbur, J. (1989). Consensus and difference in collaborative learning. *College English, 51*(6), 602–616.

Vygotsky, L. S. (1962). *Thought and action* (E. Hanfmann & N. Vakar, Eds. & Trans.). Cambridge, MA: Harvard University Press.

Wales, C., & Stager, R. A. (1978). *The guided design approach.* Englewood Cliffs, NJ: Educational Technology Publications, Instructional Design Library.

Wiener, H. S. (1986). Collaborative learning in the classroom. *College English, 48*(1), 52–61.

Chapter Six

Assessing Student Involvement in Learning

Robert C. Froh, Mark Hawkes
Syracuse University

Assessing how students benefit from postsecondary education can be done in many ways. One approach, which has received insufficient attention, is the assessment of student involvement in learning. Pascarella and Terenzini (1991), using Tinto's theory of student attrition, find that various forms of involvement have substantial effects on student retention and development. Astin's (1975) study of college dropouts concludes that virtually every significant effect of college could be related to student involvement. Yet most assessment efforts have been directed toward cognitive outcomes or toward indicators of student satisfaction. Focusing on student involvement in order to determine the impact of the college experience rests on the simple notion that students learn what they are involved in.

Student involvement refers to the intellectual and interpersonal activities that students choose to engage in as a part of their higher education experience. In the classroom, involvement has been linked to the concept of active learning, defined by Bonwell and Eison (1991) as "anything that involves students in doing things and thinking about what they are doing." Outside the classroom, involvement includes the variety of ways students direct their efforts in developing interpersonal and intellectual skills. It includes developing skills in such areas as study, informal discussion, time organization, establishing relationships, and academic and career planning.

What are some indicators of student involvement in learning? Highly involved students reply "often" or "very often" to items such as the following (items are taken from four scales of "Student Perceptions of Student Life," Center for Instructional Development, 1994, Syracuse University, p. 13):

- Participated in class discussions. Met with other students to work on class-related projects or assignments. Talked with instructors regarding course-related issues. (academic involvement, in class)

- Talked informally with faculty outside of class time. Sought advice regarding what courses would be most appropriate in academic plans. (academic involvement, out of class)

- Discussed important issues with students holding viewpoints different from your own. Discussed career plans and ambitions with university staff or faculty. (personal social involvement)

- Attended speeches or presentations on topics of interest to you. Helped to organize an activity or event. (cultural social involvement)

Assessing student involvement in learning can provide information that enhances the range of interactions, events, and programs that facilitate learning. In this chapter, we refer to research literature that supports this approach, and we describe assessment practices that maintain ownership by faculty, staff, and administrators. Most of our examples come from our own institution. Syracuse University is a large, private research university that has developed an assessment agenda to help faculty and administrators decide how different programs enable student involvement in campus life.

Importance of Student Involvement in Learning

Why has the assessment of student involvement in learning received so little attention? For one thing, the concept of involve-

ment may not be well understood. From their inte ____
ulty, Stark and her collaborators found that for m ____
volvement appeared to be synonymous with list ____
attention, or being alert rather than signifying engager ____
material being learned" (1988, p. 95). This limited u ____ ____anding
of involvement persists in the face of national studies such as
Involvement in Learning (Study Group, 1984), which encouraged faculty to use more active modes of learning. Other studies, including
Campus Life: In Search of Community (Boyer, 1990), suggest that we
need to view student life from the perspective of involvement in
community. They recommend that we strengthen community
through involving all members of the community: counselors, chap-
lains, residence hall staff, deans, and "faculty who care about students and engage them in active learning" (p. 12). This vision of
community requires that faculty and staff encourage students to be
creative and get involved in learning across all facets of campus life.

Assessing student involvement can draw together faculty and
administrators across a range of academic and nonacademic programs. Too often, faculty focus almost solely on academic performance and ignore student interpersonal needs and the ways that
interpersonal needs connect to intellectual and academic needs.
Student affairs administrators, on the other hand, attempt to
strengthen the quality of out-of-class life and fail to create opportunities for communicating with faculty about how students perform academically.

Collaborative and cooperative learning actively involve students in improving their learning and building their community
membership. Collaborative learning recognizes that both academic
and interpersonal involvement are essential to student learning and
development. Tinto (1993) cites many examples of institutions
where students with common academic interests enroll in a common set of courses as a means of "encouraging the formation of self-
sustaining student communities that have an academic focus"
(Tinto, 1993, p. 168).

Focusing on student involvement helps us understand how students spend their time. Recent reports indicate that the time students spend in study is insufficient. In a national survey of incoming freshmen conducted in 1989 (cited in Erickson and Strommer, 1991), less than half of the students said they had spent six or more hours per week studying and doing homework during the previous year in high school, and only 10 percent reported they frequently did extra reading or work for a course. Most freshmen indicate they study about two hours a night or about one hour outside class for each hour in class (Erickson and Strommer, 1991). These authors suggest that "If we want students to study more on a more regular schedule and in more productive ways, we need to reconsider the assignments we give and create others more suited to those goals" (p. 123).

Thus at our university, we encourage the following kinds of student involvement:

- Finding an appropriate balance between academic and social activities
- Spending a sufficient amount of time in study, and managing time effectively
- Attending class regularly
- Approaching learning actively (particularly for lecture classes) while in class and while studying
- Working with peers in study and other learning activities

Students tell us that they appreciate faculty and peers who stimulate involvement. (Most of the following comments come from focus-group discussions by first-year students.)

I had COM 107 (Introduction to Communications) last semester and we handed [the professor] a card with all our information on it, and the next day he knew all our names. It was like the greatest feeling! He took time out and made an effort to learn our names. At times, it's going to be impossible for a professor to have a smaller class, but when he takes time out to make sure that you know that he cares that you are individuals, that shows a lot of effort on his part.

Our Freshman Forum advisor was great. It has been really wonderful to have a faculty member you could go one-on-one with. And I'll have him for the next four years or so, and that makes it a little more personal.

We went to GOLD (a student leadership program) retreat last weekend and it was one of the best weekends I've had since I've been here. It was great! I know so many more people, and we've gotten very close. It was definitely worthwhile, and the camp was very nice.

There's a lot of influence from your peers and friends. There's people who don't want to study, and you'll see their friends come out and scream at them to get to work. I have friends who will wake their friends to make sure they get to class. I think they're afraid of their friends not doing well and failing out. I've been yelled at a couple of times.

I went to an all-black high school and lived in a predominantly black neighborhood. To me coming here was a big thing because I was exposed to all these different people from different places. Listening to all these different things, I think it's a good thing for me. I get the feeling that a lot of people coming here don't feel the same way.

The last person quoted above indicated during a follow-up conversation that "there's just not much for us multicultural blacks to do." She has gotten to know students in both the African-American community and the European-American community, but she has some difficulty crossing easily between the two groups. Students in each group have their own insecurities that prevent them from mixing as much as she does. This woman left the university because she could not resolve how to interact and learn from a range of people and still receive approval and acceptance from her African-American friends.

These comments point to the breadth of involvements that students need. They also suggest that involvement in learning within the classroom needs to be complemented with nonclassroom experiences that enable students to develop intellectually and interpersonally during their college years.

Research on student motivation offers other reasons to focus on student involvement. McKeachie (1994) cites research showing that students who fear failure improve their performance when they can attribute their failure to lack of effort or to not setting reasonable standards rather than to lack of ability. For students who work hard yet still do not do well, he notes that attributing failure to ineffective strategies actually improves motivation for success. Pace (1983) suggests assessing "quality of effort" as the way to get at both quantitative and qualitative issues of student involvement.

Philosophers have called for a deeper understanding of participation and involvement. Parker Palmer puts it this way: "Knowing and learning are communal acts. They require many eyes and ears, many observations and experiences. They require a continual cycle of discussion, disagreement, and consensus over what has been seen and what it all means" (1987, p. 24).

Finally, focusing on student involvement can suggest changes and improvements that are nonthreatening. They do not threaten faculty because the selection of content of academic courses and curriculum is left in the hands of individual faculty. They do not threaten administrators because responsibility for nonacademic programs is left with administrators who have the appropriate expertise. Instead, all are asked to work together to determine if their efforts truly engage students in learning.

Conceptual Base for Student Involvement in Learning

Our conceptual base for assessing student involvement in learning rests on three major sources: Tinto's (1987, 1993) theory of student attrition from college, Astin's (1985) theory of student involvement, and Pace's (1990) definitions and measures of the "quality of student effort."

Retention as an Indicator of Involvement

Vincent Tinto's (1987, 1993) theory of student attrition describes a longitudinal model in which students' preentry attributes (background, skills, abilities, and prior education) and their initial academic goals and commitments to a given institution interact with campus experiences in the academic and social systems. Each student's experiences, as indicated by their academic and social involvements, continually modify their goals and institutional commitments.

Integrative academic and social experiences reinforce retention at an institution. Astin (1985) and Pascarella and Terenzini (1991), using Tinto's theory, find that various forms of involvement have substantial effects on student retention and development. Astin's (1975) study of college dropouts concludes that virtually every significant effect of college could be related to student involvement.

Astin's Theory of Student Involvement

As Pascarella and Terenzini (1991) describe it, Alexander Astin proposed one of the earliest college impact models. They summarize Astin's description of a theory of student involvement that contains "elements of the Freudian notion of cathexis (the investment of psychological energy), as well [as] the learning theory concept of 'time-on-task'" (Pascarella and Terenzini, 1991, p. 50).

Astin (1975) describes an input-environment-outcome model. Input variables include family background, skills and abilities, prior schooling, and academic goals (Tinto's preentry attributes). Environment variables include institutional experiences and what he calls "intermediate outcomes" of student involvement with these institutional experiences. (Intermediate outcomes include aspects of involvement that can be known only after a student has been in college for some time.) Outcome variables include grades, tests of cognitive and affective knowledge and skills, and retention.

Astin finds that learning, academic performance, and retention are positively associated with student involvement. Astin (1993) categorizes measures of student involvement into five areas: academic involvement, involvement with faculty, involvement with peers, involvement in work, and other forms of involvement. Academic involvement, for example, includes items about time allocation, courses taken, specific learning experiences, and specific pedagogical experiences. Involvement with faculty, on the other hand, includes items such as "being a guest in a professor's home, working on a professor's research project, assisting faculty in teaching a class, hours per week spent talking with faculty outside of class" (p. 383).

Although Pascarella and Terenzini (1991) question whether Astin's propositions truly constitute a theory, they agree that the institutional environment offers students opportunities for encounters with ideas and people, and students must actively seek these opportunities to become involved. The "individual plays a central role in determining the extent and nature of growth according to the quality of effort or involvement with the resources provided by the institution" (p. 51).

Astin (1978) suggests that conceiving student involvement as an intermediate outcome invites some causal questions for future research, such as, "Does interacting with faculty result in greater satisfaction with faculty, or are more satisfied students more likely to interact?" (p. 187). However, he points out that "the fact that these associations [between involvement and satisfaction] remain even after entering-freshmen characteristics are controlled suggests strongly that the student's general satisfaction with the undergraduate experience can be enhanced by more direct involvement in various aspects of the college environment" (p. 187).

Judging the Quality of the Educational Process

Robert Pace argues that in thinking about the quality of programs we should give due attention to how students experience education. In measuring the quality of the experience, he postulates that "all learning and development requires an investment of time and effort by the student. Time is a frequency dimension. Effort is a quality dimension in the sense that some educational processes require more effort than others. It's fairly easy to look up a given reference in the library. It's more difficult, takes more effort, to develop a set of references for a report. . . . The activity requiring the greater effort is also potentially more educative" (Pace, 1984, p. 5). Pace suggests that having a high-quality experience depends on investing high-quality effort. Pace's conceptualization provides a vehicle for determining both how colleges and faculty are accountable for programs and resources and for how students are accountable for the "amount, scope, and quality of effort they invest in their own learning and development" (p. 6).

Pace (1983) built a framework for measuring students' "quality of effort" in various aspects of campus life using the College Student Experiences Questionnaire. Each scale contains approximately ten activities where students' responses ("never," "occasionally," "often," or "very often") reflect both frequency and quality of involvements in campus life. These scales include use of college facilities and use of opportunities for personal experiences and group association. The college facilities scales are: course learning, library, activities related to science-technology, cultural facilities, student union, athletic and recreation facilities, and dormitory or fraternity-sorority. The scales for personal experiences and group association are: experiences with faculty, experiences in writing, clubs and organizations, personal experiences, student acquaintances, topics of conversation, and information in conversations. Each scale contains from six to ten items.

Pace (1990) argues that a dimension of quality underlies each set of activities. "Activities that reflect greater effort are ones that are more likely to have a greater influence on student learning and development" (p. 18). For example, the course-learning scale contains a range of questions, from those representing lower quality of effort such as "taking notes and underlining" to questions representing such higher-level cognitive activities as efforts "to explain and organize."

Assessment Programs Focusing on Student Involvement

When we follow Tinto, Astin, and Pace's conceptualizations, and when we use measures of student involvement or "quality of student effort," we are able to extend the range of assessment goals and activities used to judge the quality of educational processes and outcomes.

From an assessment point of view, Pace's way of defining and measuring student involvement is attractive. It produces scale scores for various areas of student involvement that can vary from one time to another and from one group to another. This increases the likelihood of finding how different academic and nonacademic programs or specific student characteristics influence student involvement. For example, in one research study Pace (1990) finds selective liberal arts colleges superior to other types of institutions (research, doctoral, general liberal arts, and comprehensive colleges and universities) on a number of involvement scales.

A much shorter questionnaire designed at our institution, the "Student Perceptions of Student Life Survey," used Pace's conceptualization. We found differences on four scales among various student populations and various academic and nonacademic programs. The questionnaire includes a range of involvement questions in four scales: academic involvement, in class; academic involvement, out of class; personal-social involvement; and cultural-social involvement. (The response scale is "never," "occasionally," "often," and "very often.")

Student responses to these items and to open-ended questions reveal strengths and weaknesses in programs. For example, African-American students showed higher levels of involvement than other groups of students in a number of academic and social areas. Although they represent only about 10 percent of the total population, African Americans have a very active subcommunity, and they take advantage of an academic support structure that apparently serves them well.

As an indicator of course and program effectiveness, student involvement appears to be less constrained than other forms of outcomes assessment. Precise measures of student learning and satisfaction are difficult to develop. Faculty are often dissatisfied with standardized achievement tests that assess what they believe to be the most important learning outcomes of their courses and curricula. While the strongest achievement measures look at general education knowledge and at skills such as writing and critical thinking, these measures are too far removed from what faculty are actually teaching. Measures of student satisfaction often show very little variation over time despite programmatic changes. Satisfaction measures may be significantly influenced by extraneous matters, such as coverage of issues in the student newspaper or how peers describe their reactions to various experiences, rather than by individual students' respective summations of the quality of their experiences. Measures of involvement, on the other hand, have strong content validity and are easy to administer and score.

Assessment of Student Involvement at the Course Level

Examining student involvement at the course level is a form of "classroom assessment." Classroom assessment consists of small-scale assessments conducted continuously within courses to monitor student progress in class (Angelo and Cross, 1993). Classroom assessment techniques are not tests; they are intended to determine to what degree and in what manner students are acquiring knowledge or skills. Classroom assessments look at the intensity of student involvement and at the process of learning in order to provide feedback to teachers and students, rather than looking at particular content that has already been learned by students. In this way, assessment is formative rather than summative. Several examples of course-level assessments follow.

Course-Specific Surveys. John Olmsted of California State University at Fullerton uses in-class questionnaires to engage students more directly and actively in the learning process (see Angelo and Cross, 1993). The questionnaires ask how students intend to be involved in the course: how they will use office visits with him, what strategies they have in mind for the study of chemistry, what strategies they will employ to use tests as learning experiences, and what self-analysis they will undergo to determine which concepts were difficult for them and how they overcame those difficulties as they completed homework assignments. Olmsted concludes that this process turns students into active learners who consider how creative solutions might be employed to improve their learning.

Surveys Based on Seven Principles of Good Practice. Many faculty believe that most students define learning as going to class, taking notes, and reproducing newly acquired insights on a test. To help students broaden their perspectives, several faculty at Syracuse University have adapted *Seven Principles of Good Practice in Undergraduate Education* (Chickering and Gamson, 1991).

A professor of public affairs worked with our evaluation and research office to develop an inventory through which students report their involvement in the seven areas defined by the principles: student-faculty contact, cooperation among students, active learning, prompt feedback, time-on-task, high expectations, and respect for diverse talents and ways of learning.

Here are examples of items:

- I list questions that I have from class or readings and follow them up by consulting with peers, my professor, or on my own.
- I identify areas where I am weak and seek extra help to strengthen them.
- I try to get clear information about my instructor's goals.

The inventory is intended to help students see how their involvement enables them to take responsibility for their education and to use faculty and other students as sources of support for their learning.

The professor of public affairs then illustrated the extent of involvement this activity encourages:

> A student made an appointment to tell me that he was disappointed in the decision to grade only certain exercises in a paper instead of the whole paper. He told me he did not care about the grade but only the principle of the matter. I think from his demeanor that he was sincere.

Research by Oberst (1994) indicates that these principles, particularly the time-on-task principle, are associated with better academic performance.

Student Journals.   Faculty in the School of Nursing at Syracuse use student journals on the premise that students' interpersonal skills are enhanced by the reflective self-assessment that journals require. A number of courses in the college require students to write in their journals at least weekly, although faculty report that most do so more frequently. Students are encouraged to analyze personal experiences and to express feelings that cause them to feel a part of the nursing profession or estranged from it. Faculty view the journals as windows into students' lives through which they can determine the level of physical and emotional investment each student is willing to make in the program. By understanding this level of involvement, faculty can better assist students to reach their personal and academic goals. Journals are consistent with Pace's (1990) "quality of effort" concept, in which he suggests that activities reflecting greater effort from students are more likely to have a greater influence on learning and development. In universitywide surveys, nursing students consistently demonstrate comparatively higher levels not only of academic performance but also of satisfaction, sense of community, and involvement.

Midsemester Course Evaluations. Students in various courses are asked to evaluate at midsemester the utility and effectiveness of the course and instructor. These formative evaluations give students the opportunity to elaborate on their classroom experiences and to suggest ideas that they feel would enhance their involvement, as well as the involvement of future students in the course.

In a focus group, one communications instructor spoke of how she persuaded students to critique the class and think about what was most helpful to their learning. She listed ideas the students had suggested on a short survey. Then they discussed how they could work together to make the class better. "When we talked about organizing our thoughts and putting them down on paper," she reported, "one student would say, 'I spend a couple of hours writing a speech and I don't think it is a problem,' but another student would say, 'I spent eight hours writing a speech and I think it is a problem.'" In that way, the dialogue turned to levels of student involvement in their learning.

Fieldwork Experiences. A junior-year theory course in dietetics is being improved by incorporating fieldwork experiences of seniors who completed internships after taking the theory course. Four team leaders who are seniors receive an honorarium for collecting, synthesizing, and processing information from the fieldwork experiences of other seniors. To strengthen the integration of theory and practice in the course, team leaders work with course professors to revise textbook readings, assignments, lecture content, and exam questions. They also design questionnaires to obtain feedback from current dietetics class members. This creates a more student-responsive curriculum and builds tools that give instructors frequent feedback, thereby increasing students' involvement in the course. Seniors, both the team leaders and other seniors who are asked to examine the impact of their fieldwork experiences, get more invested in their curriculum. These seniors also model how students in the junior dietetics course might get more involved in their curriculum through student-designed classroom assessment.

Assessment of Student Involvement at the Academic Program Level

Assessment should also be carried out at the program and department levels (Tinto, 1993). At these levels, assessments enable faculty to inquire about the net effect of courses that make up programs or departments. When viewed as an intermediate outcome, student involvement provides a common metric for comparing the effects of individual courses and sets of courses.

Cumulative Student Portfolios. Sociology majors and minors develop a cumulative portfolio of their analytic and research accomplishments though the duration of program course work. The project is being piloted with seniors and will be the foundation of a longitudinal study to investigate the impact of the student portfolio on course development, student skills, and advising and graduate-placement processes within the college. As part of the portfolio, students write analytically about the involvements they have had and about how they are developing as a result. Thus both students and faculty can judge which involvements appear to be most valuable in contributing to students' learning.

Diagnostic Testing. Diagnostic tests for foreign languages and writing place students into appropriate courses. A number of other programs, including economics, retailing, and mathematics, use diagnostic testing to determine whether students have the prerequisite skills to complete a course. Students judged incapable are offered a "quick tune-up" of remedial material to refresh their skills, or they are referred to prerequisite courses. Diagnostic testing and remediation focuses student involvement at the level most appropriate to their skills, producing a higher level of engagement in their learning. It also saves valuable class time from being diverted to reviews of prerequisites.

Midsemester Progress Reports. Midsemester progress reports provide first-year students with feedback about their learning and classroom participation. Students get a midterm picture of how instructors perceive their progress in four categories, each of which is critical to a good learning experience and indicative of personal involvement: attendance, participation, work submitted, and quizzes and exams. Instructors also assign a midsemester grade, if they choose.

The midsemester progress report is a valuable motivator for students to become more directed in their involvement and committed to their academic work. These reports also enable academic advisors to work with students who are having difficulty before it is too late. Students find the reports valuable. One said, "I'm glad there were categories, because it's important to know what areas you need to improve on in class instead of just an overall grade." Another appreciated the timeliness of the feedback: "I was used to progress reports in high school, and as a first-year student I think this has made the transition smoother. It's nice to know grades before it's too late to change them."

Assessment of Student Involvement at the Institution Level

Faculty often hear students complain that their lives out of class interfere with their academic lives. Students who live in residence halls sometimes say they cannot study because of noise levels on their floors or general noise levels. Students who live in fraternity or sorority houses say they cannot study because of social gatherings or because of obligations during the rush period. Students may have problems with roommates, friends, and parents impeding their academic endeavors.

Assessing student involvement across programs and departments gives faculty ways to determine the impact of students' out-of-class life on their learning and personal development. These assessments are highly varied:

- Attrition and retention reports. Every year we look at cohort and fall-to-fall statistics for student retention at the institution level and at the school or college level, as well as by gender and ethnicity.

- First-year-student focus groups. Groups of eight to twelve students are conducted at least three times a year. They provide information about student involvement in areas such as "making academic and social connections," "being shaped by your campus experience," and "the influence of Greek life on academic involvement."

- Student Perceptions of Student Life Survey. This survey is sent annually to a 10 percent sample of all undergraduate students and to a 20–50 percent sample of underrepresented groups. Results document involvement, satisfaction, and commitment to various components of campus life. The survey is administered again in April to the same students to examine changes in responses over the first year.

- Leavers study. Students who left the university after their first semester are interviewed to determine their reasons for leaving.

- Transfer study. Students who transfer from the institution are interviewed to determine their reasons for transferring.

- Graduate student perceptions of student life. This survey is conducted biannually.

- Quality of life in the residence hall. Students living in residence halls are surveyed annually.

- Additional studies focus on nonacademic activities such as Greek life, recreation programs, student orientation, and other special events.

What Assessment of Out-of-Class Life Tells Us. Such studies as those listed above have produced numerous suggestions regarding the first-year experience, many of which encourage opportunities for greater student involvement. A follow-up study of the Student Perceptions of Student Life Survey (Tinto and Froh, 1992) links student involvement to persistence. These assessments yield findings about the sense of community on campus, about commitment to teaching and learning, and about issues of gender and ethnicity.

Regarding the sense of community on campus:

- New students feel a strong need to establish relationships with peers, particularly at the beginning of their first year. Students stressed how important such relationships are to their succeeding academically and socially.

- Transfer students need more help in getting connected to the campus culture. They feel somewhat out of place in orientation efforts designed primarily for new first-year students.

- New students are idealistic about interacting with students from different cultures and backgrounds; they often find such interactions more difficult than they anticipated.

Faculty can respond to some of these issues by encouraging interaction among students within their classrooms on course-related topics.
Regarding commitment to teaching and learning:

- Students said that, on average, faculty need to work harder at making lectures more interesting and involving. Students recognize they need to contribute more of themselves by attending all classes and participating more actively.
- Even more important than having smaller classes is faculty showing that they want to get to know students as individuals. Students want more contact with faculty.
- Students in fraternities and sororities want faculty to recognize that they regard academics as important. They also realize that they need to facilitate more interaction between faculty and the members of their organizations.
- First-year students want more help in organizing their time.
- Students would like more involvement in the process of campus decision making.

Thus the campus community needs to find more ways for students and faculty to establish and strengthen informal relationships. Regarding issues of gender and ethnicity:

- Women have gotten more involved in campus programs and have sought more help in improving their academic performance than men, except for in-class involvement, where men and women participate equally.
- African-American students have gotten more involved in campus life and have sought more help than other ethnic

groups, except for in-class involvement, where their effort has been similar to that of European Americans.

- Asian-Pacific students have preferred to work and study on their own, but they use personal and academic support services more often than European-American students.

These findings have influenced programs and services, particularly for first-year students. To cite examples, new resources have reduced class sizes in introductory courses, first-year student seminars are being led by faculty in all colleges in order to ensure more contact with faculty early in the student's academic career, midsemester progress reports are given to all first-year students, and early alert reports in residence-hall settings indicate how students are adjusting to nonclassroom life. With regard to class size, either large classes have been reduced to sections of no more than fifty students, or more sections for recitation/discussion have been added to ensure a maximum of twenty-five students per section.

The Compact.   The University Compact gets to the very essence of student involvement, where integrative academic and social experiences combine to elicit institutional commitment (Tinto, 1987). The Compact also addresses the ideas of communal learning as envisioned by Palmer (1987) and encouraged by The Carnegie Foundation report, *Campus Life: In Search of Community* (Boyer, 1990), where student learning is seen as springing from involvements of all members of the community: students, faculty, administrators, and staff. The Compact was developed by students, staff, faculty, and administrators and consists of statements that participants agree can encourage a "strong learning environment."

The Compact has four themes: (1) supporting scholarly learning, (2) promoting a culturally and socially diverse climate that supports the development of each member of the community, (3) upholding the highest ideals of personal and academic honesty, and (4) maintaining a safe and healthy environment for each member of the community. Under the theme of supporting scholarly learning, for example, a document accompanying the Compact encourages self-assessment by all members of the learning community. It asks students to examine whether they "participate as constructive and active members in their classes," and it then asks faculty members to examine whether they "involve students as active participants in their own learning through class discussion and group activities." Administrators and staff are asked to examine whether they "facilitate the pursuit of scholarship by establishing a climate and a physical environment that supports this endeavor." The companion self-assessments identify subthemes of the four general areas. Through discussion and self-assessment, members of the community can periodically examine whether their involvements are consistent with the Compact and support a learning community.

In conclusion, this chapter has presented examples of using assessment of student involvement in learning as an intermediate and easily measurable outcome. Focusing on involvement enables students, faculty, and administrators to collaborate in determining the net effect of students' in-class and out-of-class involvements on their learning and development.

References

Angelo, T. A., & Cross, K. P. (1993). *Classroom assessment techniques: A handbook for college teachers.* San Francisco: Jossey-Bass.

Astin, A. (1975). *Preventing students from dropping out.* San Francisco: Jossey-Bass.

Astin, A. (1978). *Four critical years: Effects of college on beliefs, attitudes, and knowledge.* San Francisco: Jossey-Bass.

Astin, A. (1985). *Achieving educational excellence: A critical assessment of priorities and practices in higher education.* San Francisco: Jossey-Bass.

Astin, A. (1991). *Assessment for excellence: The philosophy and practice of assessment and evaluation in higher education.* New York: Macmillan.

Astin, A. (1993). *What matters in college: Four critical years revisited.* San Francisco: Jossey-Bass.

Bonwell, C. C., and Eison, J. A. (1991). *Active learning: Creating excitement in the classroom.* ASHE-ERIC Higher Education Reports.

Boyer, E. (1990). *Campus life: In search of community.* The Carnegie Foundation for the Advancement of Teaching.

Center for Instructional Development (1994, May). Student perceptions of student life, Fall 1993. Report prepared for the Syracuse University Campus Study Executive Committee, Syracuse, NY.

Chickering, A., & Gamson, Z. (Eds.). (1991). *Applying the seven principles of good practices in undergraduate education*. New Directions for Teaching and Learning, no. 47. San Francisco: Jossey-Bass.

Erickson, B. L., & Strommer, D. W. (1991). *Teaching college freshmen*. San Francisco: Jossey-Bass.

Light, R. (1990). *The Harvard assessment seminars: Explorations with students and faculty about teaching, learning, and student life*. Harvard University Graduate School of Education and Kennedy School of Government.

McKeachie, W. J. (1994). *Teaching tips: Strategies, research, and theory for college and university teachers*. (9th ed.). Lexington, MA: D. C. Heath.

Oberst, J. (1994). *Seven principles student inventory: An indicator of success?* Doctoral dissertation draft, Syracuse University.

Pace, C. (1983). *College student experiences: A questionnaire* (2nd ed.). Los Angeles: University of California, Higher Education Research Institute.

Pace, C. (1984). *Measuring the quality of college student experiences*. Los Angeles: University of California, Higher Education Research Institute.

Pace, C. (1990). *The undergraduates: A report of their activities and progress in college in the 1980s*. Los Angeles: University of California, Center for the Study of Evaluation.

Palmer, P. (1987, September/October). Community, conflict, and ways of knowing. *Change*, 20–25.

Pascarella, E., & Terenzini, P. (1991). *How college affects students: Findings and insights from 20 years of research*. San Francisco: Jossey-Bass.

Stark, J. S., Lowther, M. A., Ryan, M. P., Bomotti, S. S., Genthon, M., Haven, C. L., & Martens, G. (1988). *Reflections on course planning: Faculty and students consider influences and goals*. Ann Arbor, MI: National Center for Research to Improve Postsecondary Teaching and Learning.

Study Group on the Conditions of Excellence in American Higher Education. (1984). *Involvement in learning: Realizing the potential of American higher education*. Washington, DC: National Institute of Education/U.S. Department of Education.

Tinto, V. (1987). *Leaving college: Rethinking the causes and cures of student attrition*. Chicago: University of Chicago Press.

Tinto, V. (1993). *Leaving college: Rethinking the causes and cures of student attrition* (2nd ed.). Chicago: University of Chicago Press.

Tinto, V., & Froh, R. (1992, October). *Deconstructing social theory: Translating research on student persistence into policy*. Paper presented at the annual meeting of the Association for the Study of Higher Education, Minneapolis.

Part Two

Teachers and Teaching

The theme of Part Two is our belief that our knowledge of students and learning mandates new ways of thinking about and practicing instruction. These new viewpoints see teaching in broader and more detailed frameworks. From this new perspective, the role of the faculty member involves more than the transfer of information. It is a role not at the center of the instructional package but in relation to a variety of roles and activities. In this framework, the teacher functions more as a manager who triages and then monitors a variety of instructional tasks that we know are positively associated with learning.

Some of the work in this new paradigm is different. It employs strategies and orientations that are alternatives to the conventional teaching role. But much of the work is the same. Teachers still plan and organize courses. They still design assignments and assess student performance on the assignments. But even these customary instructional tasks are thought about in new ways. What we propose, then, is not more or less work for faculty but work of a different kind—work, we believe, with a clearer sense of focus and purpose. It is teaching considered principally in terms of its impact on students and learning.

The Theme in Variations: Chapter Summaries

Susan Millar, in Chapter Seven, provides a natural transition between Parts One and Two. We have detailed how students are changing and explored the implications of those changes as they link with new knowledge about learning. Millar begins simply and obviously: the changes in students require a new role for faculty.

The role she explores theoretically and illustrates with a case study is consistent with the theme of this and the previous part: students must be the centerpiece of our educational endeavors because they are the ones who do the learning. Millar addresses the radical change this shift implies for teachers. This is instruction on a whole new set of terms—terms that recognize, indeed encourage, student discovery and creation of knowledge. It involves a transfer of power and a classroom configured so that students have more of a say in its operation.

What makes Millar's chapter so convincing is the case she uses to show this new orientation in action. Many faculty see the social construction of knowledge, as the meaning-making of students is often described, as relevant only in the humanities and social sciences where terms and issues are more variable in their meaning and use. Millar's case describes efforts to construct discovery-based experiences for students beginning an engineering curriculum.

The chapter also illustrates that the case for a shift in focus from teachers and teaching to students and learning can be made in philosophical terms. There are reasons and justifications for the move based on the assumptions, principles, and premises of education. The move is more than one of political expediency.

Even in an instructional realm so transformed, many important details of good teaching remain intact. They become the objects of more concerted and focused effort. Take course planning, for example. It has always been important. With learning as the relevant outcome, the design of learning experiences, the purpose and goals of instruction, and the structure and sequence of content all grow in scope and significance.

George Geis (Chapter Eight) assumes that courses already exist and that part of this new orientation to teaching is deciding whether or not they should be revised. He writes about the "life of a course" and sees the planning process as interactive and evolving.

This chapter does not break new ground, but it does offer a systematic, ordered approach to planning that is likely to result in courses being organized so that they provide students with the structure necessary for learning to occur. The chapter concludes by recommending student feedback as part of the replanning and revising process. Geis observes, "The more fully students participate in the instructional event, the greater the chances are of them becoming learners."

In some ways, the Geis chapter anticipates Part Three. He sees planning as something more than the individual activity of an isolated instructor. Courses must be viewed in sequence, in relationship to other courses that together make up a coherent curricular experience, both within a department and across the entire course-taking experience of a student. Courses must also been seen from the perspective of future employers. Do they give students the knowledge and skills that do in fact prepare them for the world of work?

Joseph Lowman addresses another "detail" of teaching from this larger context, assignments—but assignments that promote and integrate learning. Faculty have always designed and used assignments, but often their dual purpose has been ignored. Assignments are what faculty use to ascertain levels of student mastery so that grades can be generated; that purpose is real and legitimate. But equally important is the recognition of assignments as learning opportunities.

In Chapter Nine, Lowman treats a range of assignments. He writes about reading and writing assignments, problem solving, and

observational and hands-on assignments. The point he makes so
clearly about each is that there are ways of designing and using
these assignments that do help students to learn better. There is
nothing about what Lowman proposes that cannot be used to generate grades, but his focus encourages faculty to explore the connection between assignments and learning.

Both Geis and Lowman show that all is not new under the
teaching sun but that even what is familiar and comfortable to faculty needs to be explored in new and different ways when teaching effectiveness is tied to learning outcomes. Robert Menges and
William Rando, on the other hand, do propose something new: an
eclectic model of the process of seeking and using feedback to
improve teaching and learning.

They note, in Chapter Ten, that faculty have always sought
feedback but are rarely very systematic about the collection process.
Moreover, acting on the collected feedback has been a problem.
Faculty seem more inclined to focus on the feedback itself (its
veracity, relevance, and what the institution might do with it) than
on the changes it might call for.

Part of the reluctance to deal with feedback is that often it
identifies or relates to some problematic aspect of instruction (as
in the chapter's scenario of an instructor whose students, when they
discuss, rarely incorporate ideas or information from the reading).
Instructional problems are not something most faculty are disposed
to consider thoughtfully or discuss with others.

However, in an environment where the prime concern is student learning, monitoring learning experiences is essential. You
cannot tell, by observation alone, if a student is learning. Moreover, solicitation of and response to feedback about learning shift
the emphasis, as we have already noted, making the focus of the
improvement effort not the teaching, but the learning. It is much
safer and easier for faculty to talk about improving student learning than about improving their teaching. Nonetheless, this chapter is true to the inseparability of teaching and learning. It is about

improving both, but it emphasizes that teaching gets better because faculty respond to the learning experiences of students.

Despite emphasizing challenges and problems (that is, the parts of given instructional activities such as reading assignments that might need to be "improved" because they are not working well), Chapter Ten is positive. There is a sense of mastery and control about the process it proposes. Instructional difficulties do not occur because faculty are inept or students are capricious; they occur because components of the activities don't fit the instructional circumstances in which they are used. So the faculty member must tinker, adapt, adjust, change, modify, and rethink the details. The process is actually rather intriguing, engaging, and challenging; when successfully completed, it brings a sense of satisfaction and accomplishment. In that light, the process doesn't seem all that difficult, and there certainly is little about it to make one defensive.

Geis and Lowman illustrate some of what it means for teachers to be "managers" of learning experiences and environments, while Menges and Rando show how it is that a teacher can "monitor" learning processes. Marilla Svinicki and colleagues round out Part Two with a chapter that moves away from details back to the larger context that opens this part. However, the topics in Chapter Eleven are quite different from those of Millar's Chapter Seven.

Teaching methods have long been the focus of a variety of research endeavors. As Svinicki and colleagues note, the quest has always been to find the "best" or most effective methods. These authors think the results point out the folly of the approach. Different methods seem to end up pretty much equal, but their comprehensive review identifies the circumstances and conditions under which most instructional methods do and don't work. This is the chapter that informs the managing and monitoring decisions identified in earlier chapters.

Besides its emphasis on methods of instruction, what also positions this chapter clearly in a section on teaching is its attention to learning as the basis for decisions about instruction. The authors propose that we look specifically at research on learning and extrapolate instructional implications from it. Chapter Eleven is especially valuable in its willingness to bridge the gap between research and practice. Summaries of findings are followed with concrete suggestions for teachers interested in maximizing learning outcomes.

Like others in Part Two, this chapter demonstrates how closely and inseparably teaching and learning are tied together. To consider instructional methods independently of their effects on students is to rob them of credible purpose, and to consider learning independently of the roles and functions of the teacher is to render it significantly less effective.

Advancing the Thesis

If undergraduate education is to be improved, teaching must be changed. This sections spells out the details of some of those changes. Changes begin with a different orientation to teaching, new ways of thinking about teaching roles in light of changing students and greater commitments to their learning. Changes are realized by attending to the details of instruction—including those that are comfortably part of current faculty teaching activities. But the details are important, and more essential in this paradigm; they ought to be the objects of fixed and focused faculty attention. There is also a new role for monitoring the impact of instructional efforts: how does a teaching policy, practice, or behavior affect student learning? Here is a new way of looking at the research on instructional methods and learning: what does the research tell us directly about how we should be teaching?

Part Two demonstrates the diversity of the scholarship available to improve practice. It includes summaries and distillations of research and practice, and it uses case studies to illustrate implementation. It also makes clear the complexity of the teaching-learning process, and in that way shows how the diversity of scholarship reflects the character of the phenomena in question.

Finally, this section also illustrates how a "scholarly" orientation to teaching improves practice. It demonstrates the attention to detail required by reflective practice. It shows how and why students can and should be involved in their own learning. The teacher still manages and monitors, but the students do the work of learning. They help faculty by monitoring and reporting their experiences.

Chapter Seven

New Roles for Teachers in Today's Classrooms

Susan B. Millar
University of Wisconsin–Madison

College students have changed, as Chapter Two of this volume clearly documents. They come less well prepared to handle the traditional rigors of postsecondary courses. Their learning needs are more diverse, and many of them have unrealistic expectations of the work and motivation necessary for success. Further, these diverse students find themselves in classes taught by faculty who traditionally have equated skillful, effective teaching with presentation of objective course content for students to master. Not unexpectedly, many of today's college students do not successfully master the content or achieve the standards set by such faculty.

In this chapter, I propose that the faculty role must change in order to assist students to meet academic standards. I discuss how this change has already begun, basing my explanation on Fullan's theory that it is only when the *meaning* of our experiences in educational institutions changes that significant shifts in everyday educational experiences occur (Fullan, 1991). In particular, I propose that the meaning of teaching is changing. Many faculty are altering key features of their classrooms and are providing learning environments that, for the most part, improve students' academic achievement. In doing so, these faculty cease to equate effective teaching with mere presentation of course content. Instead, they perceive teaching as a complex dialogical process.

I begin by describing a Cartesian position that takes for granted that humans are independent, atomistic agents who utilize objective knowledge in order to better control their social and natural world. For a variety of reasons, many faculty are abandoning this Cartesian position in favor of a dialogical position. Briefly, the dialogical position takes for granted that each person's very existence depends on interactions during which knowledge itself is continually recreated. A major part of the chapter is devoted to a case study that illustrates how this shift in the philosophical stance of faculty can both motivate students and help them achieve higher academic standards. Finally, I briefly critique the chapter itself in terms of the dialogical standpoint.

Cartesian and Dialogical Philosophical Positions

The Cartesian philosophical position on the nature of the self and knowledge assumes that the mature individual is an independent, atomistic agent, capable of constituting himself or herself and of controlling nature and other beings (Wertsch, 1991; Wilshire, 1990). A Cartesian conception of knowledge requires "an immense abstraction from the world as immediately lived" (Wilshire, 1990, p. 37). Cartesian thinkers thus view themselves as transcendent, independent subjects observing and acting upon an objective, passive world. Moreover, they choose to represent their capacity to control aspects of the world as a function of possessing knowledge.

Cartesian thinkers construe learning as a knowledge-acquisition process that enables a relatively empty novice to become a knowledge-full expert. By extension, teaching is construed as a process by which knowledge is unidirectionally transmitted from expert to novice. This is the "banking" idea of education developed in Freire's classic *Pedagogy of the Oppressed* (1990). The teacher who operates from within a Cartesian position is known, in Freire's terms, by his "narration":

The teacher talks about reality as if it were motionless, static, compartmentalized, and predictable. . . . His task is to "fill" the student with the contents of his narration—contents which are detached from reality. . . . [Narration] turns [students] into "containers," into "receptacles" to be "filled" by the teacher. The more completely he fills the receptacles, the better a teacher he is. The more meekly the receptacles permit themselves to be filled, the better students they are (1990, p. 57–58).

In the Cartesian view, the teacher helps students become independent, atomistic agents (like the faculty) by transmitting knowledge that students need to become agents capable of controlling situations in the world.

The Cartesian position is consistent with the idea that the role of the teacher is that of judge. In some ways, students are like course content, a kind of material which faculty—and for that matter students themselves—organize, sift, sort, and "measure" in terms of how well they meet objective standards. Moreover, Cartesian thinkers assume that the resulting sortings are a natural consequence of the precollege training, native intelligence, and motivation that students bring to their coursework. Thus students on their side are responsible only for proving that they have acquired the requisite knowledge, and faculty on their side are responsible only for transmitting the knowledge and judging the adequacy with which students have met the standards, that is, mastered the material.

Yet many well-prepared, diligent students fail to achieve academic standards, even when faculty present well-organized material. Cartesian faculty and students resolve the apparent contradiction by concluding that those who fail are not cut out for this discipline. They do not ask, By what processes do students actually make sense of and think in terms of the knowledge developed in this discipline? Rather, they assume that those who fail to meet standards are underprepared, should study harder, should change majors, or do something else with their lives.

Increasing numbers of faculty are questioning the Cartesian position. They are beginning to view their role from the significantly different standpoint referred to here as "dialogical." Four features of contemporary higher education encourage faculty to challenge the adequacy of the Cartesian position.

First, too many students are being lost in some fields—what is sometimes called the "pipeline" problem. We are warned to expect "serious problems . . . by the late 1990s" in replacing the professoriate (Bowen and Rudenstein, 1992, p. 3). In the mathematics-based disciplines in particular, policy reports discuss "leakage" in the mathematics, science, and engineering pipelines. For example, the National Science Foundation cites significant declines in the numbers of baccalaureate science degrees earned since the mid-1980s, despite an overall increase in the total number of bachelor's degrees (National Science Foundation, 1989). Moreover, since 1993 the NSF's interest in cultivating the scientific elite who get all the way through the "pipeline" has been superseded by its interest in "science for all" (National Science Foundation, n.d.). Citizens and state legislators are upset about low enrollment and retention rates in the math-based disciplines for U.S.-born students, especially women and ethnic minorities. Moreover, employers commonly complain that students in these and other majors are not prepared to work in teams and have undeveloped communication and critical thinking skills.

Second, scholars question the process by which access to higher education is being provided, particularly at public institutions. They ask, Who is served when higher education institutions enroll students whom they then allow to flounder and fail? Scholars such as Bonsangue (1992) and Treisman (1992) argue that neither students nor society at large is served by such institutions. Institutions admitting students who have little hope of meeting academic standards exact a high toll from state taxpayers (who subsidize tuition) and from students (whose self-esteem may be seriously damaged by repeated failure).

Third, although faculty efforts to investigate and make improvements in student learning are generally not equitably rewarded during promotion and salary evaluations (Fairweather, 1992), new support for faculty efforts to improve student learning is apparent at both institutional and national levels. Presidents and provosts are emphasizing the importance of improving the learning experiences of undergraduates. Professional associations are shifting their attention to teaching and learning processes. For example, the American Association of Higher Education and the Postsecondary Education Division of the American Educational Research Association have taken the teaching-learning process as themes for their national conferences, and the American Mathematics Association has begun to attach major importance to teaching issues. Federal research foundations, such as the National Science Foundation, are breaking with their own traditions and allocating a substantial portion of their funds for educational innovation. Higher education publishers, such as Jossey-Bass, Heldref Publications, Kluwer Academic Publishers, and the ASHE-ERIC Higher Education Reports, are finding expanding markets for magazines, books, and monographs focusing on teaching and learning issues.

Finally, the Cartesian theory of knowledge itself is being critiqued across the academy. In the first part of the century, physicists such as de Broglie and Heisenberg were realizing that quantum mechanics revealed the inadequacy of a Cartesian theory of knowledge. Scientists began to theorize that the presence of the knower must be taken into account in the process of knowing. Such a theory contradicts the philosophical position that knowledge is external to the knower and subject to being "uncovered" by researchers. Meanwhile, in the 1920s and 1930s in Russia, Vygotsky's explorations of child development (1978) and Bakhtin's analysis of the

role of "voice" in the creation of meaning (1986) offered compa-
rably revolutionary, but largely unheeded, challenges to the Cartesian philosophical position.

Motivated by practical, ethical, and philosophical concerns,
many academics are now asking, How does my theory of knowl-
edge-production affect my research process and findings? and How
does my theory of learning affect the teaching-learning process
experienced by my students—and by me? For example, Tobias
(1990) and Bruffee (1993) engaged these questions by proposing
that intellectually talented students are disenchanted by the "com-
pellingly certain and coherent" vision of science served up in traditional introductory science courses (Bruffee, 1993, p. 146). Their
proposal is supported by Hewitt and Seymour's research on causes
of attrition from science, mathematics, and engineering (SME)
majors, which shows that the three reasons for leaving most frequently cited by "switchers" were "non-SME majors offer a better
education with greater intrinsic interest" (64 percent), "rejection
of SME career(s) and associated lifestyle" (57 percent), and "lack
of/loss of interest in subject: 'turned off science'" (46 percent)
(Hewitt and Seymour, 1994, p. 54). Bruffee proposes that an "interdependent, interpretive, and constructive" approach to science
would retain the interest of the postmodern student (1993, p. 144).

I propose that Bruffee and others who are asking these new
questions exemplify the shift to a dialogical philosophical position
on the nature of self and knowledge. Rather than representing the
self as an atomistic agent who absorbs authoritative knowledge,
they represent the self as the complex product of interactions during which knowledge itself is continually created and recreated.
These more dialogical faculty view the teaching-learning enterprise
as a complex social system containing variables that operate at
institutional, curricular, and pedagogical levels.

At the heart of the dialogical position is the concept of "addres-
sivity," which is experienced when "the voice of a listener responds

to the voice of a speaker" (Wertsch, 1991, p. 52). Each party to an interaction thus comes with his or her own system of dialogically constructed knowledge and contributes in a reciprocal fashion to ongoing interactions. In this representation of self and knowledge, each person comes by knowledge *in the course of* addressing the other during interactions, not by absorbing transmittable, objective material. Thus learning is construed as an inherently dialogical process occurring among knowers who depend on their mutual interaction for the development of new knowledge and their own identities.

Representing the self and knowledge in this way requires that both knowledgeable experts and novices view the experts not merely as sources of knowledge but as participants in dialogical interactions. The teacher as well as the student must attend to the intentions and understandings of the other to sustain a teaching-learning interaction. Thus while teachers operating from a dialogical position expect students to attend carefully to the teachers' rich fund of discipline-based knowledge, they also expect to address students in terms of students' particular contexts. As Wertsch puts it, "Ultimately, an utterance reflects not only the voice producing it but also the voices to which it is addressed" (1991, p. 53). In other words, dialogical faculty seek to learn how their students differ from them, and moreover they value these differences.

As students' knowledge and contexts come into focus, dialogical faculty drop the assumption that student performance is a function only of student variables (academic preparation, intelligence, and motivation) and hence only the responsibility of precollege environments and of students. These faculty understand that their role as arbiter of course standards and student achievement does not require that they treat students as material to be sorted or "weeded out." Instead, they can treat students as novices seeking guidance and make themselves, *qua* knowledgeable and experienced individuals, available as key elements in the learning climate. In thus giving students opportunities to dialogically construct disciplinary knowledge in interaction with them, they play a critical role that contributes to student efforts to achieve academic standards.

As the following case study shows, shifting from a Cartesian to a dialogical position is itself accomplished through an interactive faculty process. The case features a group of engineering faculty who worked together to offer a new introductory course. They started their shift to a more dialogical position while preparing a new course: their planning process entailed listening to student complaints and evaluating the many variables that affect student learning outcomes. Seeing students in light of this new knowledge and different perspective, they were able to formulate and implement new approaches to their course. As they assessed the effects of these new variables on their curricular and pedagogical approaches and on student achievement, their shift toward a dialogical philosophical position continued to the point that it seemed "natural."

Shift to a Dialogical Philosophical Position: Case Study

This case is drawn from a site visit to an institution I will call Research State University, conducted in 1991–1992 as part of the second-year evaluation of an engineering education project funded by the National Science Foundation. Information comes from open-ended interviews with administrators, faculty, and students and from written materials provided by the principal investigator. That the case features an engineering course should not be taken to imply that engineering faculties are the only ones asking these questions. The engineering course is featured because the author happens to have studied it and because it provides a particularly good example of the shift from a Cartesian to a dialogical position. (The literature that develops this idea is immense. Key readings with which I am familiar include Jordanova, 1980; Wilshire, 1990; Wertsch, 1991; and Harding, 1986, 1991.) The focus is on efforts of four faculty members who revised the introductory engineering course required of all first-year engineering majors. At the time of the site visit, pilot sections of this revised course had been offered for three semesters. The case study took place midway through the third semester, when two pilot classes were in progress.

The Impetus for Change

Before the NSF project, engineering faculty at Research State had little reason to question their approach. They had been granting large numbers of bachelor's degrees while increasing their production of engineering research. During the 1980s, however, key administrators in the Engineering Dean's Office became concerned about the dropout rates for all students, but particularly for women and minorities. They assessed existing student support programs, studied retention programs around the country, and instituted a set of support programs for minority students.

Toward the end of the 1980s, undergraduate student complaints became more insistent, or were taken more seriously. In my interviews, students and faculty explained that the level of alienation between faculty and students had reached a critical point in the early 1990s. Students and faculty decided to establish a Code of Faculty-Student Expectations in an effort to improve relations. Each group met separately to formulate their expectations of the other. According to a student leader who attended both meetings, students expected that faculty would be involved primarily in their own research, but they also expected that faculty as teachers should "light the spark" for students. Instead, students reported aloof and sometimes disrespectful faculty attitudes. Faculty consensus was that students should show commitment and interest in their classes. Faced with students who read newspapers during lectures, skipped lectures altogether, cheated on exams, complained about grades, and failed to do homework, faculty found it difficult to maintain enthusiasm as undergraduate instructors.

At this point, a midcareer professor responded to an NSF request for proposals for a faculty-based effort to improve engineering education. In describing his involvement to us, he referred to the college's persistently low enrollment rates for women and minorities, declining enrollments for white men, and low retention rates for engineering majors. He perceived that the college administration was generally supportive of improving undergraduate education. But he described his concern about the level of alienation between faculty and undergraduates and explained how he had come to know that a small but influential group of colleagues were interested in improving undergraduate engineering courses. He realized that NSF was likely to put substantial fiscal resources into their new education initiative. In light of all this information, he convinced his colleagues and the dean's office to make a commitment to the NSF project.

The Planning Process

When the project was funded, this professor and three of his colleagues devoted themselves to the introductory engineering course. In assessing and planning revisions, they did not assume that students left or felt alienated because they were inadequate. Instead of seeking ways to "fix" the students, they focused on how students experienced the course.

What students told them indicated that some students left for an appropriate reason: they had found other fields to be more interesting. Many others, however, left or were dissatisfied for reasons that troubled these faculty. Some students left because they failed or could not tolerate the "weed-out" mentality in their prerequisite mathematics and science courses and in some of the engineering courses. Other students complained that their courses were too "theoretical" and fragmented. As one student put it, "You don't want to learn something that you can't use. There needs to be a reason behind it." Another explained, "Everyone is trying to just absorb everything, and then you take a quiz." Another common complaint—highlighted in the Code of Faculty-Student Expectations incident—was the aloof and disrespectful faculty attitudes perceived by students. Students protested, "Faculty act like they don't have time for our questions," and "They make us feel like our questions are stupid." Still other students complained that they felt discouraged and put off by the competitive attitudes of the students, attitudes that were exacerbated by faculty practices such as grading on the curve. (These reasons are confirmed in interviews with students in all seven engineering schools in the project—Millar and Fairweather, 1992—and in other recent research; see Hewitt and Seymour, 1994.)

The four faculty members interpreted these complaints as flags marking trouble spots in their traditional course and sought to design a course free of these problems. They were assisted in their efforts by an associate dean who had a broad knowledge of the teaching and learning literature. One professor took the initiative to explore this literature, noting with marked enthusiasm how much he had learned from it. (A brief guide to this literature appears at the end of this chapter.)

The Implementation Process

These faculty came to perceive three different types of variables—institutional, pedagogical, and curricular—that might be altered to improve their introductory course.

Institutional Variables. Beginning with class size, they reasoned that reducing classes to no more than twenty-five students could, by itself, alleviate student-identified problems associated with faculty "aloofness." Moreover, this change made alterations in pedagogical variables feasible. In order to teach smaller sections, they secured the dean's permission for a pilot project. They also tried to address an institutional variable over which they had no direct control, the prerequisite courses taught in nonengineering departments with a weed-out approach. They reasoned that by providing substantial hands-on engineering design experience in their introductory engineering course they could indirectly mitigate the alienating effects of the prerequisite courses. Hands-on design experience was expected to make students more aware of the relevance of mathematics and science content for engineering.

Pedagogical Variables. Faculty focused on making the new course work well for the students while also meeting academic standards. Beginning with student complaints about competing against each other for grades, they examined current grading practices. Relying mostly on individual performance on tests, grades traditionally were computed by assigning a C to the median performance and arraying the other grades on both sides of the median to achieve a normal distribution. Aware that these practices alienated many students, faculty decided to base half of each student's grade on the overall performance of his or her "project group." The other half would be based on individual performance on exams, with grading on the curve eliminated. These new practices would moderate the overly competitive atmosphere about which students complained and would accustom students to being evaluated on both individual and team performance, thereby previewing experiences of practicing engineers.

Faculty also decided to alter two other closely related pedagogical variables: the use of class time and classroom interaction processes. As faculty interviewees explained it, lecture time was decreased, project group time was added, and computer laboratory time was increased. Changes in classroom interaction processes included an overall shift toward a more informal faculty stance toward students and the introduction of three new formats: the project group format, the minilecture format, and the "roving consultant" format. The project group format involved placing four or five randomly selected students into a group that worked together the entire semester. The minilecture format involved ten- to fifteen-minute faculty lectures followed by informal question-answer sessions. When using the "roving consultant" format, the faculty member and a couple of graduate students were on hand to provide cues and clues when different groups or individuals asked for help.

Curriculum Variables. The curriculum was shifted from a format in which faculty transmit specified content to students to one informed by the idea that students learn through team efforts to solve real-life engineering problems. To accomplish this shift, they created project groups and required each group to design and build a device that solved a problem posed by the faculty. For example, in one semester the problem was to design, construct, and install a swing set in a public site at minimal cost. Another semester, it was to design and construct a solar-powered still that produced potable water from saline water, again at minimal cost. The new course design aimed to answer student complaints that the curriculum was too abstract and fragmented as well as to provide more realistic understanding of engineering work and strengthen motivation to join the profession.

The new course developed incrementally as faculty took turns offering it. At the end of each term, they assessed the overall outcomes. Were students more likely to become, or remain, committed to engineering? Did they meet faculty standards for mastering new engineering concepts and skills? In short, what were the effects of these course adjustments on students and their learning?

The Assessment Process

I gathered information about assessment from students, faculty, and administrators.

Student Assessments. My interviews included three students who had experienced the course from the standpoint of different project groups and who could compare it with a traditional version of the course. Tom had failed, and Ray had dropped out of the old version of the course. Jim, having done poorly in first-year courses at another big engineering school, had just transferred to Research State.

Students contrasted the new course with traditional courses. For example, they explained how the extended group effort to design and build tools that solve a real-life problem contrasted with the overly abstract and fragmented curricula of other courses. As Tom put it:

> Before, like when you're just learning facts and stuff, you think, "Why am I learning this? What do I need that for?" But [in this class], you're working on a project, and pulling things in from all over the place—you know, different disciplines. And you're realizing while you're studying those separate disciplines—like when you're in your chemistry class or your physics class, that, "Well yeah, this connects." You see connections between things. It's more rewarding. It's more of an education. You feel like more of an educated person. . . . You almost feel like an engineer, even though you don't have the knowledge.

Ray agreed with Tom but also expressed some ambivalence about the challenge posed by the new curriculum design. Although traditional pencil tests presented knowledge in a fragmented form, he had learned how to perform well on these tests and felt disoriented and threatened when required to solve real-life, open-ended design problems. As he explained:

> I can study in physics or something, and do very well, but it's not like that in this class. I mean, it's very different. It's not like, "Do this chapter." Instead, you have to *find* the chapter to go to for the equation that you need and then use it. It's really depressing. Because all these things I know already—I realize I've just forgotten them.

These students also drew comparisons to mathematics and science prerequisite courses. Tom explained:

> Take chemistry, for example. Chemistry is a single discipline, and this [revised introductory] course would be, like, interdisciplinary. And in chemistry, you would learn how different parts of chemistry interact. For example, atomic theory relates to bonding, but basically, it's still all just chemistry. . . . It's like little pieces. But in this class, we're putting pieces together. It gives things relevance.

The revised course also helped confirm Tom's commitment to engineering. He continued:

> It's also good because—remember when we were talking about physics as a weed-out class? I don't really think that kind of class is fair. Obviously if someone just absolutely cannot visualize it, really not capable, then yeah, they shouldn't be there. But if someone wants to decide for themselves if they want to do engineering, they shouldn't decide they don't want to do it because *physics* is too hard. It should be like, I don't really like *engineering*. And with this class, you actually find out what an engineer does.

Linked closely to assessments of the design-based hands-on curriculum structure were students' reactions to the way class time had been reorganized and how that affected faculty-student interactions. Upon being asked how the course is organized, the students said:

> JIM: Wednesday morning is engineering concepts. Thursday afternoon, the first half is more concepts, and the second half is meeting with your groups.
> RAY: Yeah, we talk about chemistry, calculus—it's all hard stuff.
> TOM: And Monday morning is all programming. Wednesday morning is like a lecture, but it's different than most

lectures. It's kind of a mixture, because we'll stop in the middle of the class and say, "Well, what about so and so?"

JIM: I think it's really helpful because we're touching on a lot of areas, like in chemistry, physics, statics—things maybe we haven't touched on yet—haven't even had those classes yet. But we need them for our projects. And you'd think you'd have a real problem, but since it's so interactive, it's really easy to understand.

Furthermore, these students explained that the faculty listened to their complaints and implemented changes in response to them. For example, early in the course they felt the faculty were demanding too much interdependence by expecting each group to improve and build the design developed by another group. "I like how they're flexible about things like this," Tom explained. "I remember walking over to the library with [the professor], explaining the problem to her." Shortly thereafter, the professor dropped the cross-group activity. Comments like these show that students felt they were being invited into the discipline.

In project groups, they felt that the continuous, informal student-student interaction built into the course was a particularly productive aspect of the learning experience. Their voices rising with excitement, they explained that their groups began with very high expectations for themselves—higher than the faculty expectations. They described how they had to scale down the plans in order to accomplish their goals in real time and with limited fiscal resources. Furthermore, all expressed appreciation for what the assignment had taught them about the division of labor—a skill actually needed in industry.

At the same time, however, Ray and Jim commented that being dependent on the performance of other members of their group for part of their grade made them feel insecure. As Ray put it:

I'm kind of worried. I'm taking, like, really hard classes, but I'm worried about this class the most because I don't have as much control over this class as I have in my other classes. 'Cause like in the other classes, I just take tests and I know what I'm doing with exams. But this class—yeah, it's a lot of fun too, to build things—but I don't have much control over my grade here.

It is clear from these comments that the course went beyond merely avoiding problems students experienced in traditional courses. On the one hand, the revised course created new problems, particularly for students who felt threatened by having to take a more active role in the construction of engineering knowledge. On the other hand, the course invited students into the "discourse community" of engineers. As Tom put it, they "almost felt like engineers."

Faculty and Administrator Assessments.   As far as the faculty was concerned, the course was too new to justify long-term assessments. However, their evaluation of student performance in terms of course content and skills and their informal assessments of their own experiences with students were strongly positive. Each of the faculty members spontaneously offered the same three assessments. First, students learned more and developed better designs than faculty had expected. In other words, standards were not compromised by the revision. Second, faculty agreed that the course was far more work for them but also far more rewarding. Third, they found that interacting with students helped them better understand student learning and highlighted the importance of context-specific student feedback in fostering high-level student performance.

The dean's assessment can be summed up simply. He decided to fund this version of the course for the entire first-year class in the semester following the case study. He planned to offer eighteen sections of the class so that class size could remain below thirty, and he requested that departments staff these sections with highly regarded senior people, thereby involving many new faculty in the course. As he explained, he had weighed the anticipated benefits in student performance and retention against possible losses to the school's research and service missions and decided that this new distribution of faculty effort would result in a net gain for the school.

Overall, the changes made in key variables in the course fostered generally high levels of student commitment and encouraged students to achieve course standards. But while the revised course alleviated problems associated with the traditional introductory lecture courses, it created its own new stresses. For example, student feedback indicated that, even as the course's collaborative and active approach to learning generated student enthusiasm and commitment, it also generated some insecurity. Were there better ways to help students shift from passive to interactive approaches to learning? Were certain types of students more likely to respond well to this approach than other types? What about long-term effects? Would students trained in their first year with interactive learning strategies be more likely to attain their baccalaureates in engineering, more likely to become creative and productive engineers as judged by industry employers, and more likely to go on to graduate engineering programs? Was the additional teaching effort required of faculty justifiable, given the goals of a research university? Would the dean continue to fund the course after external support had expired? Answers to these questions will evolve as those involved with the project continue to assess the effects of the course on students, faculty, administration, and the college.

Conclusion

This chapter seeks to provide an explanation of the changing role that faculty play in ensuring that students achieve academic standards. I started from the assumption that it is only when faculty and students give new meaning to their experiences that they are able to genuinely change their everyday educational experiences (Fullan, 1991). I then argued that many faculty are questioning the Cartesian position that has long informed academic practices and are shifting to a dialogical position that gives new meaning—and new shape—to their teaching. I then presented a case that illustrates changes in the philosophical stance of faculty and the attendant effects on students.

I bring the story full circle by noting that I learned, through writing this chapter, that Cartesian habits of mind are persistent. Precisely because I remained largely Cartesian in my own perspective, I failed until now to perceive how much the faculty's capacity to make curricular and pedagogical changes depends on student-initiated interactions. It was Research State students, not faculty, who were the first to chafe against the Cartesian position. In typical Cartesian fashion, I missed this crucial element by implicitly assuming that only the faculty would be sufficiently knowledgeable and able to initiate the change.

I now perceive that the students in the case study are not generic "students." They are *today*'s students, some of whom resist and complain. Implicitly, they expect to be able to make connections between their course material and other experiences. They expect to engage in a kind of dialogue—in their own minds, if nowhere else—about how course material is related within and across courses and how it is related to their own experiences. They strive to match their teachers' words with their own "counter words." Similarly, these students complain of being treated like raw material to be sorted and of being forced to outperform their fellow students on exams on pain of being "weeded-out." They reject faculty whose behavior communicates that the "good" student is the one who passively produces the right answers on tests. They expect to be treated "addressively," to be affirmed for asking questions.

While my critique of the overly Cartesian interpretation of this chapter is warranted, the chapter's emphasis on the initiative that the Research State faculty took is also warranted. Unlike many of today's faculty, these four *listened* to today's students. They sought external funds to support improved teaching and sampled the literature on teaching. They changed their minds and their behaviors.

Freeing themselves from the Cartesian assumption that faculty must be independent experts who transmit knowledge, they planned, implemented, and assessed their new course—together. They adopted pedagogical practices that required them to interact with their students—informally, and often on the students' turf. And they developed a curriculum that required students to interact and depend on each other to meet the academic standards.

I conclude by noting that not only is the meaning of teaching changing for some faculty but the meaning of learning is changing for some students. Faculty and students are together altering key features of college classrooms. Responding to these more dialogical learning climates, both students and faculty find the teaching-learning process inherently more rewarding. And in the process, students are achieving academic standards.

Resource: Guide to the Literature on Teaching and Learning in Postsecondary Education

The higher education teaching and learning literature may be organized as follows:

- *Single case studies*, which provide examples of how other faculty altered and improved specific courses. Commonly found in discipline-specific journals, for example, *Educational Studies in Mathematics, Engineering Education, Science and Education, Contributions from History, Philosophy, and Sociology of Science and Mathematics*, and *Teaching Sociology*, and in general publications devoted to teaching (for example, *College Teaching*), these studies are most useful for faculty who teach courses in the same discipline and type of institution featured in the case study.

- *Multiple case study analyses*, which profile the larger contexts within which particular institutions, disciplines, or courses are situated. These studies identify trends not possible to perceive in single case studies. For examples, see Tobias (1992), Hewitt and Seymour (1994), and Conrad, Haworth, and Millar (1993).

- *Theoretical analyses of teaching-learning processes*, developed by using the tools of a particular discipline. Examples include books by Palmer (1983), Lave and Wenger (1991), Elbow (1986), Langer and Applebee (1987), and Walvoord and McCarthy (1990). Theoretical analyses also appear in journals such as *Instructional Science: An International Journal of Higher Education* and *Educational Planning*.

- *Practical guides for improving teaching*. Some of these, including works by Angelo and Cross (1993), Goswami and Stillman (1987), and Weimer, Parrett, and Kern (1988), present ideas and techniques for improving one's own classes. Others highlight general approaches to teaching that have been found effective. Examples include Bonwell and Eison's book on active learning (1991), material on collaborative learning from the National Center for Postsecondary Teaching, Learning, and Assessment (Goodsell, Maher, and Tinto, 1992; NCTLA, 1994), Gabelnick and others' work on learning communities (1990), Edgerton's piece on teaching portfolios (1992), Weimer's treatment of classroom methods (1990), Svinicki's collection of articles on teaching (1990), and Austin and Baldwin's book on faculty collaboration (1991).

References

Angelo, T. A., & Cross, K. P. (1993). *Classroom assessment techniques: A handbook for faculty.* San Francisco: Jossey-Bass.

Austin, A. E., & Baldwin, R. G. (1991). *Faculty collaboration: Enhancing the quality of scholarship and teaching.* (ASHE-ERIC Higher Education Report No. 7). Washington, DC: George Washington University, School of Education and Human Development.

Bakhtin, M. M. (1986). *Speech genres and other late essays.* (C. Emerson & M. Holquist, Eds., V. W. McGee, Trans.). Austin: University of Texas Press.

Bonsangue, M. V. (1992). *The effects of calculus workshop groups on minority achievement and persistence in mathematics, science, and engineering.* Unpublished doctoral dissertation, Claremont, CA: The Claremont Graduate School.

Bonwell, C. C., & Eison, J. A. (1991). *Active learning: Creating excitement in the classroom.* (ASHE-ERIC Higher Education Report No. 1). Washington, DC: George Washington University, School of Education and Human Development.

Bowen, G. B., & Rudenstein, N. L. (1992). *In pursuit of the Ph.D.* Princeton: Princeton University Press.

Bruffee, K. A. (1993). *Collaborative learning: Higher education, interdependence, and the authority of knowledge* (pp. 142–154). Baltimore: Johns Hopkins University Press.

Conrad, C. F., Haworth, J. G., & Millar, S. B. (1993). *A silent success: Master's programs in the USA.* Baltimore, MD: Johns Hopkins University Press.

Edgerton, R. (1992). *The teaching portfolio: Capturing the scholarship in teaching* Washington, DC: American Association for Higher Education Teaching Initiative.

Elbow, P. (1986). *Embracing contraries: Explorations in learning and teaching.* New York: Oxford University Press.

Fairweather, J. F. (1992). *Teaching and the faculty reward structure.* University Park, PA: Center for the Study of Higher Education, Pennsylvania State University.

Freire, P. (1990). *Pedagogy of the oppressed.* New York: Continuum.

Fullan, M. G., with Stiegelbauer, S. (1991). *The new meaning of educational change.* New York: Teachers College Press, Columbia University.

Gabelnick, F., MacGregor, J., Matthews, R. S., & Smith, B. L. (Eds.). (1990). New directions for teaching and learning: No. 41. *Learning communities: Creating connections among students, faculty, and disciplines.* San Francisco: Jossey-Bass.

Goodsell, A., Maher, M., & Tinto, V. (1992). *Collaborative learning: A sourcebook for higher education.* University Park, PA: National Center on Postsecondary Teaching, Learning, and Assessment.

Goswami, D., & Stillman, P. R. (1987). *Reclaiming the classroom: Teacher research as an agency for change.* Upper Montclair, NJ: Boynton/Cook.

Harding, S. (1986). *The science question in feminism.* Ithaca: Cornell University Press.

Harding, S. (1991). *Whose science? Whose knowledge? Thinking from women's lives.* Ithaca: Cornell University Press.

Hewitt, N. M., & Seymour, E. (1994). *Talking about leaving: Factors contributing to high attrition rates among science and engineering undergraduate majors* (Final report to the Alfred P. Sloan Foundation on an ethnographic inquiry at seven institutions). Boulder, CO: University of Colorado, Bureau of Sociological Research.

Jordanova, L. J. (1980). Natural facts: A historical perspective on science and sexuality. In C. MacCormack & S. Strathern (Eds.), *Nature, culture and gender, a critique* (pp. 42–69). Cambridge: Cambridge University Press.

Langer, J. A., & Applebee, A. N. (1987). *How writing shapes thinking: A study of teaching and learning* (NCTE Research Report, no. 22). Urbana, IL: National Council of Teachers of English.

Lave, J., & Wenger, E. (1991). *Situated learning: Legitimate peripheral participation.* New York, NY: University Press.

Millar, S. B., & Fairweather, J. F. (1992). *Engineering coalition of schools for excellence and leadership (ECSEL), report on the second year of activities: 1991–92.* University Park, PA: Penn State Center for the Study of Higher Education.

National Center on Postsecondary Teaching, Learning, and Assessment (NCTLA). (1994). *What works: Building effective collaborative learning experiences.* University Park, PA: National Center on Postsecondary Teaching, Learning, and Assessment.

National Science Foundation. (1989). *Meeting the national need for scientists to the year 2000.* Washington, DC: National Science Foundation, Commission on Professionals in Science and Technology.

National Science Foundation, Directorate for Education and Human Resources. (N.d; identified as NSF 94–121). *Foundation for the future: The systemic cornerstone, scientific literacy, and mathematical power for all.* Washington, DC: National Science Foundation.

Palmer, P. (1983). *To know as we are known.* New York: HarperCollins.

Svinicki, M. D. (Ed.). (1990). New directions for teaching and learning: No. 42. *The changing face of college teaching.* San Francisco: Jossey-Bass.

Tobias, S. (1990). *They're not dumb, they're different.* Tucson, AZ: Research Corporation.

Tobias, S. (1992). *Revitalizing undergraduate science: Why some things work and most don't.* Tucson, AZ: Research Corporation.

Treisman, U., Speaker, (1992). *Increasing minority participation in math-based disciplines* [Videotape]. Los Angeles: California State System, Office of the President.

Vygotsky, L. S. (1978). *Mind in society: The development of higher psychological processes* (M. Cole, V. John-Steiner, S. Scribner, and E. Souberman, Eds.). Cambridge: Harvard University Press.

Walvoord, B. E., & McCarthy, L. P. (1990). *Thinking and writing in college: A naturalistic study of students in four disciplines.* Urbana, IL: National Council of Teachers of English.

Weimer, M. G. (1990). *Improving college teaching.* San Francisco: Jossey-Bass.

Weimer, M., Parrett, J. L., & Kern, M. M. (1988). *How am I teaching? Forms and activities for acquiring instructional input*. Madison, WI: Magna.

Wertsch, J. V. (1991). *Voices of the mind: A sociocultural approach to mediated action*. Cambridge: Harvard University Press.

Wilshire, B. (1990). *The moral collapse of the university: Professionalism, purity, and alienation*. Albany: State University of New York Press.

Chapter Eight

Planning and Developing
Effective Courses

George L. Geis
Ontario Institute for Studies in Education

What is the role of a teacher? For many of us the first picture that comes to mind is standing-up, face-to-face contact with students, usually lecturing to them. Dressel (1971) notes: "Too often no clear distinction is made between teaching and the broader concept of instruction. Teaching refers to the activities of the teacher in direct contact with students. . . . [The] concept of instruction extends the concept of teaching to include the teacher's preplanning and preparation. . . ." (pp. 177–178). This chapter explores the latter role mentioned by Dressel: the role of developer of the course.

This chapter discusses a series of "decision points" in the development or revision of a course, as illustrated in Figure 8.1.

After discussing the concept of planning, I examine influences on the critical first decision: to develop, or revise, the course. Then the broad outline and context of the course is discussed. Following

Figure 8.1. Decision Points.

1 Deciding to → 2 Clarifying → 3 Determining → 4 Specifying and
develop or   purpose of   general   organizing the
revise   the course   orientation   goals

5 Deciding → 6 Mapping → 7 Sequencing → 8 Student
what to   influences
include

I would like to thank my colleague Michael Skolnik for comments and suggestions upon reading a draft version of this chapter.

179

that, this chapter deals with providing more detail of possible goals, and some ways of selecting from them and arranging them into a pattern or sequence. Finally, I offer brief comments on how the content, students, and other course characteristics interact.

Planning

In the opening quotation, Dressel uses the terms *preplanning* and *preparation*. The literature on course and curriculum development assumes a planning stance: the professor will undertake systematically a series of decisions before the course is offered and, usually, produce an explicit statement of those decisions, that is, a plan. Such a model makes eminent sense in some situations, for example, when uniform instruction is being developed by a team for use in various sites employing instructors who act as conduits for the preplanned course; when universal certification tests are used at the end of a course; or in self-instructional situations, as when materials will be used by isolated learners at a distance from the course developers. The model of systematic instructional design (see Gagne, Briggs, and Wager, 1988; Dick and Carey, 1990) that emphasizes such detailed preplanning has been implemented successfully in large areas of instruction in industry, vocational and distance courses, and the military.

On many college and university campuses, in contrast, the professor is usually not only the creator of the course but also its deliverer and facilitator. In these situations, the course is likely to unfold or evolve, with planning and implementation interacting dynamically *during the life of the course*. This is possible because the students and course developer are present during the whole course and decisions can be made in real time. "Planning" for such situations is often only at the macro level, perhaps a course outline. The more microscopic levels of the course emerge from information gained during the course, for example revelations of students' interest, preparation, and problems with the course. Details of the course can easily be fine tuned while maintaining a fair degree of correspondence to the original, holistic, macro plan.

In addition, different professors take different approaches. Some opt for an analytic approach to course design while others proceed more intuitively. The first kind of course developer will feel comfortable with extensive preplanning, and with a heuristic for systematic instructional design. The second will rely upon the spontaneity and reactivity of an evolving process of course development. In fact, many professors combine both analytic and intuitive approaches. Since inspiration favors the prepared mind, acquaintance with the decisions that can and should be made (explicitly or implicitly) and the influences upon them should be of use to anyone undertaking the development of a course.

Decision One: To Develop (or Redesign) a Course

The first decision that must be made regardless of one's stance with regard to planning is *whether or not to develop (or revise) a course*. Revisiting the reasons for developing or revising a course makes the parameters of the nature and content of the course clearer. Influences on the decision may be divided, somewhat arbitrarily, into those that are external and those that are internal.

External Influences: The Needs Analysis

A large amount of instructional development in industry, the military, the professions, and service groups is driven by demonstrable needs. A new piece of equipment requires skills the workers do not have. Sales are down in a chain of stores, and the evidence is that salespeople do not effectively promote products. Patients complain about the care they are receiving in a clinic. A vocational-community college learns of the increasing use of computers by local businesses but that there are few well-trained computer personnel to fill available jobs.

Learning about and responding to these external influences involves needs analysis, a technique well described elsewhere (Rossett, 1987; Rothwell and Kazanas, 1992; Kaufman, Rojas, and Mayer, 1993).

One interesting aspect of needs analysis is that it not only indicates when new instruction should be developed, but it also defines the content of that instruction and may even suggest instructional methods. Here is an example.

Assume that it has been discovered, through interviews and surveys with physicians and patients, that doctors often fail to interact with long-term chronic-care patients in a supporting way. Such interaction would not only comfort the patient but might also attenuate some symptoms of the illness. Having discovered this "need," the instructional developers proceed to develop some kind of learning experiences (perhaps a "course") which would address the need; concurrently, they would develop some evaluation instruments. The outcomes are evident, although not very easy to measure—for example, if the course is successful the student physician will provide psychological support; the physician will consult and inform the patient about possible next stages of the illness and suggest ways of dealing with them; patients and their families will report more positively about their relationships with the physician.

The needs analysis has provided a picture both of the content *and* the evaluation for this "course." Furthermore it offers some hints about the kinds of learning experiences that would be good bets to try out. For example, instructors might experiment with simulations and role-playing peer exercises; they might include clinical visits as part of the experiences in the course; they might have patients attend some of the classes as guest speakers and tell their stories.

Although the applications of needs analysis and the related instructional implementation process model have been predominantly in nonacademic settings, numerous academic writers specializing in curriculum and instruction have proposed similar models for school, college, and university course development (for example, Taba, 1962; Dressel, 1963). Many professors almost automatically consider at least some of these sources when developing courses.

Other External Influences

Potential employers, "users" (clients, patients, buyers), and students are typical sources of statements of "needs" that generate instruction. But there are other external influences as well.

Accrediting or Licensing Agencies. These include government or professional bodies that license or certify graduates.

Various Groups in Society. As an example, we have recently seen the effects of women pressing for inclusion of women's perspectives in history, science, and literature. The result has been a broadening of content and perspectives in courses, and in some cases the setting up of women's studies programs.

Experts in the Profession, Vocation, or Discipline. An example would be curricula prescribed by professional associations. Experts may not only inform the developer about existing needs but also offer predictions of what the knowledge needs will be in the future. We often teach for the next generation and so must project what skills and knowledge will be needed a decade or so from now.

Internal Influences

Unlike many trainers and instructional designers, professors often develop a course for reasons that might be called internal to the system, in contrast to the external influences just discussed.

The Department. According to Wood and Davis, "[We] know that most curriculum change is piecemeal, incremental, and unplanned with respect to the total curriculum" (1978, p. 3). Nevertheless, there is a rough structure that the department refers to when deciding whether a new course should be mounted. In some departments (for example, the physical sciences), the set of offerings and their sequence is often dictated by traditions (programs in similar departments elsewhere, by professional associations, or by existing textbooks). In other departments (the humanities), courses tend to be arranged as a horizontal menu, cafeteria-style rather than in a linear sequence.

In times of strained financial resources, an important departmental consideration in devising new courses may be the need to recruit students. Or development of specific courses may reflect the attempt of the department to gain some kind of accreditation or to respond to reviewers' criticisms. Of course, there may be the drive in some departments for aggrandizement and status. As Dressel says: "Competition plays a major role in increasing the number of courses. Departmental course listings are a source of pride to faculty members, admissions officers, deans and presidents, who like to refer to the richness and variety of their institution's offerings" (1971, pp. 231–232).

The Discipline and its Content. This can be a major influence in decisions about generating or revising a course. Professional associations often have a section devoted to the teaching of the discipline (see Division Two of the American Psychological Association). Some have developed curricular guidelines and sets of objectives for the curriculum (Mathematics Association of America, American Physiological Society, American Sociological Association). When a professional association issues new curriculum recommendations, the department or program may respond by developing or revising courses. Similarly the appearance of new materials for teaching, particularly new textbooks, may lead to course development.

Students. Students can be an important influence on the initiation decision. The requests or demands of students for a new course in an area may persuade the department or professor to mount one. This is somewhat similar to responding to a needs assessment, as discussed earlier. Students' feedback during and after a course is often important in persuading the professor to make revisions in the course. Student complaints to the department may also initiate changes. A more detailed discussion of the student as an influence on course development is offered at the end of this chapter.

The Professor. The professor's own body of knowledge, areas of expertise, interests, and perspectives are likely to define the content and how it appears in the course. As the professor acquires new areas of expertise or enriches existing ones, she or he is likely to consider initiating or revising a course. Professors frequently report that they develop new courses or redesign old ones for one of two reasons: exploration or renewal.

Developing or revising a course offers the opportunity to explore, synthesize, and organize the new area, subjecting it to the rigors of being taught to others. In addition, the professor may find redoing or developing a course refreshing and a way to overcome the boredom accumulated after having taught the same course many times. Diamond (1989) calls this the "academic seven-year itch."

Finally, the professor's interest in technology may prompt development or revision of a course. A professor may change the course in order to experiment with and use, say, computers or simulations.

Whatever the reasons, professors do repeatedly undertake the design and redesign of courses. The results are sometimes extraordinarily innovative. For example, Keller and Sherman's course revisions evolved into the Personalized System of Instruction (Keller, 1968; Sherman and Ruskin, 1978). Postlethwaite, beginning from a revision of his own biology course, created the Audio-Tutorial Method (Postlethwaite, Novak, and Murray, 1972).

Decision Two: Purposes

In some cases, the purpose(s) of the course may emerge naturally from reflection on the influences that led to its development; in others the influences and purposes may not be clear. Before launching into the development of the course, the purposes should be made explicit. Finer tuning will occur when the course objectives are clarified (a matter to be discussed later in the chapter). The purpose of the course may be to enable learners to develop specific job skills; or it may be seen as producing more sophisticated critical thinking. The course may be a way for students to learn research techniques, gain a greater appreciation of music, or become acquainted with alternative explanations of phenomena.

Returning repeatedly to the original purpose can and should influence later decisions about details of the course.

Decision Three: Orientation of the Course

Having decided that a course will be developed or revised and having clarified the purposes of the course, the professor is tempted to start to think about content and format. But before moving to that level of specificity—to what Stark and others (1988) call the "learning plan"—he or she would be wise to consider the general orientation for the course.

Several authors have proposed spectra of orientations (Posner and Rudnitsky, 1986). Dressel (1971) offers these questions as a starting point (pp. 15–39):

- Should the course emphasize the discipline or the interests, needs, and motivations of the individual, for example, letting the students select the topics from a menu?
- Should it be theoretical and abstract, or should it confront current issues and problems?

- Is the course's perspective on the discipline that the discipline is an accumulation of knowledge, or a mode of thought?

- Is the course designed to prepare people for a career? As a prerequisite or foundation for career preparation? As a pure, abstract treatment of a body of knowledge? As a part of a general liberal arts sequence, not aimed at specialists but at the development of an informed, intelligent, well-rounded citizen?

- Given the choice between depth and breadth, which is appropriate for this course?

Decision Four: Greater Specificity Through Goals and Evaluation

Producing broad topic statements and selecting a general orientation are essential steps on the way to developing a more specific course description. However they are not in themselves sufficient. For example, topics such as the Civil War, atoms and molecules, the concept of positive reinforcement, and deconstructionist theory stand for very large areas of content and fail to indicate what anticipated learning or student outcomes will be encouraged. Gilbert has noted that: "The foremost unresolved issue in education is subject matter—how to define one. When we decide we want to teach history, say, the first problem is define what history is. . . . We could, for example, define history as the written record of past events. Or . . . as what historians do . . . or as what those do who make history. . . . We might even define history as a source of predictive power" (Gilbert, 1976, pp. 29–30). In this process of increasing specification, the professor should describe (1) what the student will learn (what Gilbert, 1976, calls *acquirement*) and (2) what the student will be able to do as a result of having learned that (Gilbert calls this *accomplishment*).

Aims and Objectives

Often misunderstood, misused, and much maligned, objectives are a critical concept in discussing course "content." The idea is simple: one should have a clear idea of what the intended outcomes of the course are if one is to rationally develop it.

In the literature, stress on details of goal definition (for example, the constraint to use specific words, the prohibition of nonobservable outcomes) has led some thoughtful educators to reject completely a valuable step and aid in course development. It is true that "objectives can . . . get in the way of effective instructional performance if followed with the rigidity of theory rather than practice" (Bergquist and Phillips, 1977, p. 133). Pressure to formulate specific objectives can lead to development of trivialized outcome statements, since the most superficial and obvious ones are the easiest to come up with. As Bergquist observed, objectives can overly constrain the course, preventing the professor and class from taking advantage of unique, serendipitous occurrences, special class interests, or recent events.

Despite the criticisms, most educators would agree with Dressel that "Objectives are the basis for the selection of materials and for the organization of the course" (Dressel, 1971, p. 178). There are many benefits of well-stated objectives:

- Such specification assists the professor-designer in ordering or structuring the course.
- Objectives keep the professor "on target," reducing the risks of redundancy, omission, or irrelevancy.
- Good objective statements can assist in communications with others (such as describing to colleagues what your course is about so that other courses can be aligned with it).
- Objectives can inform students about the course in more detail than a brief note in a course catalog.

- Importantly, objectives can set up guidelines for evaluations of learners and of the course, a point we will return to shortly.

Specific predetermined objectives that must be matched—to the letter—by learners may be appropriate when the outcomes are standardized and must correspond to externally determined requirements, as in training users of hazardous materials, or in teaching a learner to use a computer-based statistical package. But professors who teach other kinds of courses, even though they do have in mind some goals, may have concerns about providing such precise detail.

The professor may, correctly, feel that some outcomes of a course should be and will be determined by the dynamics of the course itself. And the professor may want to leave open the opportunity for original creations and divergent outcomes. These concerns need not in fact preclude development of rather precise outcome statements. With a little reflection and imagination, a clear and useful statement of the aims of any course can be generated, for example, "The students will produce an original work of art combining at least three different media and demonstrating the basic principles learned in the course, such as balance and unity." Many such academic goals involve outcomes that cannot be stated in exact form but can be described in terms of critical attributes (Geis, 1978).

Numerous references can assist in clarifying content in terms of goals and then objectives. A classic is *Preparing Instructional Objectives* (Mager, 1984). Interested professors might consult Dick and Carey (1990), Cohen (1970), the useful exercise on goals in Bergquist and Phillips (1977, pp. 142–143), or Newble and Cannon (1989). In *On College Teaching* (Milton and Associates, 1978), Robert Barry takes the reader on a personal journey through a year of teaching a course and describes some revelations that stating objectives produced, which not only influenced his planning of the course as it unfolded but also affected classroom discussions with learners.

Producing explicit statements of objectives before considering content in detail may seem a bit foreign to many professorial course developers. Even more unusual may be the next suggestion: that evaluation materials be sketched out at this time.

Evaluation and Alignment

As one states specific objectives with greater precision, the statements begin to resemble evaluation items. For example:

Topic: World Wars

General goal: Students will understand the major variables that produced the world wars.

More specific objective: Students will be able to describe the critical variables that led to World War I.

Test item: "Discuss at least five major causes of World War I, indicating the contributions of each to the conflict."

Convergence of the goals of the course and the "examination" is often illustrated by students' questions early in the course, such as, "What do you expect us to do on the exam?" This inquiry can be easily dismissed as an almost blind fixation on grades, but one reason that students are asking the question is, very reasonably, to organize and focus on features and concepts in the course. They are asking, "What is the course really about?" and "What should I expect to get from the course?" Two legitimate questions.

Newble and Cannon (1989, pp. 77–86) offer a simple and excellent aid for developing evaluation materials as part of the early stage of course development. It consists of three columns, labeled Objectives, Activities, and Assessment. For each objective or "content concept," the professor indicates what the learner activity will be and how mastery of that bit of knowledge or skill will be measured. Using this simple format, the designer-professor can *align* the three major components of the course—what is to be taught, how and when it is to be taught, and how achievement will be measured—so that they present a coherent whole and reflect and complement each other.

Decision Five: Including and Excluding

The content of the course (what the course will be about and consist of) has been somewhat delimited by the decisions discussed so far. Now the developer needs to sort through the many potential inclusions, selecting those that will in fact be included, and order them in some way.

Criteria for Inclusion

Systematic selection of objectives, content, and activities can be aided by using specific criteria for inclusion. For example, Lowman (1984) suggests starting with a large list of objectives and selecting on the basis of two criteria: *student interests* and *importance in the discipline*. Gilbert (1976) offers three criteria for selection: (1) does the content item have generalization power (will it answer or help to answer other questions)? (2) is it important (admittedly a subjective decision)? and (3) does the student already know it (a check on previous student learning and other courses, to eliminate redundancy)?

Dressel and Marcus (1982, pp. 164–165) offer a slightly more elaborate set of criteria. The concepts to be included in a course should:

- Be important, central, and fundamental
- Be transmittable through planned education experiences
- Be based on or related to research
- Stimulate search for meaning and encourage further investigation

- Interrelate facts and lower-level concepts
- Be useful in decision making
- Be directive, cumulative, and integrative

Newble and Cannon (1989, pp. 72–73), taking a somewhat different perspective, offer five sets of criteria:

- *Philosophical criteria* test whether the content is a means of enhancing the intellectual development of students and not an end in itself.
- *Professional criteria* ask such things as whether the content provides the kinds of theoretical and practical experiences required for registration, and whether attention is paid to professional ethics. As noted earlier, course developers should be sure to examine existing mandates, requirements, and guidelines from licensing agencies and professional groups.
- *Psychological criteria* ensure the selection of content that is carefully integrated to avoid fragmentation, that provides opportunities to emphasize and develop higher-level intellectual skills, and is related to process activities and to the development of attitudes and values.
- *Practical criteria* lead the course designer to consider the resources available for implementing that piece of the course.
- *Student criteria* reflect the importance of taking into account learners' needs, interests, levels of maturity and intellectual development, and diverse backgrounds.

Decisions to include or exclude specific content are probably the most critical and difficult ones the professor will have to make in developing the course. The sets of criteria presented here can help in those decisions, as can repeated reflection on purposes. Without a clear picture of the purpose, good course development is likely to be serendipitous.

Taxonomies

Since a course involves many different goals and types of content, some sort of system or template can be used to assist in organizing the content, activities, and evaluations. Over the years, researchers and educators have developed a number of taxonomies that may be useful in clarifying and sorting the many possible candidates for the course's content. Taxonomizing can be thought of as making decisions about the level for each "content item."

Course content falls into three major categories: knowledge, skill, and attitudes. Taxonomies have been developed for each of these domains (Bloom, 1956; Krathwohl, Bloom, and Masia, 1964; Simpson, 1955). The taxonomy of the cognitive or knowledge domain developed by Bloom locates content and objectives within one of several categories: recall and recognize; comprehend; apply; analyze; synthesize; evaluate (see also Clark and Peterson, 1986). Dressel and Marcus (1982, p. 162) provide a somewhat different but useful list of types of concepts with examples of each type.

Whereas Bloom-type taxonomies emphasize content categories, the one developed by Robert Gagne (1977) co-relates *kind of learning and learning outcomes* with *appropriate instructional environment*. He suggests that course developers consider concurrently the type of objective or performance desired (say, skill development) and the conditions of learning which will most effectively assist in development of those outcomes (modeling, guided practice).

Decisions Six and Seven: Mapping and Sequencing

These decisions involve visualizing the major concepts of the course and placing them in a meaningful sequence.

Mapping

Most professors have some idea of how the major objectives and concepts in a course relate to each other and to the course as a whole. Visualizing the major concepts and segments of the course assists in locating parts of the content and reviewing the inclusion decisions. Several authors suggest that the professor should actually draw a picture of the course. This provides a holistic view and allows checking for content redundancies and omissions. (It can also provide students with a useful overview of the course.)

One of the best ways to do this is to name, in a word or two, the major ideas, concepts, skills, and information segments of the course and then try to produce a map of these pieces. By assembling the terms visually on paper and trying to indicate relationships, the professor produces a course "concept map" for reflection and revision. A similar method, suggested by Rowntree (1981), involves placing each topic, theme, activity, or major concept on an index card and moving the cards around until related items are clustered.

Posner and Rudnitsky (1986, especially pp. 25–35), Cross and Angelo (1988), and Rowntree (1981, pp. 81–85 and 118–224) offer practical advice on, and examples of, mapping concepts and ideas, and ways of constructing flowcharts to help in describing course elements and sequences. Janet Donald (1983) has carried out a series of interesting studies in which both professors and students developed maps of key concepts in their courses. She provides descriptions of the techniques as well as the results obtained in a variety of disciplines. She comments, "The findings of this study have implications for course improvement and for curriculum development in the discipline. To the professor, consideration of the key concepts in a course and their relationships can provide information about how to structure a course, where to concentrate attention to alleviate learning difficulties, and how to judge student achievement in the course" (pp. 39–40).

Even a sketchy map illustrates the relationships of key concepts, displays what the content of the course will be, and helps the professor order the flow of the course.

Sequencing

What would be the optimal order of events in the course? Even when a sequence is imposed by the textbook, examining and developing a rationale for it is an important step (see Ramsden, 1992, pp. 138–141).

Sequencing the body of knowledge as it is arranged in the discipline may not be the optimal teaching sequence. According to Glaser: "Often, the requirements of the subject matter have dictated [the organization of the course, but] it would seem best if the organization of the instruction were a joint function of *both* the structure of the subject matter and the characteristics of the instructional sequence which best facilitate retention, concept manipulation, generalizability of knowledge and so forth. The distinction I wish to make here is between what can be called the logical and epistemological arrangement of a subject matter on the one hand and the 'learning structure' on the other" (1968, p. 158).

Rowntree (1981, p. 107) offers a variety of ways of sequencing the course:

- *Topic by topic*. In this sequence there is no particular dependency of one topic on another and the sequence is therefore random. For example, courses on "current issues" are typically sequenced this way.
- *Chronological*. The course is arranged along some time continuum.
- *Causal*. The course presents a series of events or phenomena which lead to a conclusion or solution.
- *Logical structure*. The course involves a cumulative series of prerequisites.
- *Problem-centered*. Here the course is built around questions or cases.
- *Spiral*. In this kind of course the same concept is revisited

repeatedly as the course progresses, each time with more knowledge and insight.

- *Backward chaining.* The course begins with acquiring mastery of final performance and works backwards to previous required performances. For example, a writing course might begin with learning to edit the work of others before producing original materials.

Newble and Cannon (1989) make a number of interesting, somewhat different, suggestions about sequencing. For example, the course developer should first group related objectives and activities and then sequence them. This is much like mapping and then sequencing. Examples of sequencing strategies they propose include:

- Proceeding from what the student knows to what he or she does not know
- Proceeding from concrete experiences to abstract experiences
- Following the logical or historical development of the field
- Employing as course foci important themes or concepts.
- Starting from unusual or novel situations and working backwards to understanding

Student sequencing of the content is another possibility. In Hypertext computer environments, for example, the student "browses" through concepts and information, selecting his or her own path to pursue. More traditional courses may partially simulate this design by offering reading lists from which each student may select a different book, or a menu of assignments one of which is chosen by each student. If the schedule of the course is accompanied by a commentary on the *rationale* for the sequence, students can see better the whole course and relate each week's events to a larger picture.

Decision Eight: Fine Tuning
Through Interaction with Learners

A number of other influences affecting the development of the course should be mentioned, for example such characteristics of the course as class size, media of instruction, format, and the like.

To examine the variety of possible class formats, the interested reader should consult Beard and Hartley (1984), Lowman (1984), McKeachie (1994), Rothwell and Kazanas (1992), or Weston and Cranton (1986). Designers of courses that involve a large degree of student control of content and learning activities might consult Knowles (1986), who discusses learning contracts, self-instruction, and peer teaching.

The most important influence is often the students in the course. The course comes alive and evolves as it is taught. The interaction with students often determines major content inclusions and exclusions, and it almost always produces some fine tuning of the course plan. As Lowman (1984) says, "[It] should be emphasized again that although thoughtful selection of content and objectives contributes significantly to a course, still, as in warfare and athletics, the value of the battle or game plan depends most on how well it is executed and whether it is flexible when surprises occur" (p. 147).

Some knowledge about students can be gained ahead of time through student records and enrollment information. But much may have to await their presence at the first class meeting. A variety of techniques can be used to discover such things as students' learning styles, methods of studying, and interests. Numerous instruments are available to elicit such information. Of importance also is the student's entry knowledge of content and knowledge about what skills are needed to learn in the course, for example, ability to read information from graphic displays (see Lindquist and others, 1978; Cross and Angelo, 1988, pp. 90–93). Students may not have the assumed prerequisite knowledge needed to understand certain concepts in the course. Or the amount of content to be examined in the course may be too large a workload for a particular set of students (see Ramsden, 1992). The textbook may be above the class's reading level. Or some of the material to be covered may prove to be redundant (perhaps students have already dealt with it in another course).

An explication of student interests is important (Ramsden, 1992, pp. 90–93). It may reveal that some of the course objectives are not shared by them; conversely, some student goals may not have been included in the course. At a less global level of course design, examples may be tailored to students' interests and backgrounds when they have been made explicit. Newble and Cannon (1989, pp. 73–75) offer a brief but interesting examination of different kinds of students and how they might influence course content and methods.

Lindquist and others (1978) suggest interviewing the students, whether in the course of academic advising, during classes, or in informal contacts, as a readily available technique for gaining much useful information. Rowntree (1981) suggests asking students at the beginning of the course to write down two or three questions they expect the course will deal with. Analysis of their responses can suggest some additional goals, a change in sequence, or the addition of particular examples or cases.

A variety of other useful techniques and instruments for checking on students' preparedness and progress are available (as in Cross and Angelo, 1988) and can guide the ongoing redesign of the course. For example, students might be asked at the close of each class to write on an index card one or two matters covered in the class that remain unclear. The next class can begin by addressing those things that remain unclear to many students.

Probably one of the few principles that most educators agree on is that learning is an active process; the more fully students participate in the instructional event, the greater the chances of their becoming learners. Increasing the amount of class activity through such things as discussions, role-plays, simulations, games, and student presentations is not only good pedagogy, but also it will provide the professor with more information about what and how students are learning and thus allow the professor to adjust the course class-by-class in order to increase its effectiveness.

Many adult educators (Knowles, 1986) would assign the learner a much more proactive role in developing course content and designing class activities. Partnerships and contracts recast the dynamics of the course so that a less hierarchical pattern is established. In the eyes of these educators, the influence of the students in deciding what the course should be about would be direct, continuing, and of primary importance.

Conclusion: Planning for Student Learning

In the beginning of this chapter, it was noted that professors often have a different view of course development than do "planners." Many of the decisions discussed in this chapter can be made in close proximity to actual implementation, that is, what has been described need not be completed as a plan before a course starts. Rather, the purpose has been to provide an awareness of decisions and influences that the professor can return to as the course unfolds.

The Scylla and Charybdis of determining content for a course are clear. If too little planning time is spent and the decisions about content are whimsical, the course may not serve the students (or the discipline) well. If the content is rigidly determined before the class begins, the major benefits of a live classroom—spontaneity, responsiveness and flexibility—are lost.

Joy Rogers, Professor of Education at Loyola University in Chicago, told of an interesting way she has taught an introductory statistics course. The course is carefully designed with clear objectives and ample opportunity for student activities in mastering, discriminating among, and applying statistical techniques. But for

each class, Professor Rogers appears with a box of materials—
overheads, exercises, examples, brief handouts, and so forth. As the
session unfolds, the particularities of the class at that moment
determine what the next "content item" will be. Should she show
an illustration? Should the class engage in a self-instructional exercise? Are more examples needed? Part of the "content" of the
course *for any one meeting* emerges from the file box (personal communication with Professor Joy Rogers, June 12, 1989).

This chapter has suggested that course preplanning is important and that course development should be carried out systematically. At the same time, it has attempted to emphasize the need
for responsiveness to the unique features of live classroom teaching and to the true goal of all good teaching: assisting the learner.
As Dressel and Marcus say (1982, pp. 13–14): "The success of
teaching must . . . be determined by whether and what students
learn, not by what the teacher does or asks students to do, and most
certainly not solely by [the professor's] scholarly precision and
verve. . . . This is not to say that the materials, content and forms
of presentation are unimportant or irrelevant; rather, it emphasizes
that these are subject to choice by the teacher guided by a concern
for their effectiveness in promoting learning by students."

References

Beard, R., & Hartley, J. (1984). *Teaching and learning in higher education* (4th ed.).
    London: Harper & Row.
Bergquist, W. H., & Phillips, S. R. (1977). *A handbook for faculty development*
    (Vol. 2). Washington, DC: Council for the Advancement of Small
    Colleges.
Bloom, B. S., (Ed.). (1956). *Taxonomy of educational objectives: Classification of
    educational goals. Handbook 1: Cognitive domain.* New York: David
    McKay.
Clark, C., & Peterson, P. (1986). Teachers' thought processes. In M. Wittrock
    (Ed.), *Handbook of research on teaching* (3rd ed.). New York: MacMil-
    lan.
Cohen, A. M. (1970). *Objectives for college courses.* Beverly Hills, CA: Glencoe
    Press.

Cross, K. P., & Angelo, T. A. (1988). *Classroom assessment techniques: A handbook for faculty*. Ann Arbor, MI: University of Michigan, National Center for Research to Improve Postsecondary Teaching and Learning.

Diamond, R. M. (1989). *Designing and improving courses and curricula in higher education: A systematic approach*. San Francisco: Jossey-Bass.

Dick, W., & Carey, L. (1990). *The systematic design of instruction* (3rd ed.). Glenview, IL: Scott-Foresman/Little, Brown, Higher Education.

Donald, J. (1983). Knowledge structures: Methods for exploring course content. *Journal of Higher Education, 54*, 31–41.

Dressel, P. L. (1963). *The undergraduate curriculum in higher education*. Washington, DC: Center for Applied Research in Education.

Dressel, P. L. (1971). *College and university curriculum*. Berkeley, CA: McCutchan.

Dressel, P. L., & Marcus, D. (1982). *On teaching and learning in college: Reemphasizing the roles of learners and the disciplines in liberal education*. San Francisco: Jossey-Bass.

Gagne, R. (1977). *Conditions of learning* (3rd ed.). Troy, MO: Holt, Rinehart & Winston.

Gagne, R., Briggs, L., & Wager, W. (1988). *Principles of instructional design* (3rd ed.). Troy, MO: Holt, Rinehart & Winston.

Geis, G. L. (1978). Three kinds of behavioral objectives: total, sample, and consequence statements. *Educational Technology, XVIII*(1), 28–31.

Gilbert, T. F. (1976). Saying what a subject matter is. *Instructional Science, 5*, 29–53.

Glaser, R. (1968). Ten untenable assumptions of college instruction. *Educational Record, 49*, 154–159.

Kaufman, R., Rojas, A. M., & Mayer, H. (1993). *Needs assessment: A user's guide*. Englewood Cliffs, NJ: Educational Technology.

Keller, F. S. (1968). "Goodbye, teacher . . ." *Journal of Applied Behavior Analysis, 1*, 79–89.

Knowles, M. J. (1986). *Using learning contracts: Practical approaches to individualizing and structuring learning*. San Francisco: Jossey-Bass.

Krathwohl, D. R., Bloom, B. S., & Masia, B. B. (1964). *Taxonomy of educational objectives: Classification of educational goals. Handbook 2: Affective domain*. New York: David McKay.

Lindquist, J., Bergquist, W., Mathis, C., Case, C., Clark, T., & Buhl, L. (Eds.). (1978). *Designing teaching improvement programs*. Berkeley, CA: Pacific Soundings Press.

Lowman, J. (1984). *Mastering the techniques of teaching*. San Francisco: Jossey-Bass.

Mager, R. F. (1984). *Preparing instructional objectives* (2nd, rev. ed.). Belmont, CA: Davis S. Lake.

McKeachie, W. J. (1994). *Teaching tips: Strategies, research, and theory for college and university teachers*. (9th ed.). Lexington, MA: D. C. Heath.

Milton, O., & Associates. (1978). *On college teaching: A guide to contemporary practices.* San Francisco: Jossey-Bass.

Newble, D., & Cannon, R. (1989). *A handbook for teachers in universities and colleges.* New York: St. Martin's Press.

Posner, G. J., & Rudnitsky, A. N. (1986). *Course design: A guide to curriculum development for teachers* (3rd ed.). New York: Longman.

Postlethwaite, S. N., Novak, J., & Murray, H. J., Jr. (1972). *The audio-tutorial approach to learning* (3rd ed.). Minneapolis, MN: Burgess.

Ramsden, P. (1992). *Learning to teach in higher education.* London: Routledge.

Rossett, A. (1987). *Training needs assessment.* Englewood Cliffs, NJ: Educational Technology.

Rothwell, W. J., & Kazanas, H. C. (1992). *Mastering the instructional design process: A systematic approach.* San Francisco: Jossey-Bass.

Rowntree, D. (1981). *Developing courses for students.* London: McGraw-Hill.

Sherman, J. G., & Ruskin, R. S. (1978). *The instructional design library: No. 13. The personalized system of instruction.* Englewood Cliffs, NJ: Educational Technology Publications.

Simpson, E. J. (1955). The classification of educational objectives: Psychomotor domain. *Illinois Teachers of Home Economics, 10,* 110–144.

Stark, J. S., Lowther, M. A., Ryan, M. P., Bomotti, S. S., Genthon, M., Haven, C. L., & Martens, G. (1988). *Reflections on course planning: Faculty and students consider influences and goals.* Ann Arbor, MI: National Center for Research to Improve Postsecondary Teaching and Learning.

Taba, H. (1962). *Curriculum development: Theory and practice.* New York: Harcourt, Brace & World.

Weston, C., & Cranton, P. A. (1986). Selecting instructional strategies. *Journal of Higher Education, 57,* 259–288.

Wood, L., & Davis, B. G. (1978). *ASHE-ERIC Higher Education Research Report: No. 8. Designing and evaluating higher education curricula.* Washington, DC: Association for the Study of Higher Education.

Chapter Nine

Assignments That Promote
and Integrate Learning

Joseph Lowman
University of North Carolina, Chapel Hill

This chapter deals with the many tasks instructors ask students to do outside of class and how they can be used to maximize learning. Fortunately, no serious conflict exists between what is presented here and in the other chapters in this volume dealing with improving classroom instruction, because the real issue is not whether in-class or out-of-class activities are more important but how they can best be integrated toward meeting a common set of ends.

When a few illustrative statistics on a typical college course are calculated, the importance of outside assignments becomes clearer. Consistent with regional accrediting guidelines, most three-credit-hour courses meet for two and a half hours during each of the sixteen weeks in a semester. This means a total of forty hours (2,400 minutes), or one work week, are available for class sessions. Actually, even fewer hours are available for class instruction because of exams, the first and last class sessions, and the few minutes usually spent on administrative matters during each class session. These data surprise most college teachers when they see how little actual class time they have to meet course objectives. But by adding in the two hours or so students can be expected to spend on their

---

Note: My son Campbell Lowman contributed many insights and suggestions to the section on problem solving. Many of the outside assignments described in this chapter can be organized as group rather than individual projects. See Chapter Five on collaborative learning for suggestions and for research evaluating group approaches.

assignments outside of class (per class hour), we come up with a more comfortable figure of 100 hours per course. Although even experienced college instructors find it challenging to integrate those outside hours with what is planned for class meetings, a variety of learning objectives are best met using outside assignments.

What Is Best Accomplished in Class?

To understand how to integrate outside assignments, instructors need to look first at the intellectual (or cognitive) and at the emotional (or affective) objectives that can be met in class.

A primary intellectual objective is to cover course content: the specific facts, theories, or procedures under study. Students, to be sure, learn some content by attending class alone, but what they can absorb in a few hours of class is extremely limited, and designing class sessions primarily to transfer information wastes precious time as well as opportunities for more complex learning. Given the higher-order intellectual objectives of application, analysis, synthesis, and evaluation, it is more important that instructors use classes (1) to clarify especially difficult concepts or procedures, (2) to illustrate content using engaging examples, and (3) to emphasize the connections among different concepts. Research on human cognition during the last few decades has strongly demonstrated the potency of efforts to help students better organize what they are studying (Weinstein, Goetz, and Alexander, 1988; McKeachie, 1986). Students who have learned specific concepts within a meaningful context have many more ways of retrieving information about the concepts than when they attempt to learn them in isolation. In effect, studying trees during class has the most value for what it can teach students about the forest.

As important as class meetings are to promoting an organizing intellectual perspective on course content, they promote learning most by meeting affective objectives, by stimulating positive emotions in students about the domain of ideas under study so as to help them see the importance of learning it well (Lowman, 1984), and by increasing students' motivation to do so (Lowman, 1990). (The importance of affective objectives is illustrated well in a 1992 article in the *Chronicle of Higher Education* about Jerry King, a Lehigh University professor who speaks eloquently of his efforts to help students see the beauty and elegance of mathematics; see Wheeler, 1992.) The best college classes are also those in which instructors promote positive emotions about the course as an interpersonal setting in which students see that their instructor is concerned about their learning and likely to evaluate their work fairly (Lowman, 1984). Students who feel positively about the content of a course and the instructor are most likely to be motivated to take book, calculator, or computer keyboard in hand on their own and get down to the often difficult business of solitary study.

A final purpose served by class meetings is the pacing, structure, or discipline that comes from regular reminders that one has considerable work to complete in a finite amount of time. Many students who have difficulty keeping up with their work during a semester report that the daily schedule of a summer session helps their performance by making it harder for them to forget their obligations. From this vantage point, coming to class, like attending religious services regularly, has a positive impact on students' behavior during the rest of the week by reminding them of their obligations and commitments.

Although this pacing effect of class attendance is more mundane than the intellectual and emotional ones discussed previously, it is strongly connected to the effectiveness of outside assignments. Outside assignments should be spaced out over a course so as to motivate students to work on them steadily rather than to cram them into a few days of frenetic activity at the end. Assignments should also be handled in ways that encourage students to do them for what they will learn from them, or to prepare for exams rather than mainly to avoid punishment for not doing their homework.

In summary, outside assignments are more likely to promote learning if they integrate with class sessions that engage students, offer an intellectual perspective on the subject, stimulate positive emotions about the subject and the instructor, and motivate students to work steadily over the term.

Educational Value and Motivational Strategy: Key Issues in Assigning Work That Promotes Learning

The two major issues concerning assignments deal with (1) the ticklish relationships among the difficulty, enjoyment, and educational value of the work instructors ask students to do outside class and (2) the methods used to motivate students to complete it. Research has consistently suggested that these general issues contribute a great deal to how much desired learning actually results from specific types of outside assignments (Baird, 1987).

Student motivation for and enjoyment of assignments are greatly affected by their educational value and how they are integrated with what happens in class. Unfortunately, some instructors seem to equate educational value with how much effort or time assignments require; thus they may unwittingly resemble the middle- or high-school teachers who brag about how many hours of homework—much of it mindless—they assign. It is much easier to assign work that is overly time-consuming or frustratingly difficult than that which is designed to accomplish clear course objectives. It is also much easier simply to make assignments and rarely mention them again in class than to draw connections regularly between topics in class presentations and outside assignments. If college teachers design assignments that are closely connected to their overall course objectives and integrate them with what is happening in class sessions at the time, students are much more likely to find the required effort worthwhile, the final product satisfying, and the motivation to tackle the next assignment forthcoming.

Motivation is such a critical issue to the effectiveness of outside assignments because students need internal discipline to complete them. Class meetings are social, externally structured events in students' lives that require minimal self-discipline. Students need only arrive on time, stay awake, and take notes to give them the illusion they are meeting their academic responsibilities. In contrast, outside assignments usually require students to choose among competing activities—many of them more inherently pleasurable for the typical student than schoolwork—and to schedule periods for solitary concentration and effort. Because reading and rereading challenging text, solving complex problems, or crafting one's words and thoughts on a computer screen or piece of paper are difficult and solitary activities, the methods instructors use to motivate students to complete assignments are critical to how much students apply themselves and to what they learn from the assignments.

The motivational strategies used to promote student completion of the reading or homework problems routinely assigned in college courses vary along two broad and related dimensions: (1) structured versus unstructured leadership (Baba and Ace, 1989) and (2) grading versus learning orientation (Milton, Pollio, and Eison, 1986). When planning their courses, many instructors simply adopt the leadership techniques they experienced as students without ever thinking much about the implications of various strategies for the kinds of motivation stimulated in students or for what they may be learning from assignments. Research suggests that different leadership styles do make a difference in student learning (Baba and Ace, 1989).

The structured-unstructured dimension is illustrated at its laissez-faire extreme by instructors who simply announce assigned chapters, problem sets, or papers in the syllabus and rarely mention them again, assuming college students are—or should be—mature enough to take responsibility for doing the suggested work and seeing how it relates to what is happening in class. This approach may work well with those students in every class who are internally motivated to keep up with their work despite little external encouragement and to see the connections between assignments and class topics on their own. Such an unstructured regime ensures, however, that many students will inevitably fall behind in their work, as competing social and academic pressures build up over a semester; consequently they will do less well than they might have on assignments and exams. Even highly motivated students may have difficulty keeping up without any acknowledgment of the reading or problems in class. Although it requires less effort and responsibility for instructors, a laissez-faire approach sets up many students to achieve far less in a class than they might have under more engaging and sophisticated instructor leadership.

At the other extreme of structure are instructors who have daily quizzes or unannounced pop quizzes on assigned reading, or who grade homework problems rigorously, usually based only on whether students get the correct answers. Although these procedures are likely to produce more short-term compliance among students than unstructured methods, they also often create student anxiety and an adversarial relationship with instructors, with consequences for the kind of orientation students bring to their learning (Lowman, 1990). Many instructors use structured control strategies because of the belief, now questioned by many (McKeachie, 1986; Milton, Pollio, and Eison, 1986), that they are the only way to ensure that students will actually do the assigned work. In fact, students can be motivated to do outside work using a variety of creative structured techniques that minimize grades as a means of behavior control. Chapter Five, on collaborative learning, presents a number of structured techniques that will motivate students to prepare for class carefully, even enthusiastically. In addition, the specific sections of this chapter on reading, problem-solving, and writing assignments offer a number of motivational techniques that involve giving ungraded feedback on students' initial performance to prepare them for subsequent graded work.

The sets of homework problems universally assigned in mathematics, physics, or engineering courses provide an illustrative example here. A common objective for assigning such problems is to teach students to use higher-order cognitive skills to decide (1) how to formulate problems initially and (2) when to try other approaches should initial attempts fail, as they usually do for most students (Woods, 1987). To solve such problems, students must learn to be flexible in their thinking and to remain confident that, with persistence and an openness to creative "ah-ha" insights, they can eventually succeed. Instructors typically assign a series of increasingly difficult problems to give students practice in using the problem-solving processes under study in class, so they will be able to do them successfully on subsequent exams.

What are some of the likely effects on students' learning when they are required to turn in homework sets to be graded based only on whether they got the correct solutions? Some, if not most, students are understandably more likely to focus on getting the correct answer than on experimenting with the problem-solving procedures under study. Their anxiety about receiving a low grade for unsolved or incorrect problems is sure to interfere with their confidence, persistence, and the relaxed mental attitude needed to be open to creative insight. The section of this chapter dealing with problem-solving assignments describes alternative ways of motivating students to complete and to learn from such assignments.

The second leadership dimension, grading versus learning orientation, speaks to the complex relationship between grades and learning and is closely related to the structured-unstructured dimension. For any course, using grades to motivate compliance with routine homework or reading assignments has the unintended side effect of orienting students more toward the external grades they receive than toward internal intellectual satisfactions (Lowman, 1990; Milton, Pollio, and Eison, 1986). Students' intrinsic curiosity and pleasure from learning can be diminished considerably by too much emphasis on grades as an exclusive motivational technique. Instructors who assume students are interested only in the grade they receive and who design their leadership strategies accordingly help produce, ironically, the very grade-oriented behavior they disdain. Fortunately, there are effective motivational options occupying a middle ground between laissez-faire and grade-oriented strategies.

For example, something as subtle as the language that instructors use when talking about assignments in class communicates powerful expectations about what kind of attitude they expect students to show when completing their assignments. Rarely mentioning assignments, as in a laissez-faire approach, may give students an unintended message that instructors do not consider them worth talking about and lead to students' not taking them seriously. Or talking about assignments frequently while using phrases such as "I require," "I demand," or "You must" connotes an image of the instructor as powerful authority and students as underlings who can be expected to do only what they are forced to do. In contrast, phrases such as "I think you will find," "I hope you will see," or "I will be interested in what you think" imply a less vertical power relationship between students and instructor and raise the possibility that students may sometimes want to complete assignments for *their* sake. The keys to motivating students to complete assignments with an attitude more toward learning than grading are (1) to avoid using overly structured carrot-and-stick inducements, (2) to talk about assignments in ways that communicate an assumption that students will want to do them and will find them interesting, and (3) to provide feedback on assignments that will help students learn the information and skills they will need on later evaluated work.

In summary, then, outside assignments should be designed to accomplish educational objectives that are clear to the instructor and students alike, that are integrated with what is happening during class, and that do not require student time and effort for its own sake. Students should be motivated to complete assignments if in giving them the instructor (1) avoids language that emphasizes a role as formal authority, (2) uses language that attributes intrinsic motives to students and suggests they will find the assignments intellectually satisfying, and (3) uses creative classroom exercises and ungraded feedback designed to help prepare them for subsequent graded work.

Reading Assignments

In the same way that reading remains the primary means by which educated people gain information, it is difficult to imagine a college course without reading assignments, almost always via the printed word. Even in today's computer-rich times, when every college student must achieve a modicum of skill and comfort with computers as aids to writing or calculating (Herman, 1988), the importance of books in their many contemporary forms is undiminished. Wilbert McKeachie writes: "But each of the new media has settled into its niche in the educational arsenal without dislodging the textbook. In fact, the greatest revolution in education has come not from teaching machines or computers, but from the greater availability of a wide variety of printed materials" (1986, p. 148). He goes on to illustrate this greater access by noting the open library stacks, the large number of paperback editions and reprint series, and, most importantly, the ubiquitous photocopy machines now scattered around every college campus and neighboring commercial area. Without doubt it is easier than ever for teachers to make assigned readings available for students.

When selecting readings, instructors should begin by asking themselves how readings contribute to the intellectual and emotional objectives around which they are organizing their courses. Does a reading present desired content, does it stimulate students to apply general course concepts to an engaging example, or does it prompt them to think critically about an issue? Instructors should also ask how much students are likely to enjoy reading the assignment. To be sure, some classical texts and technical materials are difficult—even a bit forbidding—to students initially and should be assigned nonetheless. But all readings need not be that demanding. When available, readings should be selected that engage students easily as well as serve instructors' intellectual ends.

An initial decision concerns whether college teachers use a prepared text or something put together on their own. Some instructors

may avoid texts, believing students will learn more from reading original sources. Actually, research indicates that the structural organization (headings, summaries, key questions, figures, or graphs)
characteristic of modern texts aids learning, especially for less able
students (Wilhite, 1983). But instructors should not avoid putting
something together on their own if they do not find a suitable text.
The extra time required initially may be more than offset by a better fit with an instructor's specific course objectives, especially if they
envision using the materials for more than one term. In introductory
courses where helping students master a large basic vocabulary for
the discipline is a major objective, prepared texts are usually preferable. And in more advanced courses aimed at promoting critical
thinking and independent analysis, reading in original sources may
fit better. Even though few texts or customized sets of readings are
likely to fit one's needs perfectly, instructors who ask themselves how
they will integrate readings with their course will be able to decide
more easily which readings to select or adopt. This will also help
avoid assigning any readings that will not be used.

Unread assignments are unlikely to contribute to student learning. Two practical considerations affect the probability that students will actually do the reading we assign: access to the material
and cost. An initial question is whether instructors should ask each
student to buy a personal copy of a reading, or instead put it on
reserve for shared use. If the reading material is going to be used by
every student and is too long to be easily and legally photocopied,
it is usually preferable to order personal copies in addition to placing copies on reserve. Owning personal copies means students can
do their reading when and where they wish. This makes it more
likely that students will actively grapple with the text, underlining
key points and writing in the margins, which promotes understanding and retention (McKeachie, 1986). Unfortunately, some
students may be unwilling (or unable) to buy readings they see as
excessively expensive—$75 and $100 texts are not uncommon—
and their learning may suffer from having to borrow others' texts

or do all their reading in library or instructor copies of texts placed on reserve. Because instructors receive complimentary copies of books, it is easy for them to be ignorant of how much texts cost students. Before making final decisions on which readings to assign and how to make them accessible to students, instructors should find out how much texts or course-packs will cost; this may help them choose between equal or nearly equal alternatives. At the very least, it may help them empathize with what students or their parents have to pay for a college education.

Once readings are assigned and available to students, how can they be integrated into what is covered in class? Most importantly, how can students be motivated to do the readings when they are assigned? Referring to readings in class frequently is probably the best single option. For example, when an instructor comments, "Your text gives a number of reasons for the decline of the British Empire, let's look at only the two most compelling," students who have read the assigned chapter beforehand will hear an organizing reminder; those who have not will get a brief foundation for what they will learn when reading later. Another option is to use discussion to encourage students to think critically about a topic discussed in the text. Giving a brief summary beforehand serves as a reminder for those who have read it, while preventing others from being left out of the discussion completely. Critical questioning in class promotes students' understanding and retention; it also models the mature attitude we want to encourage students to bring to all the reading they do. Integrating readings into class presentations and discussions is the best means of motivating students to read beforehand, not out of anxiety at the prospect of receiving a low grade on a pop quiz but out of response to an instructor who gives them an intellectual reason and the freedom to do so.

A very effective instructor I once observed began her freshman course with a discussion of the teaching and learning process, in which she asked students to construct metaphors that capture how they viewed teachers, students, and learning. The resulting discussion produced a wide range of possible images that gave her a foundation for a short presentation on her vision of learning as an active process highly dependent on students' taking personal responsibility for it, beginning with doing assigned work before-hand. She went so far as to make the following proposition to her class: if her students would commit themselves to always read the assignments before coming to class, she promised to organize every class so as to reinforce them for having done so. Additionally, if students noticed any class in which she failed to incorporate assigned readings, she promised to bake them cookies for the next class. (Incidentally, she brought them cookies on a few occasions anyway.)

Thus ready access to the written word remains the greatest technological aid to learning. Reading assignments are most likely to promote student learning if they closely fit instructors' learning objectives, are integrated with classroom activities, and are made readily accessible to students.

Problem Solving

Instructors of technical courses in engineering, mathematics, and other sciences usually make frequent use of problem-solving home-work assignments. One study of a four-year engineering curriculum, for example, found that students observe faculty solving over one thousand problems of various types on the board and work over three thousand themselves out of class (Woods, 1987). Woods's study also found that simply solving many problems does not ensure that students will learn problem-solving skills they can apply in new situations. For students to make the most of these assignments, the problems must be selected carefully and integrated closely with classroom activities.

What kinds of objectives can problem-solving assignments meet?

1. Students are much more likely to learn the general principles or structure of a scientific discipline if they have close contact with specific examples, and solving problems can give them that intimacy.

2. Problems can also help students learn a number of explicit thinking skills associated with problem solving. Students can learn how to analyze a problem conceptually, to formulate and evaluate various ways of seeking solutions, and to put potential solutions into operation and evaluate their effectiveness.

3. Students can learn a number of implicit attitudinal components to problem solving. Students must learn to have confidence in their problem-solving abilities and to be unafraid of making mistakes, to be willing to postpone judgments and to be open to insight, and, most importantly, to be persistent in the face of ambiguity and frustration.

4. Students can learn about problem solving as an explicit topic of study to help them solve problems they have not encountered before. Research suggests, however, that most of the problems instructors assign serve to illustrate discipline concepts and that few are aimed at problem solving per se (Woods, 1987).

Donald Woods, a chemical engineering professor who has written extensively on problem-solving instruction, suggests instructors use the following steps to create assignments that are likely to teach disciplined problem solving as well as illustrate concepts (1987).

First, ensure that students gain a fundamental understanding of their disciplines. As Woods notes, "Research in problem solving has shown that 'good learning' is vital to effective problem solving" (p. 66).

Second, require students to memorize the tacit knowledge of the sort that usually comes from years of experience and is required to make probable decisions about how well a given solution will work.

Third, sensitize students to the cognitive processes they use when solving problems and the importance of learning general problem-solving skills as well as how to solve specific types of problems.

Fourth, begin by teaching students how to solve particular kinds of problems, but gradually shift toward a focus on higher-order problem-solving skills, especially with more advanced students.

Woods's suggestions illustrate well that the way problems are treated in class and the techniques used to motivate students greatly affect how effectively they enhance student learning. For example, it is essential that problems be discussed in class before and after students tackle them. Although a few instructors believe it is so important that students learn how to approach and set up problems from scratch that they rarely go over them in class beforehand, more effective teachers of technical subjects aim for a better balance of frustration and helpful hints on homework and go over at least an abbreviated example or two beforehand. This lets more students gain the cognitive skills and required confidence from homework that they need when asked to solve exam problems on their own.

It is always advisable to go over problems after they are due in ways that emphasize the critical steps in setting up and solving a problem. Not only does this reinforce students who solved problems correctly, but it makes it more likely they will learn *why* they got the correct answer. Some may fail to understand the problem but get it correct nonetheless. More importantly, it gives students who were not successful initially a second or third chance to experience the flash of insight so essential in this kind of problem solving. Every student also needs a completed example of each problem in their notes for study before exams, and going over the homework in class is the best way of ensuring that they have it. Going over work in class clearly aids students' intellectual understanding of principles and problem-solving procedures.

Going over work also meets a number of emotional objectives. The concentration and mental effort required for most students to master technical material is extremely vulnerable to interference from their emotions. Although too much frustration can lead to the debilitating anxiety that leads some students to avoid courses requiring, say, calculation, some anxiety is so inevitable in these subjects that students must learn how to handle their frustration as well as specific procedures. As much as anything, students need to remain confident in their abilities if they are to keep trying when they get stuck and to be open to the solutions that may come to them eventually. Sometimes the insight does not occur until after they see their instructor show them how to set up and solve home-work problems afterward. If students know that their instructor will take time to go over homework and answer their questions in class, as well as welcome them genuinely during office hours if they still do not understand, students are far less likely to feel overwhelmed when working on problems independently. Few instances in college teaching better illustrate how important it is for instructors to acknowledge students' emotional needs when they plan outside problem-solving assignments.

It is easier to motivate students to complete homework problems beforehand than it is to motivate them for reading, because the work is so clearly connected to class content and what students know they will be asked to do on exams. Going over homework early in class emphasizes to students the importance of what they were asked to do outside. In contrast, waiting until the end of a class and asking casually, "Does anyone have any questions about the homework?" makes it unlikely that very many questions will be asked; instead, it makes it easy for an individual student to assume the instructor did not expect anyone to have had difficulty—or that he or she is the only one who did not understand. If an instructor is able to define the homework role with students as a coach who is trying to get them prepared to meet difficult problems on exams, he or she has tremendous power to motivate students to work hard on assigned problems. As was mentioned earlier, collecting homework and grading it based mainly on whether correct answers were obtained unduly raises students' anxiety, narrows their focus to the end product rather than the problem-solving process, makes it unlikely they will have their homework in hand when problems are discussed, and lowers the probability students will experience much personal satisfaction from successfully mastering the kinds of problems under study.

In summary, homework problems designed to illustrate content and teach problem-solving skills are an integral part of technical subjects such as engineering and other sciences. Choosing increasingly complex problems that let students gain confidence and tolerance for ambiguity as well as learn important problem-solving skills is more important than assigning large numbers of problems for their own sake. Going over similar problems in class beforehand makes it less likely students will feel overwhelmed when trying them on their own. In addition, it is essential to go over problems afterward if students are to learn the underlying processes needed to solve problems on subsequent exams.

Writing Assignments

When most college students and instructors think of written assignments, they imagine the traditional library or research term paper that was once an almost universal assignment in college courses. Such papers often produce much frustration and little satisfaction in students and teachers alike, probably because independent thinking and clear writing are difficult for most students and because many instructors eventually conclude the low quality of student papers fails to justify the time required to grade them. Fortunately for all us, we know a lot more about how to use writing assignments in college classes than we did two decades ago. For example, research has demonstrated that using several focused writing assignments promotes more active reading, critical thinking, and regular study over a term than traditional term papers (Erickson and Strommer, 1991). The options for assigning written work presented in this section are much broader than the limited range of objectives possible with the traditional term paper. From these more varied assignments comes written work that promotes more learning and is more satisfying for everyone. As Kenneth Eble notes, "Good assignments elicit good work; bad assignments, bad work" (1988, p. 132).

Objectives for Formal Written Assignments

Too often college teachers have overly broad objectives when they assign formal written work and assume that an interesting and informative paper will result if students are simply asked to search library resources for information on a topic and write up what they have found. In addition, instructors often assume that students will both know what we want when we ask them to "discuss" or "compare and contrast" and be able to execute it well. Some students, to be sure, are able to produce well-focused work from vague assignments. But the key to getting good work from an entire class is to focus the assignment sufficiently to let students know what we want them to gain intellectually from the experience and to give them explicit practice in doing so. Targeting more specific writing assignments makes it much more likely that students will hit the mark and that we will be able to judge easily when they have done so.

A selection of specific objectives and writing assignments selected to meet them follows.

Example #1.

> *Objective*: Students will develop skill in searching library collections and databases for articles or books on a subject.

Assignment: Distribute a list of topics relevant to current research or scholarly topics in your course and ask students to write up a two- or three-page description of relevant references they found in your school's library and databases. Because the objective is to learn to use the local resources, avoid asking them to summarize or critique what they found. That would be a good assignment for a different objective.

Example #2.

Objective: Students will see how course concepts are illustrated in specific works of art, literature, or research studies.

Assignment: Distribute lists of key concepts and target examples; ask students to write a four- or five-page paper showing how they are illustrated in one or two of the examples.

Example #3.

Objective: Students will reflect intellectually and emotionally on what they are reading in a course and on what occurs to them during class sessions.

Assignment: Ask them to keep a log or journal of personal reactions to course readings, meetings, or outside events (for example, films, concerts, or lectures) they have been asked to attend; ask them to use their log to write a short essay near the end of the course that gives an overview of how their thinking or aesthetic sensitivity has progressed over the term.

Example #4.

Objective: Students will question the validity of theories or concepts under study and form an argument presenting their position.

Assignment: Distribute descriptions (or original text) of several studies, critical essays, magazine articles, newspaper editorials, and so on. Ask students to choose one and write a one-sentence argument about some controversy or limitation in what they read. Have them illustrate their argument with two or three illustrations from the text. (See Cuddy, 1985, for a description of this one-sentence technique.)

Example #5.

Objective: Students will see the similarities and differences between two literary works, compositions, elections, scientific studies, and so on.

Assignment: As in Example #4, give them descriptions or copies, but this time ask them to write a short paper presenting similarities and differences.

Example #6.

Objective: Students will discover the joy of using their imagination and creativity to understand better the human side of some of the events under study.

Assignment: Give students a list of several brief fantasy scenes or news stories relating to your course. Ask them to write a three-to-five-page narrative they might attribute to one of the characters, giving what the person is thinking or feeling about what is happening and the student's speculation about what might happen next. For example, a vignette in a political science course might deal with an unsuccessful political candidate who ponders how to win next time.

These examples vary from quite short to moderate in length and from the concrete to the imaginative; each of them illustrates how specific objectives help shape focused writing assignments. These examples could, of course, be given sequentially or combined to form a single ambitious project. See Durkin's *Writing in the Disciplines* (1986) and Connolly and Vilardi's *Writing to Learn Mathematics* (1989) for descriptions of many focused writing assignments for use in the humanities, mathematics, and social and natural sciences.

Objectives for Informal Written Work

One of the most useful discoveries about writing assignments in recent years has been the many ways instructors can use nongraded writing informally, often during class via methods called classroom assessment (Angelo and Cross, 1992). For example, instead of stopping during a lecture and asking students to discuss some aspect of what has been covered, an instructor can ask them to take a few minutes to write their reactions, suggestions, comparisons, or other critical comments. A few students can then be asked to read their comments, or you can ask everyone to pass them in for you to read. An enjoyable group variation is to ask students to exchange comments with a neighbor and discuss them briefly together. Brief writing like this takes only a few minutes of class time (and review, if collected). If informal writing is also returned to students, a short comment or two but no grade should be added. Students could be asked to complete brief informal writing assignments out of class, but this usually fails to capture the informal, spontaneous quality of in-class writing and to provide immediate feedback to instructors that can help them modify their presentations.

A popular in-class option is the "minute paper," in which students are asked during the last minute of a class session to list the point or procedure they are most confused about or to comment on what part of the preceding class they found most stimulating or meaningful. Even experienced instructors are often surprised by what they learn from minute papers. These and other variations on informal writing assignments not only stimulate student involvement and critical thinking; they also give college teachers feedback on what students are thinking without the anxiety of formal graded work.

Using Writing Assignments

The most important consideration in using written assignments is to be sure everyone is clear about an assignment's purpose. Giving students instructors' objectives in writing as well as discussing them in class makes it more likely that everyone will write the kind of paper envisioned rather than the kind they believe—or have been told by high school teachers or other students—that college professors want. Unfortunately, even if an instructor carefully designs a focused assignment asking students to show a lot of their own thinking, distributes a written description, and spends part of a class session answering questions about the papers, a few students are still likely to write the immature cut-and-paste paper they learned to write in high school. To make it more likely every student will understand what is expected, give examples in class of what to avoid as well as what to aim for. Put exemplary papers from previous classes on reserve as models.

Instructors must also decide how many written assignments to use in a course, how long they should be, and when they should be due. The objectives for an assignment guide the number of papers and how long they should be, and experienced instructors usually give a range rather than a specific number of expected pages. Assigning a single broad paper without giving students practice with shorter papers aimed at focused objectives runs the risk of students' not meeting the specific objectives instructors have for them. Although research (see Erickson and Strommer, 1991; Meyers, 1986) suggests two smaller papers create less anxiety among students than a single longer one (perhaps because the stakes are not as high on any one piece of writing), multiple assignments may create more administrative work for teachers than a single one. Although instructors' objectives will also influence when they want papers submitted, having them turned in early enough to be able to read them carefully, return them promptly, and allow students to revise and resubmit their work if they so desire is always preferable to letting papers come in at the very end of the term. Unfortunately, no simple answers exist to these scheduling dilemmas.

Instructors most often assign written work for their course alone. But increasingly many schools offer courses that integrate or link writing assignments between composition and general education courses. These so-called "writing across the curriculum" programs typically bring together faculty of English and other disciplines to design writing assignments jointly that will increase content mastery as well as expose students to the kind of writing desired in that discipline (McGovern and Hogshead, 1990; Zinsser, 1988). Although evaluation studies suggest that it has been difficult to demonstrate that linked programs improve writing or content mastery (Madigan and Brosamer, 1990), students and faculty who participate in them generally report success and satisfaction.

Evaluating Written Assignments

The substantial liability of writing assignments is the difficulty of grading them fairly and in ways that improve students' course knowledge, writing skill, and confidence. Differences among students in the complexity of their thinking, and in the clarity, smoothness, and artfulness of their writing, make evaluative comparisons a subjective task highly vulnerable to a variety of distortions (Cronbach, 1970). Even though there are no widely accepted formulas or guidelines for how to assign grades or numbers to written work, there is a growing literature on how to assign grades in ways students see as fair and that promote better writing.

Fair grading is usually defined as giving a grade that is objective, valid, and reliable. Objective grading is based on qualities of the writing, not of the writer. The best way to be objective is to be blind to authorship when grading. Valid grading occurs when the criteria used in assigning grades fit the objectives students thought they were seeking. Even if students are given a clear statement of an instructor's objectives, evaluating their papers would be invalid if grades were based on criteria unconnected to the objective. For example, grading papers based on stylistic features such as economy or maturity of expression would be considered an invalid assessment if these features were not connected to the original objectives as communicated to students (Zinsser, 1988).

Reliable grading refers to the probability we would give the same grade to the same paper if we read it again independently. Experienced teachers know all too well that their concentration and grading standards can tend to drift up or down over time, especially when they are tired. Research conducted over a fifty-year span has repeatedly demonstrated that the grade a specific paper receives can be influenced by the context in which it is read (see Jacobs and Chase, 1992). For example, the quality of papers read immediately preceding a given paper can influence evaluation, such that if a paper of average quality comes after two or three poor ones it can seem better than it is (McKeachie, 1986). Students usually feel very strongly about fairness in how their work is evaluated and have every right to expect instructors to strive for the reliability everyone would equate with fairness.

Several well-established techniques can ensure that instructors' evaluation of students' writing is objective, valid, and reliable. Reading students' papers without knowing their names is an easy way to remain objective. This could mean using the last four digits of students' social security or school identification numbers or some other system in lieu of names. Grading work while blind to authorship also impresses upon students that it is their work and not their relationship with the instructor that is being evaluated. Valid grading comes from constructing criteria for different grades that are tied to instructors' specific objectives for the assignment and that are communicated clearly to students beforehand. Early in the writing process, some instructors take class time to ask students meeting in small groups to apply the scoring criteria to sample papers, ensuring that students are familiar with the criteria to be applied to their work later. Such so-called holistic scoring of papers has been found to increase grading reliability as well as validity (Madigan and Brosamer, 1991). Reliable grading comes from reading papers in small batches and being alert for shifts in grading standards over time. These techniques for fair grading do take a bit more planning and effort, but the improved accuracy of instructors' grading and satisfaction with the evaluation process among students make them worth doing.

An objective for every writing assignment should be to help students increase their skill at using writing to clarify and communicate their thinking. Returning a paper with only a letter grade jotted on the title or last page has far less power to shape a student's writing than returning one with notes or reactions from instructors scribbled throughout and a brief overview written near the grade that shows how well the paper was judged to have met the various evaluation criteria the class was working toward. Comments that are a good balance between encouragement and criticism are most likely to motivate students to try their best next time (McKeachie, 1986). Learning to write well is a continuing and never-ending process. Just as professional writing is improved by editors' notes and suggestions, students' writing is more likely to improve from seeing written comments from a careful and helpful reader.

Observational and Hands-On Assignments

Laboratory experiences so universally accompany science-course lectures in part because science is based on empirical investigations and the application of general principles to real-world examples. It is not surprising that laboratories are such a well-established part of science instruction. Similarly, studio courses in the visual and performing arts and applied professional courses in health or business-related fields or journalism universally give students direct contact with projects or activities out of class. But other disciplines can also benefit from assignments that ask students to work on projects or make systematic observations outside of class and to integrate them in class discussion or written work. The final section of this chapter deals with these nonlaboratory and nonstudio uses of observational and hands-on assignments.

Instructors teaching a variety of college courses occasionally ask students to observe activities or phenomena outside of regular class meetings. For example, history courses take students on field trips to local sites or ask them to conduct oral-history interviews with elderly or influential citizens. Students in abnormal psychology courses may visit mental hospitals, and students taking sociology or criminology courses may visit prisons. Fine-arts courses routinely expect students to attend exhibits or concerts. Government or political science courses may ask student to visit local municipal council meetings or court proceedings. (Spending a Monday morning observing local criminal court proceedings is guaranteed to be a civic eye-opener for almost anyone!) Finally, business or engineering courses often encourage students to visit local offices or manufacturing plants. Observational assignments are not uncommon in many lecture-discussion courses.

Other observational assignments are more unusual and may not occur to instructors whose objectives could be met by them. For example, students studying controversial issues in a religion or philosophy course might be asked to attend a local meeting of a group whose aims they strongly disagree with and to use their observations in a subsequent class presentation or writing assignment. Meetings of either an abortion rights or right-to-life group will give almost any student an opportunity to meet people strongly holding philosophical positions different from their own. Students taking statistics, business, or accounting can be asked to collect observational data on students frequenting popular campus night spots to be used in various quantitative analyses under study. Students taking foreign language courses can be asked to visit local support groups or festivals for immigrants whose native language students are studying.

These examples illustrate the many possibilities for using outside visits, which are limited only by instructors' imaginations.

Options for giving students hands-on experiences with relevant course materials or concepts outside of class are greater than ever, largely through the use of computer and video-recording technology. Since 1985 or so, the explosion of small computers on campuses has opened a wide range of engaging computer-based assignments that can be used outside of classes to meet a variety of objectives in almost every discipline (Graves, 1989; Herman, 1988; McGraw-Hill Primus, 1992). Most of these are tutorials designed to help students with repetition and drill of basic information, especially in foreign languages, or simulations in which students apply general principles to interactive case examples. Almost all computer-assisted instruction supplements what is happening in the classroom.

Another type of hands-on assignment involves the use of modern videotape technology, which is now so convenient that objects or activities can be videotaped more easily than photographed with a still camera. Students can, of course, be asked to view traditional videotaped materials, such as films or documentaries, that are on reserve in the library or media center. But instructors can also put together their own short tapes to illustrate course concepts, or for students to analyze as case studies. For example, an ecology professor can videotape a favorite forest stream at several different times of the year and during different weather conditions to illustrate a variety of phenomena. Similarly, an animal behavior course can be enriched by homemade videos of neighborhood dogs of various ages at play or animal behavior clips taken during trips to a local zoo. In effect, some instructors who mainly want students to see the phenomenon under study, as opposed to manipulating it actively, may find video recordings are more cost effective than organizing traditional field trips.

Another use of video technology involves asking students to make their own recordings for classroom showings or submission to the instructor as part of a written assignment. For example, a sociology class can ask students to make their own short documentaries to illustrate how homeless individuals live, conspicuous consumption at a local shopping center, or the class markers that distinguish different neighborhoods. Or political science students can be sent out on election day with camcorders to conduct exit interviews at different polling sites to illustrate demographic or attitudinal variables that are related to how individuals report they voted. Whether students are asked to watch or make video recordings, using this technology builds on the traditional use of the written word for presenting information to students and asking students to prepare materials for others.

At the very least, observational and hands-on assignments can enrich students' experiences with regular course content and help them to see the course's relevance to real-world issues and human experiences. But if students are encouraged to integrate their experiences intellectually with course content, such assignments can also help students analyze, synthesize, and evaluate course concepts. As is true with the many other types of assignments discussed in this chapter, observational and hands-on activities will have more educational value if they are planned so as to be integrated with overall course objectives and actively connected to what is happening in class. Taking the educational value of outside experiences for granted is a danger in any subject, even in the sciences, where students sometimes complain that laboratories and lecture sections are often unconnected to each other. Instructors who discuss the purposes of observational assignments beforehand and give students an opportunity to discuss them afterwards in class or in writing recognize what research has consistently demonstrated (Meyers, 1986): that active processing of educational experiences increases the number of students who incorporate them into what they are learning.

Except for studio art classes and laboratory courses, outside observational or hands-on experiences are likely to be only a small part of most college courses. Increasingly, however, students are spending more time on outside assignments using computers in ways other than as calculators and typewriters. But even when these activities represent only a small part of a course, like spices in food they can greatly enrich it if they are blended thoroughly.

References

Angelo, T., & Cross, P. (1992). *Classroom assessment*. San Francisco: Jossey-Bass.

Baba, V. V., & Ace, M. E. (1989). Serendipity in leadership: Initiating structure and consideration in the classroom. *Human Relations, 42*, 509–525.

Baird, J. S. (1987). Perceived learning in relationship to student evaluation of university instruction. *Journal of Educational Psychology, 79*, 90–91.

Bloom, B. S. (Ed.). (1956). *Taxonomy of educational objectives: Cognitive domain*. New York: Longmans, Green.

Connolly, P., & Vilardi, T. (Eds.). (1989). *Writing to learn mathematics and science*. New York: Teachers College Press.

Cronbach, L. J. (1970). *Essentials of psychological testing* (3rd ed.). New York: Harper & Row.

Cuddy, L. (1985). One sentence is worth a thousand: A strategy for improving reading, writing, and thinking skills. In J. R. Jeffrey & G. R. Erickson (Eds.), *To improve the academy: Resources for student, faculty, and institutional development: Vol. 5. Professional and organizational development network* (pp. 185–194). Stillwater, OK: New Forums Press.

Durkin, D. B. (1986). *Writing in the disciplines*. New York: Random House.

Eble, K. (1988). *The craft of teaching: A guide to mastering the professor's art* (2nd ed.). San Francisco: Jossey-Bass.

Erickson, B. L., & Strommer, D. W. (1991). *Teaching college freshmen*. San Francisco: Jossey-Bass.

Graves, W. H. (1989). *Computing across the curriculum: Academic perspectives*. McKinney, TX: Academic Computing Publications.

Herman, B. (1988). *Teaching and learning with computers: A guide for college faculty and administrators*. San Francisco: Jossey-Bass.

Jacobs, L. C., & Chase, C. I. (1992). *Developing and using tests effectively*. San Francisco: Jossey-Bass.

Lowman, J. (1984). *Mastering the techniques of teaching*. San Francisco: Jossey-Bass.

Lowman, J. (1990). Promoting motivation and learning. *College Teaching, 38*, 136–139.

Madigan, R., & Brosamer, J. (1990). Improving the writing skills of students in introductory psychology. *Teaching of Psychology, 17*, 27–30.

Madigan, R., & Brosamer, J. (1991). Holistic grading of written work in introductory psychology: Reliability, validity, and efficiency. *Teaching of Psychology, 18*, 91–94.

McGovern, T. V., & Hogshead, D. L. (1990). Learning about writing, thinking about teaching. *Teaching of Psychology, 17*, 5–10.

McGraw-Hill Primus. (1992). *101 success stories of information technology in higher education.* Hightstown, NJ: McGraw-Hill Primus.

McKeachie, W. J. (1986). *Teaching tips: A guidebook for the beginning college teacher* (8th ed.). Lexington, MA: Heath.

Meyers, C. (1986). *Teaching students to think critically: A guide for faculty in all disciplines.* San Francisco: Jossey-Bass.

Milton, O., Pollio, H. R., & Eison, J. A. (1986). *Making sense of college grades: Why the grading system does not work and what can be done about it.* San Francisco: Jossey-Bass.

Weinstein, C. E., Goetz, E. T., & Alexander, P. A. (1988). *Learning and study strategies: Issues in assessment, instruction, and evaluation.* San Diego: Harcourt Brace Jovanovich.

Wheeler, D. L. (1992, July 29). Championing the philosophy and beauty of mathematics. *The Chronicle of Higher Education*, pp. A6–A7.

Wilhite, S. C. (1983). Prepassage questions: The influence of structural importance. *Journal of Educational Psychology, 75*, 234–244.

Woods, D. (1987). How might I teach problem solving? In J. E. Stice (Ed.), *Developing critical thinking and problem-solving skills.* San Francisco: Jossey-Bass.

Zinsser, W. (1988). *Writing to learn.* New York: Harper & Row.

Chapter Ten

Feedback for Enhanced Teaching and Learning

Robert J. Menges, William C. Rando
Northwestern University

As mayor of New York City, Ed Koch was fond of asking people on the street, "How am I doing?" When constituents enthusiastically expressed their views, politician Koch learned a great deal. As professors, we too solicit information about how we are doing. This chapter reviews the process of seeking feedback, focusing specifically on professors' work as teachers.

Professors are naturally inclined to seek feedback, and we do it continually throughout our careers. Nevertheless, feedback seeking is fraught with practical questions. What information is most likely to be useful? How should information be gathered? What are the best sources of useful information? What guides interpretation of the information? How does the information make a difference? How can it be turned into specific intentions and actions? These are some of the questions addressed in this chapter.

In the following pages, we present an eclectic model of the process of seeking and using feedback to improve teaching and learning. It draws on Bandura's (1991) social cognitive theory of self-regulation, on cybernetics (Richardson, 1991; Menges 1991), on studies of experiential learning (such as Kolb, 1984), and on literature from organizational behavior (Ashford and Cummings, 1983; Cusella, 1987; Ilgen, Fisher, and Taylor, 1979; Locke and Latham, 1990). Our model includes four phases: (1) seeing and gathering, (2) interpreting and valuing, (3) planning and building, and (4) doing and checking. These phases themselves form a feedback loop: after information is gathered, some of that information is subsequently fed back as input for further interpretation. Then the cycle begins again.

Before describing the model in detail, we ask that you consider "The Case of the Disconnected Discussion." In this case, Professor Hugh Hall is faced with a fairly common teaching-learning situation, and he uses feedback to understand and resolve the dilemma he faces. After describing the model, we will return to Professor Hall to examine alternative paths that he might have taken.

The Case of the Disconnected Discussion

Professor Hall notices that his students rarely use ideas and concepts from assigned readings in their daily class discussions. Instead, they offer personal anecdotes and unsupported generalizations. Despite his attempts to focus on readings, the content of discussion is usually disconnected from the content of readings. Discussions are sometimes lively, but he is worried about what students actually learn.

Professor Hall knows that today's students are not as well prepared for college as students used to be. He decides to investigate how well they comprehend the material. At the beginning of class, he asks each student to write a short paragraph answering basic questions about the content of the previous night's readings.

The paragraphs suggest that students are somewhat familiar with assigned readings. The problem is not lack of effort. Still, the paragraphs reveal many flaws and misconceptions. Students seem to understand the specifics of what they read, but they don't understand the broader context. Most do not connect ideas or see their relationships. He decides that the problem is not information but context.

Hall reviews his options. He could replace these readings with a textbook that provides more explanation and context, but textbooks on this topic are somewhat shallow. He considers hand-outs, extra readings, and videos as other ways to introduce contextual information. In the end, he decides to provide the context himself through occasional minilectures. This may reduce time for covering content, but what good is content if it is being incorrectly stored and retrieved?

He implements this plan at the very next class and observes that students are unusually attentive during the minilecture. Apparently, they have recognized the importance of context. The real test of the technique comes in the next discussion meeting. Hall notes with pleasure that students take his cue and begin to use the readings as they propose arguments and reach conclusions. In the next few weeks, their ability to discuss material from the readings improves greatly along with their overall performance in the course.

A Four-Phase Model

Our feedback model includes four phases. Phases one and two deal with the teacher obtaining and understanding informational feedback. Phases three and four deal with the teacher using that information in order to improve instruction. For each phase, we pose procedural questions that must be answered in order to determine next steps. Also for each phase, we raise questions about quality that must be answered to determine how successful that phase has been.

Feedback seeking may be prompted by something general— vague puzzlement about how things are going—or by something more specific, such as low student ratings on particular course evaluation items. Our model is issue-centered (see Rando and Lenze, 1994), focusing on challenges, puzzles, dilemmas, or any discrepancy between what is intended and what is actually happening. The four-phase model helps to analyze the issue and to stimulate change.

Phase One: Seeing and Gathering

The major tasks in phase one are seeing the problematic instructional issue clearly and gathering information needed to resolve it.

Procedural Questions

What information should be gathered? To guide information gathering, we use the Four Ps Model (Menges, 1990), which differentiates four components of instruction: preconditions, plans, procedures, and products. Distinguishing these components helps to identify the issue for which feedback is needed and to determine what kind of information is most pertinent.

First, the problematic issue may be related to *preconditions*. The term refers to circumstances that precede actual events of instruction, including background characteristics of students, knowledge and skills of the teacher, the place of the course in the curriculum, and physical facilities. Some of this information is archival, and some must be newly gathered.

Second, the issue may be related to *plans*, that is, to the instructor's goals and objectives. Are course objectives clear? Have all relevant objectives been considered by the teacher? Are they appropriate for these students? Has the teacher conveyed their relative importance to students? The Teaching Goals Inventory (Angelo and Cross, 1993) differentiates six clusters of goals and helps teachers reflect about their own goals and objectives.

Third, the issue may be related to *procedures*, that is, to events that occur when learners are interacting with teachers and with subject matter. Information on procedures may be gathered about the materials students study, about teacher presentations and other classroom activities, and about the ways students assess their progress prior to receiving grades. Many of the "tools for teaching" in Davis (1993) suggest ways that feedback about procedures can be pursued.

Fourth, the issue may be related to *products*, that is, to the course's more enduring effects on students. As the course ends, what do students know, what can they do, and what reactions do they have about the subject and about the course and teacher? To what extent are their knowledge, skills, and attitudes a direct result of the course rather than attributable to other influences? How closely do these products match the teacher's plans (course objectives) and procedures (teaching activities)?

Using the Four Ps framework helps the teacher see the issue more clearly. It also prompts questions about who is in the best position to supply that information.

From Whom Should Information Be Gathered? Obviously, the most useful information comes from those who are best informed. On the topic of plans, for example, the teacher is the primary source, although it may help to know how students and colleagues perceive course goals and objectives. Procedures can be illuminated by information from students, from colleagues, and from trained observers who visit a class, as well as from videotapes or other recordings of classroom events. Information about products usually comes from students, either as the course is ending or as delayed evaluations.

Chairs and other supervisors may be less helpful. Although responsible for reviewing a professor's teaching, they may not be well informed about the teacher's day-to-day interactions with students. They are better regarded as interpreters of information from students, classroom visitors, and others than as sources of raw data about teaching.

In What Form Should Information Be Gathered? Information should be in a form that focuses on the problem of interest and that can be obtained with a minimum of difficulty. But care must be taken that convenience does not replace relevance and meaning.

Surveys of students are easily carried out, and results can be conveniently summarized (Theall and Franklin, 1991). Patterns of teacher-student communication can be captured through classroom interaction data (Lewis, 1991). Classroom events can be recorded on videotape, preserving qualitative and contextual information about interpersonal interactions. Discussions with students during or after class permit the teacher to probe issues more thoroughly.

The National Center book *Learning from Students: A Source Book for Early-Term Student Feedback* (Rando and Lenze, 1994) includes examples of questions (both open-response questions and closed questions) for gathering feedback from students during a course. It also describes feedback mechanisms other than student surveys, including teacher-student dialogues and group interviews of students. Another National Center publication, *Instructional Consultation in Higher Education: Handbook of Principles and Practices* (Brinko and Menges, in preparation), discusses how to use videotaping and expert consultants as vehicles for feedback.

What Is the Best Time for Feedback?   The best time for *gathering* information is as soon as possible after events of interest occur. The best time for the teacher to *review* feedback depends on whether the information describes successful performance or whether it reveals discrepancies between actual and desired performance. Information about successful performance is best reviewed shortly after the activity, since its function is to confirm and maintain performance. Information that reveals discrepancies will be most effective just prior to the next performance, since it is then that changes are most likely to be considered and implemented (Keller, 1983).

Quality Questions

Having decided what information to gather, from whom, and when, we now assess the quality of the information. According to our model, information gathered for feedback should meet at least three quality criteria: relevancy, accuracy, and manageability.

How Relevant Is the Information?   Feedback is relevant if it pertains to the problem at hand. Course evaluation items about how promptly the teacher returns graded work to students may yield little relevant information for an instructor who uses essay examinations to assess higher-order thinking. Nor is information useful if it conveys a need for change but fails to indicate what kind of change is needed (Johnson, Perlow, and Pieper, 1993).

How Accurate Is the Information?   Accurate information is complete and free from bias. Incomplete feedback comes when the problem is specified prematurely or when data are too narrowly focused. Bias results from using too few informants, and sources who are inadequately informed.

How Manageable Is the Information?   End-of-course evaluations summarized in tables that are difficult to read and understand will be discarded after only cursory attention. A videotape may hold relevant and accurate information but be ignored because so much time is required to review it or because the teacher feels overwhelmed by the amount of information it contains. As Ashford and Cummings (1983) point out, the effort needed to infer meaning from data may discourage persons from using potentially powerful feedback.

Transition to a New Phase

Sometimes the feedback process does not move beyond seeing and gathering. The problem may remain opaque. Collecting information may be too difficult. Information may be poorly organized; its meaning may be ambiguous; or its implications may be uncertain. Even when conditions are otherwise favorable, the process may end because feedback carries emotional risk. Potential embarrassment sometimes deters teachers from seeking and using feedback (Ashford and Cummings, 1983). The decision to continue to the next phase should be made deliberately and with confidence.

Phase Two: Interpreting and Valuing

Once information has been gathered, the next phase involves understanding what that information means and weighing it in light of one's values.

Procedural Questions: Where Is the Problem Located?

Is the problematic issue located primarily in the learner? Is it in the teacher? Is it in the physical or institutional environment? (Our approach in this and the following section is much indebted to the PROBE model—PROfiling BEhavior—introduced by Gilbert, 1978, 1982.)

Suppose observation data show low rates of participation in class discussion. Does this mean that students have nothing to say (probably a deficiency in student preparation)? Does it mean that students are unclear about what responses are expected (probably a deficiency in directions from the teacher)? Does it mean that students find little reward from speaking in class (a deficiency in motivation)?

Figure 10.1 summarizes these distinctions. It shows that an instructional issue may be located with students or with the teacher and that solutions may be directed at information, at instruments, or at motivation. This taxonomy should not imply that the complexities of instruction are always easily segmented. In reality, issues are seldom classified so discretely. As an analytical tool, however, the taxonomy reveals aspects of problems that otherwise would be overlooked.

What Is the Nature of the Solution? From Figure 10.1, we can infer how deficiencies might be remedied. Learners may need more knowledge (information), greater capacity to handle anxiety and manage time (instruments), or stronger motivation. More concretely, students may need to study *more* in order to attain extensive and deeper knowledge; they may need to study *better*, perhaps by mastering tools such as strategies for self-discipline; or they may

Figure 10.1.   Typology of Instructional Problems.

	Information	Instruments	Motivation
Student	Students' knowledge	Students' skills	Students' motivation
Teacher	Teacher's instructions to students	Resources provided for students	Incentives available to students
	Teacher's knowledge	Teacher's skills	Teacher's motivation

Source: Adapted from Gilbert (1982), p. 28.

need *greater motivation*, such as more realistic beliefs about the importance of course tasks.

These distinctions apply to teachers as well. The teacher may need to provide more information, such as illustrating good and poor responses to classroom questions. The teacher may need to provide better content for students to think about. The teacher may need to examine the incentive structure of the course, linking task completion more directly to grades, praise, and other significant rewards.

Quality Questions: How Accurate Are the Inferences?

Accurate inferences are drawn without bias. Viewing data selectively, for example, reflects bias when more weight is given to a few negative comments than to a larger number of positive comments. Another source of bias is the fallacy of concreteness (Eisner, 1982), a too-narrow focus on manifest behavior. Interpretations must move beyond what is observable to the level of meaning.

The best way to avoid these biases comes from asking others, "Is this the way *you* see it?" Does a colleague make similar inferences from the data? Do those who provide the information agree with the teacher's inferences about what the information means?

How Authentic Are the Interpretations?   Authenticity refers to personal values. How do interpretations of the feedback match the teacher's values? When values are contradicted by the data, it is time to reconsider expectations and standards.

Here are some examples. Increased time for class discussion is likely to remedy students' poor interactive skills and boost their motivation, but it may also violate the teacher's standards for content coverage. Better reading assignments are likely to remedy students' inadequate historical context but may also violate the teacher's standards for fair workload. Extra time spent composing comments about students' papers is likely to give them better feedback, but it may also violate the teacher's standards for scholarly productivity.

Standards have multiple determinants (including personal values, the perceived views of significant others, and the norms of the organization). The relative importance of these determinants and the perceived consequences of making changes deserve careful consideration.

Authenticating one's values is ultimately highly individual, but it should not be done in isolation from the community in which one works. Dialogue about these matters can often reduce the pain of difficult compromises.

Transition to a New Phase

Moving to the third phase requires commitment to developing a plan for change. This is a longer step than was taken in moving from seeing and gathering (phase one) to interpreting and valuing (phase two). To create a plan and to carefully build each step needed to achieve it means moving from a general diagnosis to a detailed action plan. Many projects are derailed at this point. The process may consume more time and energy than are available. Solutions may seem imperfect, requiring too much compromise. Benefits may fail to outweigh costs. A detailed plan makes it easier to assess the value of continuing.

Phase Three: Planning and Building

Phase three involves creating a plan, and building each step needed for success.

Procedural Questions: How Do I Proceed?

By this point the general approach may be apparent, but details remain to be worked out. Feedback has revealed where change efforts should focus. If, for example, the problem is students' low examination scores and if feedback points toward inadequate study skills as the reason for those scores, then something about students should change. Further investigation may be required to determine whether the change involves knowledge, instruments, or motivation. Alternatively, feedback may point to poorly designed examination questions as the cause of low scores, implying that it is the teacher who should change. Perhaps the teacher should improve skills in writing and grading examinations, or perhaps the teacher can obtain better examinations from a different source. If more than a single remedy is indicated, one must decide where to begin. In this example, it may be best first to improve the quality of the examination and then, if necessary, to work with students' skills.

What Are the Benefits and Costs?   Any plan has both positive and negative consequences. These can be viewed as benefits and costs. Ask what would be required to complete each step (costs), and ask how things would be better (benefits) if that step were completed.

At least three cost categories should be considered. Cost of materials includes paper and pencils, hardware and software, and other supplies. Cost of facilities includes space, data processing (such as scoring examinations), telephone and other communications, and so on. Cost of time includes the time of teachers, students, and others. Expenses for workshops to improve students' study skills are probably greater than costs of ready-made test questions. On the other hand, workshops are less costly than failing large numbers of students in a poorly performing class.

Benefits are enjoyed by students, teachers, and the institution. For students, benefits may be cognitive (more or better learning) or affective (greater satisfaction or motivation). For the teacher, benefits may be personal (greater self-esteem, higher morale) or professional (esteem from others, increase in salary, or advances in professional standing). Potential benefits for the institution include better student retention, a larger number of majors, enhanced reputation as a teaching institution, and so on. In the instance of poor examination scores, improving study skills is more broadly beneficial to students than improvement in examination questions. Costs and benefits should be carefully considered in light of the mission and culture of the institution. The final decision probably rests with the values of the teacher. No plan is correct unless it authenticates the teacher's own values.

What Are Specific Next Steps?   Each step in the plan should be defined in detail. What activities must be completed? In what sequence? On what schedule? How will progress be monitored and outcomes evaluated?

Quality Questions: How Consistent Is the Plan?

Consistency requires one last review of previous phases of the model. How closely does this plan match the feedback? Is there some information it fails to reflect? Is there any information it contradicts? How well does it reflect inferences drawn from the information? Does it contradict those inferences in important ways?

How Feasible Is the Plan?   Feasibility relates to focus, expense, and organizational support. Plans with a relatively narrow focus are more feasible than broader and more ambitious plans. Plans that make little or no demand for new financial support face fewer obstacles than those requiring formal budgetary authorization. Plans endorsed by key figures in the organization are more likely to be granted resources and less likely to face resistance than those without such endorsements. All persons, including students, who have significant roles in approving and implementing the plan should be consulted in order to build commitment and increase the likelihood of successful implementation.

Transition to a New Phase

Moving to implementation is actually quite easy, even exciting, given commitment to a workable plan. On the other hand, when the plan has only tentative commitment or when it is unrealistic, the move to action is the most difficult transition of all. Many plans are abandoned at this point. Committing publicly to the project increases chances of success. One might enlist a friend to whom progress is regularly reported or schedule regular discussions with others who are pursuing their own instructional projects.

Phase Four: Doing and Checking

The major tasks of phase four are carrying out each step of the plan and checking on the results.

Social scientists who conduct laboratory experiments are taught to build into their design a "check on implementation." This check determines whether the experimental manipulation was effective. For example, Latham (in press) describes a study of faculty goal setting where for one group of faculty performance goals were assigned by the chair, while for another group faculty and chairs decided on goals collaboratively. As a check on whether this treatment was implemented, faculty were asked, "Compared to your chairperson, how much influence did you have over the overall goal that was set?" Compared with those in the first group, faculty in the second group reported that they had more influence than did chairs in setting goals. Thus the researchers concluded that the treatment was successfully implemented. (Incidentally, when goals were set collaboratively they were higher, that is, they were more difficult than when the chair set goals for the faculty.)

Phase four of our feedback model includes implementing the

plan and checking on its implementation. It provides documentation that the plan has been followed. Only then can the effectiveness of the plan be assessed.

To document implementation, we look at what happened, including both intended and unintended events. The timing of events and the costs of implementation are also addressed.

Procedural Questions: What Intended Events Occurred?

Intended events can be documented through ordinary records—teacher notes, course outlines, meeting schedules and minutes, student papers, and so on. If such information is not available, plans should be made to gather it.

What Unintended Events Occurred? Sometimes unanticipated events are even more informative for reaching conclusions about a plan. It may be relevant to note fuller use of the teacher's office hours, or more students lingering after class, or fewer students taking makeup examinations. A reduction in the number of newspapers discarded in a classroom may indicate greater student attention. Such unobtrusive data are sometimes not appreciated until implementation is well under way, but one must be alert at all times for data about unintended outcomes.

What Was the Timing of Events? A detailed timeline should be developed against which activities can be recorded.

What Were the Costs? Expenditures of time and money should be recorded in detail.

Quality Questions: How Faithfully Was the Plan Implemented?

Fidelity to the plan is checked simply by comparing the documented implementation against steps in the plan. Was each step followed in the planned sequence? Were constraints of schedule and budget met?

How Fully Was the Issue Resolved? The second indicator of successful implementation concerns resolution of the problem that prompted feedback seeking in the first place. If the problem is examination performance, pertinent short-term results might include improvement of student study skills (or improvement of the quality of the examination). In the long term, results must show improvement in examination scores.

Transition to a New Phase

Although our tour of the model is now complete, the process of feedback seeking is not over. The fourth phase of this model is much like the first. During phase one, information illuminates a puzzle or a problem. During phase four, information permits us to document implementation of the plan and to judge its effects. Phase four yields information for further refinements, and this should be thought of as beginning a new stage in the model. Indeed, we believe that the model is best seen as a spiral. With each turn, it produces successively greater refinements in teaching and learning.

Questions posed in each phase of the model are listed in Figure 10.2. These questions give us a convenient checklist as we return to the case introduced earlier.

Return to the Case of the Disconnected Discussion

Let us now return to the situation faced by Professor Hall. To summarize the first scenario, we saw that Hall's feedback took the form of information from students about their mastery of course readings. From students' paragraphs, he concludes that their contextual knowledge is deficient. His remedy consists of brief presentations that put information from the readings into a broader context. As

Figure 10.2.   Key Questions for the Feedback Model.

Phase 1. Seeing and Gathering

Procedural questions:	What information should be gathered?
	From whom?
	In what form?
	What is the best time?
Quality questions:	How relevant is the information?
	How accurate?
	How manageable?
Transition question:	Am I committed to continue?

Phase 2. Interpreting and Valuing

Procedural questions:	Where is the issue located?
	What is the nature of the solution?
Quality questions:	How accurate are the inferences?
	How authentic are the interpretations?
Transition question:	Am I committed to continue?

Phase 3. Planning and Building

Procedural questions:	How do I proceed?
	What are the benefits and costs?
	What are specific next steps?
Quality questions:	How consistent is the plan?
	How feasible is the plan?
Transition question:	Am I committed to continue?

Phase 4. Doing and Checking

Procedural questions:	What intended events occurred?
	What unintended events occurred?
	What was the timing of events?
	What were the costs?
Quality questions:	How faithfully was the plan implemented?
	How fully was the issue resolved?
Transition question:	Am I committed to continue?

this plan is implemented, he finds that more and more comments during discussion are connected to the readings and that students apparently are also learning more course content.

Suppose that Hall's initial assumption about the nature of the problem had to do with students' *skills* rather than with their general knowledge. How then might the situation unfold?

Scenario Two: Students' Critical Reading Skills

In this scenario, the focus is on students' critical reading skills. Consider the following three scenarios.

Professor Hall acknowledges that the articles he assigns are tough to read and that students can get lost in their complexity. Students may give up and learn nothing. He decides that feedback about his students' reading habits would be useful. The next day in class, he asks them to write down all the strategies they use to get through the difficult reading.

Their responses do not surprise him. A few students list such strategies as "underline main ideas," "write key words in the margins," and "number key points within paragraphs." For the most part, students seem to possess few reading and comprehension techniques that help them think critically about what they read. The results are even more sobering when he surmises that some students list strategies that they know about but do not actually use.

Somewhat shocked and a bit perplexed, Hall wonders whether this problem results from basic skill deficiencies or from inadequate effort. In the end, he decides that may not matter. In either case, to progress in the course students must change their behavior by using new skills.

Hall develops a plan intended to accomplish three things. First, it should provide students with examples of effective reading strategies. Second, it should motivate them to use those strategies. Third, it should give feedback to him and to the students about how well the techniques work. The plan must also accommodate several levels of skill and experience. Hall decides to hold a one-day seminar on critical reading skills. He and a guest from the campus academic learning center use a combination of direct instruction and peer tutoring. He also plans a follow-up session in three weeks to review the skills and to discuss the success of the program.

Although announcement of the seminar produced some resistance from students, the seminar itself is well received and students subsequently report that the new techniques actually save them a lot of time and spare them unnecessary anxiety. Hall notes marked improvements in the discussion sessions and in test scores. He resolves to do a similar workshop in the next semester.

Summary. In this scenario, Hall sees the problem as a deficiency in students' critical reading skills. He gathers feedback about their reading and study practices and then organizes a seminar on critical thinking. Students learn techniques that lead to better-quality discussions about assigned readings.

Scenario Three: Teacher's Questioning Skills

In this scenario, the focus is on the *teacher's* skills, specifically his questioning skills.

Unable to determine the reason for the disconnected discussion, Professor Hall decides to talk to his class about the situation. The readings are no doubt an important part of the problem since they are quite challenging, but he suspects that there may be other issues as well. As he awaits the discussion, Hall begins to get nervous. What if *he* is the problem? What if students set out to attack him?

He cannot raise the subject in class because of this anxiety, so he decides to call in a consultant from the college teaching center for the discussion. The consultant will act as intermediary and take the brunt of hostility or criticism. The consultant might also help him make sense of the feedback.

Visiting class the next week, the consultant takes students through a small-group exercise in which they evaluate strengths and weaknesses of the course (Rando and Lenze, 1994, chapter 2). When Hall and the consultant meet a few days later, the results are not surprising. Students report a moderate level of frustration with the readings, saying that they are complex and filled with jargon. Their main problem, they say, is not the readings but the quality of class discussions. As Hall suspected and feared, students think that class discussions lack focus and coherence. They get little out of them, and in turn they put little into them. The consultant, who has done many similar exercises in the past, tells Hall that the group's comments seem sincere and that the students are not simply looking for a scapegoat.

Somewhat humbled, Hall asks for advice. The consultant comments that the students have provided some useful information, such as noting frustration when Hall begins class by simply asking, "OK, what do you think about the readings?" Perhaps he could benefit from feedback about technique and some training based on that feedback. Hall agrees and invites the consultant back.

At the next class, the consultant sits at the side of the room while Hall attempts to ask questions more clearly and to wait more patiently for students' responses. During the last ten minutes of the session, Hall leaves and the consultant takes over the class. Students say that the discussion is better focused, though no one is poised to call the school newspaper for a feature article.

Later, the consultant tells him that the day's discussion seemed to be better connected to the readings. Hall's anxiety about talking openly with the class is gone. They sit down to plan a semester-long series of observations with feedback.

Summary. In this scenario, Professor Hall suspects that students are responding negatively to something about *him*. Feedback from a teaching consultant who watches him teach and interviews the class points to deficiencies in Hall's discussion-leading skills. By learning to ask more sharply focused questions and pausing longer after the questions are asked, Hall finds that discussion quality improves and that discussions are more closely connected to the readings. He also overcomes his anxiety about discussing course problems with the class.

Scenario Four: Incentives for Students

In this last scenario, the focus is on *incentives for students*.

Hall finds the disconnected discussions truly perplexing. These are not poor students. Their tests and quizzes are some of the best he has seen. Nor is this a class full of introverts. Students have plenty to say about nearly everything except the readings. Hall decides to give students a short take-home questionnaire asking for their perceptions of the class, including the tests, quizzes, lectures, and discussions. The questionnaire also asks how much time they spend on each activity, and why.

As Hall expected, students spend little time preparing for discussion. Many indicate that they do not prepare at all. That seems to explain the disconnected discussion, but Hall is surprised by the most common rationale: "It doesn't count toward the grade," they write. Some add that there is simply too much other work to do in all their courses to waste time "preparing to talk in class." They're really not bothered by flat discussions; their primary concern is grades. Hall has a bittersweet feeling about discovering the source of this problem. At least, he thinks, they are being honest.

Blatant appeals to grademongering always leave Hall a bit exhausted, and part of him simply wants to go on with business as usual. But his more constructive mind prevails. While he prefers that students discuss for the sake of discussion, he knows that they are pulled in many different directions as they decide how to use their time. Having modified his standards in this regard, he resolves the following: if an incentive to discuss is what they need, then that is what they will get. Hall decides to allow students to add points to their final grade by performing skillfully in discussion.

The next day Hall announces details of the new plan. "There is no mystery about this arrangement," he says. "It is for the explicit purpose of encouraging you to prepare for each day's discussion by thoroughly and thoughtfully reading the text and preparing yourselves to engage in discussion." Students are pleased with the news. They realize that they do the reading for the test anyway. Now they can do it a few weeks early and get some extra points.

In the following weeks, discussion gradually improves. Toward the end of the semester, some students even thank him for saving them from "three nights of cramming for finals." These incentives apparently brought benefits other than just engaging in better discussion.

Summary. In this scenario, poor discussion is traced to students' lack of preparation. A survey of students reveals that they feel no incentive to prepare. Hall responds to this deficiency in student motivation by announcing that skillful participation is worth extra points toward the course grade. As a result, discussion becomes more connected to the readings, students feel they are better prepared for exams, and the overall attitude of the class improves.

Conclusion

Our goal for this chapter has been to provide a systematic way of confronting issues that are problematic for teaching and learning. Our attention to detail and to a myriad of small decisions is intended to demystify the problem-solving process. The most paralyzing question a teacher can ask is, But what if I do it the wrong way? This model reveals that there is no right or wrong way. Successful problem solving is about asking the best questions and staying honest in the answers.

Our approach to feedback differs from the usual treatments of that topic in the educational literature. We view feedback as initiated by the teacher for the purpose of improving teaching and learning. As explored here, feedback is not the result of an evaluation system imposed on faculty. It is not restricted to a narrow range of issues. And it is not limited to data, such as end-of-course student evaluations, that are available only after teaching-learning events have concluded. Feedback can be gathered at nearly any time, and in situations ranging from severe problems that disrupt a course to unanticipated successes that deserve to be better understood.

Feedback used in this way not only improves the experiences of students. It also enhances the teacher's sense of intentionality and control, factors essential to faculty well-being.

Given the multiple demands of academic life, teachers may find our approach somewhat cumbersome and demanding. To use our own standard, it may seem "unfeasible." But what today seems intimidating becomes second nature tomorrow. Ultimately, the model generates its own feedback, and that is what ultimately determines its value.

References

Angelo, T. A., & Cross, K. P. (1993). *Classroom assessment techniques: A handbook for college teachers* (2nd ed.). San Francisco: Jossey-Bass.

Ashford, S. J., & Cummings, L. L. (1983). Feedback-seeking in individual adaptation: A resource perspective. *Organizational Behavior and Human Decision Processes, 32*, 370–398.

Bandura, A. (1991). Social cognitive theory of self-regulation. *Organizational Behavior and Human Decision Processes, 50*, 248–287.

Brinko, K. P., & Menges, R. J. (Eds.). (In preparation). *Instructional consultation in higher education: Handbook of principles and practices*. Stillwater, OK: New Forums Press.

Cusella, L. P. (1987). Feedback, motivation, and performance. In F. M. Jablin, L. L. Putman, K. H. Roberts, & L. W. Porter (Eds.), *Handbook of organizational communication: An interdisciplinary perspective* (pp. 624–678). Beverly Hills, CA: Sage.

Davis, B. G. (1993). *Tools for teaching*. San Francisco: Jossey-Bass.

Diamond, R. M. (1989). *Designing and improving courses and curricula in higher education: A systematic approach*. San Francisco: Jossey-Bass.

Eisner, E. W. (1982). An artistic approach to supervision. In T. J. Sergiovani (Ed.), *Supervision of teaching (ASCD yearbook)* (pp. 53–66). Alexandria, VA: Association for Supervision and Curriculum Development.

Gilbert, T. F. (1978). *Human competence*. New York: McGraw-Hill.

Gilbert, T. F. (1982). A question of performance, Part I: The PROBE model. *Training and Development Journal, 36*(9), 21–30.

Ilgen, D. R., Fisher, C. D., & Taylor, M. S. (1979). Consequences of individual feedback on behavior in organizations. *Journal of Applied Psychology, 64*, 349–371.

Johnson, D. S., Perlow, R., & Pieper, K. F. (1993). Differences in task performance as a function of type of feedback: Learning-oriented versus performance-oriented feedback. *Journal of Applied Social Psychology, 23*, 303–320.

Keller, J. M. (1983). Motivational design of instruction. In C. M. Reigeluth (Ed.), *Instructional design theories and models: An overview of their current status*. Hillsdale, NJ: Erlbaum.

Kolb, D. A. (1984). *Experiential learning*. Englewood Cliffs, NJ: Prentice-Hall.

Latham, G. (in press). Teaching goals and motivations. In J. L. Bess (Ed.), *Teaching well and liking it: The motivation of faculty in higher education*. Baltimore, MD: Johns Hopkins.

Lewis, K. G. (1991). Gathering data for the improvement of teaching: What do I need and how do I get it? In M. Theall & J. Franklin (Eds.), New directions for teaching and learning: No. 48. *Effective practices for improving teaching* (pp. 65–82). San Francisco: Jossey-Bass.

Locke, E. A., & Latham, G. P. (1990). *A theory of goal setting and task performance*. Englewood Cliffs, NJ: Prentice-Hall.

Menges, R. J. (1990). Using evaluative information to improve teaching. In P. Seldin & Associates (Eds.), *How administrators can improve teaching* (pp. 104–121). San Francisco: Jossey-Bass.

Menges, R. J. (1991). The real world of teaching improvement: A faculty perspective. In M. Theall & J. Franklin (Eds.), New directions for teaching and learning: No. 48. *Effective practices for improving teaching* (pp. 21–37). San Francisco: Jossey-Bass.

Rando, W. C., & Lenze, L. F. (1994). *Learning from students: A sourcebook for early-term student feedback*. State College, PA: National Center for Postsecondary Teaching, Learning, and Assessment.

Richardson, G. P. (1991). *Feedback thought in social science and systems theory*. Philadelphia, PA: University of Pennsylvania Press.

Theall, M., & Franklin, J. (1991). Using student ratings for teaching improvement. In M. Theall & J. Franklin (Eds.), New directions for teaching and learning: No. 48. *Effective practices for improving teaching* (pp. 83–96). San Francisco: Jossey-Bass.

Chapter Eleven

How Research on Learning Strengthens Instruction

*Marilla D. Svinicki, Anastasia S. Hagen,
Debra K. Meyer
University of Texas, Austin*

The printed word on instructional methods for higher education is both vast and sparse: vast in that there are thousands of articles on ways to teach, and sparse because many of them contribute little in the way of reliable, generalizable information that has been empirically verified. Although two very fine reviews of earlier literature have recently been published (McKeachie, 1990; McKeachie and others, 1987), such summaries and overviews are the exception. Therefore, we propose to review recent trends in instructional research and theory focusing on the basic processes of learning and how they affect instructional decisions. We believe that knowing how learning occurs allows instructors to fashion instruction appropriate to the immediate needs of courses and students.

Types of Articles on Instruction

The literature contains at least five types of articles, summarized and illustrated below, which represent different approaches to understanding instruction.

Descriptive Articles

Most common are articles that describe a teaching strategy and provide information about outcomes and student reactions. These are not actually "research" articles; rather, these works illustrate how skilled teachers recognize and devise ways to overcome instructional problems. These articles implicitly recognize the "situated" nature of learning (Brown, Collins, and Duguid, 1989): the assertion that the context of the learning plays a key role.

Comparative Articles

Far more common are comparative studies, usually intended to answer the question, Which of two methods is better, A or B? Done on a larger scale, this type of research characterizes the early work in educational research and still has many proponents, particularly when a new methodology is introduced. These articles describe situations in which matched classes are exposed to either "traditional" instruction (usually a lecture) or some new instructional method.

This research is often the first accepted by those outside the educational research community. However, disappointment soon follows when seemingly clear-cut results are not readily replicated in other settings. To illustrate, a review by Dubin and Taveggia (1968) comparing lecture and discussion finds that about half the studies favored lecture while the other half favored discussion. Cynics conclude that instructional method must be irrelevant to learning when, in reality, the comparison is too simplistic to be useful. As noted, the contextual nature of learning makes it difficult to replicate the conditions of one study in another setting.

Analytical Studies

This category of research is designed not to say what method is best but to tease out the relative importance of those forces in a method's success or failure. The question here is not, Does it work? but, Why does it work? Instead of employing a control group, much of this research compares alternative versions of the same method to determine which factors are most important for success.

Derivative Studies

Certain types of studies are inherently idiosyncratic to a particular kind of instruction. For example, lecture-method studies frequently explore note taking by students, lecturer characteristics, or presentation style. Although note taking, teacher characteristics, and style may be important in other formats, they are not usually studied in those formats. In another area, studies on collaborative learning often focus on social and intellectual development, since an important component of the method is the group process.

General Learning Research

Finally, some of this literature derives from general theories of learning and may have the greatest potential benefit for instructors. If they understand the underlying principles of learning, instructors can adapt those principles to fit instructional situations. Unfortunately, because these articles are positioned in research literature, they are not well known to instructors.

Research Bases for Instructional Methods

In this section, we describe some of the empirically based findings that relate to lecture, discussion, cooperative learning, problem-based methods, mastery methods, and computer-based methods.

Lecturing

As McKeachie (1990) notes in his recent review, lecture is a relatively effective teaching method when the objective is immediate recall of basic information. It is less effective when tests measure long-term recall or affective outcomes. From the beginning, lecture has been compared with just about every new instructional method in higher education. Most comparisons find equivalent performance on achievement measures such as unit exams or final grades, while affective results usually favor the alternative approaches, particularly peer learning and self-paced methods. Computer-assisted instruction tends to produce superior results in most areas measured.

Two critical variables, the presentation characteristics of the lecturer and student performance, can help instructors improve the learning that results from listening to lectures.

Presentation Characteristics. The most frequently mentioned presentation characteristic is the *expressiveness* (often equated with the enthusiasm) of the instructor. Sometimes dubbed "educational seduction" (Perry, 1985), expressiveness appears in early research in findings that a lecture's ratings were influenced by instructor expressiveness regardless of the actual content or learning. Subsequent studies incorporated additional measures, such as student achievement and content density, and found that while lecturer expressiveness does have a slight effect on ratings, it also has an effect on achievement and interacts with other context variables (Meier and Feldhusen, 1979; Marsh and Ware, 1982; Marsh, 1987; Stewart, 1989). Moreover, psychological theory suggests that instructor expressiveness *should* contribute to better learning and not just to more satisfaction. Thus we are led to conclude that lecturers are well advised to cultivate rather than disdain expressiveness.

A more readily accepted characteristic is that of *teacher clarity and organization*, the importance of which in terms of its relationship to learning is well documented by Feldman (1989) and Pascarella and Terenzini (1991). Indicators of teacher clarity in the research analyzed included the use of examples, signaling key points and topic shifts, asking clarifying questions to check for understanding, pausing to allow thinking, use of a logical structure, and making objectives clear. Other work (Kallison, 1986) establishes a relationship between student achievement and highlighting activities such as showing the structure of the content at the beginning and leaving it visible throughout the presentation, and adding a conclusion during which relationships are reiterated.

Should general principles come first followed by examples (the expository approach), or should the lecture build from examples to the generality (the inquiry approach)? How can an instructor present materials so that students will understand the relationship between ideas? Van Patten, Chao, and Reigeluth (1986) suggested that if the ultimate purpose is application, the general principle should come first followed by the examples. Consequently, examples should precede if the goal is recognition of the principle in different situations. They also recommend that examples be arranged in increasing order of complexity to clarify the principle before it is applied in more complex situations. In sum, this work documents that as long as *something* is done to emphasize the structure of the content, learners will benefit. Exactly what is best in which situation awaits more explicit research.

Interspersed in the literature on these presentational issues are other structural modifications found to affect learning. Most of them aim to counteract the criticisms that lectures are too fast-paced, encourage student passivity, and limit feedback. The alternative goal is to support student processing of the information. For example, Ruhl, Hughes, and Gajar (1990) examined a "pause procedure," which briefly interrupted the flow of information at logical breaks. Such breaks allowed listeners to process the information more thoroughly or to catch up. These pauses helped students recall information immediately following the lecture.

A more familiar lecture modification is the "feedback lecture" (Osterman, 1984; Osterman and others, 1985), which involves the use of outlines, study guides, guided note taking, and structured small-group discussion during the lecture followed by feedback from the instructor, all of which are intended to encourage students to process lecture material accurately and actively. Active learning in the context of the lectures is ably explored in Bonwell and Eison (1991).

Student Characteristics. For the most part, studies of student behavior during lectures address the question of whether students can and do process information at the time of the lecture itself or later, usually through the medium of note taking and review. Do the benefits of note taking derive from the act of note taking itself because it forces the students to process the information better ("encoding"), or do they derive from using the notes as study aids prior to testing ("external storage")? A body of literature describes various paradigms for evaluating this question (Yu and Berliner, 1981; Carrier, 1983; Henk and Stahl, 1985; Kiewra, 1985; Knight and McKelvie, 1986; Dubois, 1986; Anderson and Armbruster, 1986; Kiewra, 1987). The results support both positions. If their notes indicate that they are indeed encoding the information rather than simply recording it, and if the way it is encoded is consistent with the way it will later be used, then the act of note taking combined with the ability to use one's own notes for review improves performance. The value of reviewing one's own notes is an important finding, since it argues against students using the notes of others, even the instructor, instead of their own. The caveat: their notes must be fairly complete and accurate if the finding is to hold.

The next step is to determine the variables that affect or *improve note taking*. Students improve their note taking or their use of notes by using a *generative process* rather than a transcribing approach (King, 1992; Kiewra, 1984). For example, King (1992) compared straight review of notes to two different generative strategies (self-questioning and summarizing) that forced more detailed processing of the information. Generative strategies also cause students to question or summarize more during the lecture. King hypothesized that generative strategies cause students to make more connections between the concepts within the lecture and between the lecture and prior knowledge; making more connections is known to enhance learning.

Similar results were achieved when students used the self-questioning strategy as a guide to discussion individually or in small, cooperative groups (King, 1989; King, 1991). Those students did better in lecture comprehension and retention than those who simply reviewed the material alone or in groups. Results from Rickards and McCormick (1988) supported this finding. Interjecting conceptual questions throughout a lecture presentation resulted in better note taking by the students and more recall of information.

Kiewra and others (1988, 1991) have researched various *kinds of notes*: (1) the usual verbatim notes, (2) notes in the form of a linear outline, and (3) notes in a matrix format that stressed connections. They found that the matrix notes outperformed conventional verbatim notes and the linear form of notes.

The available research on learning from lecture suggests that it is no better or worse than other methods on a very gross level. Supplementary work suggests that instructors should encourage students to take and review notes in a generative manner. The more connections students build, the better they will perform and retain the information.

Discussion

Olmstead (1974) observed that for such a long-established instructional method, discussion has not been the object of much direct research, either in comparison to other methods or in terms of the factors that influence its effectiveness. McKeachie (1990) reported that lecture and discussion were comparable on immediate-recall tests, but discussion was better for long-term retention and for other outcomes such as attitude change and positive affect toward the subject. More analytic are those studies of discussion that attempt to determine the factors that influence its success, with group characteristics and teacher questioning being the most commonly studied.

Group Characteristics. Gall and Gall (1976) provided an extensive summary of group processes applied to discussion by identifying four aspects of group research relevant to the classroom: (1) group size, (2) group composition, (3) group cohesiveness, and (4) communication patterns. They concluded that five-member groups received the most support in the literature in terms of the level of individual participation. In larger groups, the dominant member (usually the instructor in a classroom group) continues to respond at about the same percentage of the overall response rate. They advise teachers to break larger groups into smaller ones. Also, larger groups with their greater diversity lead to more task-irrelevant behavior, and therefore less time is spent on crucial learning.

As for group composition, Gall and Gall (1976) concluded that homogeneous groups are more cohesive but may reach agreement prematurely. Heterogeneous groups, on the other hand, make more accurate judgments and produce significant conceptual reorganizations. Heterogeneous groups are advisable when the development of critical thinking skills is an instructional objective. Group cohesiveness does improve group relationships and increase participation and communication, so some attempts to achieve it are appropriate.

Gall and Gall (1976) explained that group members need to be able to see one another. Whenever possible, all members should have access to all others rather than having to go through a gatekeeper (like a teacher). Thus, typical row-arranged seating may sabotage discussion attempts.

Teacher Questioning, Student Responding. The nature of the interaction is another important dimension of discussion. In reality, Ellner and Barnes (1983) reported, very little use is made of questions in the college classroom, and what questions are asked tend to cluster at the low end of the cognitive continuum. According to conventional wisdom, the types of questions used and the kinds of responses offered have a huge influence on the learning that results from discussion. Unfortunately most of the research on questioning has been conducted in primary- and secondary-school classrooms.

Carlsen (1991) challenged some of the accepted wisdom on questioning. For example, the idea that the cognitive level of teacher questions has an impact on student achievement has yet to be demonstrated convincingly (Winne, 1979; Redfield and Rousseau, 1987; Samson and others, 1987). Carlsen suggests that expecting a simple one-to-one relationship between teacher question and student response ignores the rich complexity of communicative context. The same question may be interpreted at very different levels by different students.

At first glance, the lack of relationship between teacher questioning and student learning is disconcerting. However, we believe this general conclusion exposes the misconception that a teaching method can promote successful learning simply through careful application. Simply asking good questions is not enough. Given the dynamic and evolving nature of the teaching-and-learning process, factors such as how participation is structured, how class performance is assessed, or how learning is measured affect the success of any tool or method.

Paris and Turner (1990) raise a key question: if higher-level questioning is used during instruction, but not assessed, then why should higher-level questioning be associated with achievement? Furthermore, existing participation patterns must change to realize the effects of higher-level questions. Sadker and Sadker (1992) reported that only 10 percent of the students were involved in 25 percent of college classroom interactions; over half of the students remained silent.

The role of teacher silence, known as "wait time," also plays a key role. In a review of the research from kindergarten through twelfth grade classes, Tobin (1987) concludes that longer wait times are associated with higher-quality responses and higher-cognitive-level learning. He believes that longer pauses allow teachers time to think and produce higher-quality exchanges. They also give the *students* more time to think about their responses. Although the majority of this work was done with basic-education students, the logic holds even more strongly for college level instruction, where the questions should be at the higher cognitive levels that require more thinking time.

Cooperative Learning Methods: A Better Method of Group Instruction

Having made great inroads in the elementary and secondary levels, cooperative learning is now appearing in higher education settings as well. Chapter Five, on collaborative learning, summarizes research and findings pertinent to the effectiveness of this instructional method. We highlight additional cooperative methods in this section.

Problem-Based Learning Methods

Growing out of several traditions, problem-based learning techniques put students in the center of a problem and force them to analyze it to find a solution. The process draws on their existing knowledge, identifies areas where information is missing, formulates and evaluates solutions, and critiques decisions, all of which result in learning. Problem-based learning is most widely used in the fields of medicine, business, and the social sciences, where problems often have very complicated solutions. This approach parallels the inquiry methods used in science education. Two categories of problem-based methods, case studies and simulations and games, are the focus of our review.

The many versions of case methods, from video vignettes to long, complex, data-filled descriptions developed from the study and documentation of actual business decisions, continue to gain favor in higher education. Most give students an opportunity to read or view the material, after which the instructor directs the discussion through a Socratic dialogue of questions that build on student responses to previous questions (Christensen, 1981).

Strangely enough, however, actual research documenting the effectiveness of the method is meager, as others have noted (Bonwell and Eison, 1991; Olmstead, 1974; Masoner, 1988). According to Masoner (1988), little evidence suggests that students learn any more information from case studies than they would from lectures, nor has the impact on decision-making ability been documented. However, students exposed to case studies do have a slight edge in problem identification and diagnosis, do have a better appreciation of real-life situations, and were more likely to show a change in attitudes or beliefs.

With regard to these last findings, Masoner (1988) observed that cases based on real-life situations were preferable to what he called "armchair" cases. Two other studies, by Burger (1992) and Kleinfeld (1992), confirmed that the situated nature of the case content turned out to be critical to the success of the method.

Of interest since the 1970s, simulations and games put students in a "real-time" problem-solving situation, where their decisions affect the course of the simulation. Add a competitive component, as when teams compete, and it is called a game. The increasing sophistication of computer simulations has renewed interest in this problem-based method. The early research work occurred in the human relations fields (Seidner, 1976). Little has been done to analyze the elements of simulations, and results of their effectiveness have been somewhat equivocal. Perhaps current computer simulations will rejuvenate research interest as well.

However, the wide diversity of definitions, formats, and uses of simulations impedes research work. Dorn (1989) notes that there are so many variables in the research on simulations and games that it is amazing any consistency can be found at all. Seidner (1976) observed that the usual pencil-and-paper achievement test is inappropriate for performance-based instructional methods. Simulations should be assessed on performance measures that reflect a more applied orientation. We recommend using the class rather than the student as the unit of analysis, using a "conceptual module" as described by Bereiter (1990) rather than discrete facts as the measure of learning, or using an ethnographic approach to determine important variables rather than global comparisons of effectiveness.

Nevertheless, several literature reviews offer some conclusions about simulations (Seidner, 1976; Wolfe, 1985; Smith, 1986, 1987; Dorn, 1989). Most reported that simulations and games are effective on the whole in increasing student interest and motivation. They do not differ from other methods in helping students learn basic content, but they have some impact on attitudes. The learning emphasizes application of principles rather than the acquisition of facts (Dorn, 1989). Dorn also concluded that skill learning is enhanced through simulations and games, particularly interpersonal skills.

Debriefing at the end of the game has been singled out for attention. Dorn (1989) claims that "one-third or more of the total time should be devoted to debriefing; 80 percent of the value of gaming lies in the postgame discussion because the simulation only generates experience" (p. 11). Similarly, Seidner (1976) holds that the postgame discussion clarifies what is to be learned from the experience. The degree to which these statements have empirical support is somewhat unclear, but the advice appears well founded.

Individual and Group Mastery Instructional Methods

The application of behavioral research to instruction during the 1960s and 1970s resulted in such methods as the Keller Personalized System of Instruction (PSI) and Bloom's Learning for Mastery (LFM), which successfully challenge the standard models of lecture and discussion. Comparative and analytic research summarize what is known about these approaches.

Comparative Studies. In PSI instruction, the material is broken down into small units that students study at their own pace. Students decide when to take unit exams. Those are promptly scored and reviewed with the student, who is allowed to retake the test after further study. Movement to the next unit occurs after mastery of a minimum set of requirements. In the studies reviewed by Kulik, Kulik, and Cohen (1979), achievement was higher in the PSI classes; grades were moderately higher. Improved performance was experienced by students at all aptitude levels. Student ratings of PSI were significantly higher than for conventional instruction. Time required of students and instructors was about equal under both conditions. To summarize, the PSI system produced results that were both significantly better and preferred by the students.

More recently, Kulik, Kulik, and Bangert-Drowns (1990) have analyzed the research on mastery learning. In mastery learning the content is also broken into smaller units, but the work can be done individually or in groups under an instructor's direction. The instructor sets the pace and method of study, but students must still meet mastery levels on practice exams before they are allowed to take the summative exam on which their grade is based. Likewise, the meta-analysis of research found that mastery learning methods had positive effects on students and learning. Guskey and Pigott (1988) found that students in mastery classes spent more time actively engaged in learning than did students in conventional classes, and their teachers used class time more efficiently and spent more time on task, a factor consistently associated with better learning. In addition, students in mastery classes were absent less often.

Analytical Studies. Despite research demonstrating that the mastery systems in their various forms are effective in producing higher achievement levels than conventional methods, a lot of skepticism remains in the higher education community. The doubts have stimulated a variety of follow-up and analytical research. For example, Leppmann and Herrmann (1981) compared four different classes to test PSI, mastery, weekly exams, and traditional conditions against one another. They found the PSI class to receive the highest final exam scores, followed by weekly testing with mastery, then testing without mastery, and finally the conventional class.

Another set of studies attempted to deal with the problem of procrastination in PSI classes. Wesp (1986) found that daily quizzing effectively overcame the procrastination problem. Roberts and Semb (1989) allowed students to choose between deadlines set by the instructor or managing their own schedules; they found that although more students chose to have the instructor-imposed deadlines, those who set their own deadlines missed fewer of them and rated the course more favorably. The finding was also confirmed by Lamwers and Jazwinski (1989), using a different research design.

The students who benefit from mastery systems have also been of interest in subsequent analytical work. Very early on, Van-Damme and Masui (1980) tried to explain the effectiveness of PSI methods by looking at student locus of control, presuming that students with an external locus of control would do better in structured systems while those with internal locus of control would be able to function effectively on their own. Herrmann and Leppmann (1981) questioned how student study habits might influence performance in PSI courses. They found that those who were successful in PSI classes were fairly orderly and systematic in their study habits, while those who did well in lecture courses needed more assistance in organizing their work.

Despite substantial research support documenting the positive effects of PSI and mastery learning approaches, and continuing work on specific variables, given how very different these models are from customary instructional models in higher education it is unlikely that mastery learning will be adopted unconditionally in the near future.

Computer-Based Instructional Methods

Beginning as a glorified page-turner in the days of programmed instruction, the computer has developed so quickly and in so many different ways that it is almost impossible to keep up with its instructional uses. We predict this instructional tool will continue to outpace our ability to design uses for it and conduct research to test its effectiveness. Nonetheless, research inquiries have begun to lay a foundation as to the effects of this powerful learning tool.

Kulik, Kulik, and Cohen (1980) conducted one of the early meta-analyses of computer-based instruction and found that student achievement was superior to conventional instruction in a majority of studies, even though the effect sizes were not large. (For more recent research reviews, see Hasselbring, 1984; Roblyer, 1988; Kulik and Kulik, 1991; and Kozma, 1991).

However, despite gains in achievement, students do not always prefer computer-based approaches. Sawyer (1988) compared computerized and conventional study guides containing the same basic material and found that performance was the same and that the students preferred the convenience of the conventional guide, a result confirmed in another study of psychology undergraduates (Lowman, 1990).

Initially used primarily for drill, practice, and other mundane purposes, expanding capabilities have allowed instructional designers far greater creativity. For example, the use of computer conferencing and networking makes possible communication between instructors and students, and between students in real time or across time or distance (Hiltz, 1986; Albright and Graf, 1992). Computer bulletin boards are an asset for busy instructors who are trying to communicate with large classes (Kahn and Brookshire, 1991).

Computer-based instruction allows for greater study of the learning process itself. It raises intriguing questions. For example, is it necessary for every learner to be exposed to every item in the program, or can the sequence of instruction be tailored to the prior knowledge and preferences of each learner? Although some studies seem to favor allowing learner control over the sequence (Gray, 1987; Litchfield, Driscoll, and Dempsey, 1990), a recent analysis (Lee and Lee, 1991) cautioned that this effect may vary according to the amount of prior knowledge that a learner has. They found that learner control worked better for those who were reviewing information they had just learned, while program control was better for those just beginning. The differential effects diminished in proportion to the amount of prior knowledge.

Examples abound of how computer-assisted instruction has been used to investigate student learning itself. Browning and Lehman (1988) used a computer program on genetics to monitor and identify student misconceptions and difficulties in learning the material. With these data they could then produce instructional materials to counter student difficulties before they became real obstacles to learning. Stokes, Halcomb, and Slovacek (1988) investigated the effects of enforced delay before response in computer-generated test items. They found that students who were forced to wait for thirty seconds before responding did better, both on the immediate test and over the course. Tudor and Bostow (1991) used computers to study the effects of having to supply answers to questions rather than passively reading them or covertly responding to items. Learners who could either construct an answer by typing or who had time to covertly respond to the items did better than those who were passive readers of the material.

This type of classroom research is possible primarily because of the computer's capacity to monitor and control learners' responses. While the examples cited focus on the individual learner, the rise of computer networks makes it possible to study cooperative learning via computers as well.

Research on General Principles of Learning and Their Relationship to Instruction

An alternative to reviewing the research literature on teaching is to consider what we think we know about *learning* and then design instructional strategies and interventions in light of that knowledge. Instead of trying to follow a prescribed formula for a particular method of teaching, we can make modifications in *any* instructional format to accommodate the learning process. Learning models can be the basis for implementing these modifications.

A Model of Learning

Most models assume that the purpose of learning is to incorporate new information or skills into the learner's existing knowledge structure and to make that knowledge accessible. Knowledge structures consist of a wide range of information, some factual, some relational, some procedural, and some that helps regulate learning. All are connected and networked, we hope in ways that facilitate access.

To integrate information and skills, the learner engages in several overlapping processes. Learning begins with the need for some *motivation*, an intention to learn. The learner then must concentrate *attention* on the important aspects of what is to be learned and differentiate them from noise in the environment. While those important aspects are being identified, the learner accesses any *prior knowledge* that already exists in memory, because a key to learning is connecting what is known to what is being learned. New information must be processed, structured, and connected in such a way as to be accessible in the future; this process is known as *encoding*. The deeper the processing of the information in terms of its underlying organization, the better the learning and later retrieval of that information. This processing requires *active involvement*. The learner must verify an understanding of the structure by receiving *feedback*, from the internal and external environments, on the encoding choices made. Finally, the whole process of information intake, processing, organizing, and storage should be *mindful and self-regulated* by the learner.

Even this brief and simplified overview of learning allows us to suggest some ways of integrating these ideas into teaching.

Motivation

Motivation is whatever activates and sustains goal-directed behavior in the learner. Goal-directed, active involvement focuses and maintains attention on learning, thus making the learner sensitive to relevant environmental changes that signal learning (Reed and Schallert, 1989).

Motivation is affected by the *qualities of the task* itself. Ames (1992) suggested that tasks involving variety, diversity, and relevance are more likely to foster a mastery orientation. Other theorists (Eccles, 1983) hold that such characteristics enhance the perceived task value and thereby increase motivation. For example, motivation will be much higher:

- If the goals of a course are consistent with the immediate or long-term goals of the student (for example, majors are more highly motivated than nonmajors in most courses)
- If the students see an immediate application of the content (they will be more motivated to learn statistics when they are trying to analyze some real data for a project than when it is presented as abstract, disconnected content)
- If the task itself represents a challenge (it is more satisfying to get an A on a tough test than on an easy one)
- When the method of presenting the task is novel or interesting (it is more interesting to solve puzzles than to repeat well-practiced drills)

Another important aspect of motivation relates to *goal congruency*. Ames (1992) discussed how classrooms often mix mastery and performance-oriented goals (for example, encouraging discussion and disagreement, but grading on a curve based on content knowledge). Fairly common practices such as giving students a challenging problem to solve and then asking for volunteers to provide the answer seems mastery-oriented on the surface. But even this practice highlights the ability of some students compared to others. To communicate a clear mastery goal orientation, have pairs of students discuss their respective solutions; this will minimize student comparison but promote understanding by everyone.

Motivation is also affected by the *characteristics of the learners*. Most important is expectancy of success. If a student believes a task can be accomplished, then the student has greater motivation to try. Part of that belief results from a history of successes, at this or a similar task or of success in general. Another part of that belief is based on an assessment of the learners' skills and the task demands: the closer the match, the greater the expectancy of success. Finally, learners are influenced by perceptions as to the causes of events: if they believe that causes are beyond their control or that causes are arbitrary or capricious, motivation declines.

Most instructors understand the value of enhancing student motivation. Most often, they try to foster motivation by making the content relevant. They use up-to-date or personal examples; allow students to select topics of personal interest for discussion, projects, or papers; and use their personal experiences or guest speakers to show content applicability.

Another way to foster motivation is to specify clear, explicit learning goals. Such goals are motivational because they help learners see and assess their progress. Although many instructors make general statements about course goals at the beginning of a semester, more explicit descriptions of the purposes of individual assignments should be made regularly. Goals should be included in the written instructions for an assignment or even at the outset of a discussion ("Our goal in this discussion is to identify the primary themes of *Gulliver's Travels* that can be tied to current events").

More recently, researchers and theorists in motivation have begun to encourage instructors to help students learn to set their own goals. Not only does this provide all the general benefits of clear goals, but it enhances students' perceptions of environmental control, another source of motivation.

A less-well-known way to enhance motivation involves raising student expectancies for success and helping them see the relationship between their efforts and that success. For example, by making explicit what skills students already have that will be helpful in a new assignment, instructors help students see that they have the capability of completing the new work based on what they already know. And by arranging for some successes early in the learning sequence, instructors build student expectancy of future success. A closely related instructional goal involves convincing students that their success is related to their effort or strategy rather than to chance (Weinstein, Meyer, and Hagen, 1991).

Attention

If something is to be learned, attention must be focused on it; therefore, instruction must direct student attention to critical information. There are a variety of ways to direct attention; despite differences, they do share some common characteristics.

Variety. Projecting a new transparency on an overhead projector, changing voice and speech patterns, physical movements, or other types of activity can result in increased attention at the moment they occur and maintain an overall general increase in attentiveness.

Novelty and Interest Value. Information that is presented in a new way or that is incongruous draws attention (Iran-Nejad and

Ortony, 1982). By preceding the information to be learned with questions or paradoxes, attention can be enhanced. Using humor or cartoons to make a point has the same effect. The more time a learner devotes to a given topic, the more interest value in general increases (Hidi, 1990).

Highlighting. Verbal cues such as "The first point is . . ." highlight information they precede. Visual aids, including writing on the chalk board, also highlight material. Texts are highlighted through changes in typeface, the use of bullets, or underlining, among other techniques.

Time. The amount of time spent on a topic draws attention to it, as does repetition. Including the topic as a main point in an initial outline of the day's content or asking a question about it also increases attention.

Context. Less obvious but no less effective is gaining attention by virtue of establishing a context before presenting information. The context can change the salience of information to increase or decrease attention. In the famous "old hag-beautiful girl" ambiguous figure, a subject's initial interpretation of the figure can be influenced if its presentation is preceded by a homogeneous series of other pictures (context) of either old or young faces.

Activating Prior Knowledge

What we learn is retained as a framework of interconnections between ideas, skills, procedures, impressions, facts, and all manner of information. When new learning occurs, this existing framework (or "prior knowledge") influences what the learner pays attention to, how new information is perceived and interpreted, and the degree to which it is processed. The more prior knowledge learners have about a given topic, the more sophisticated will be their (1) analysis of it, (2) ability to pick out important details, and (3) ability to interpret what they receive.

Prior knowledge affects new learning in potent ways. For example, individuals with little prior knowledge of an area spend a great deal of initial learning time acquiring information rather than structuring it; their attention often is fixated on gathering details rather than understanding their significance (Shuell, 1990). Students who hold misconceptions (faulty prior knowledge) have a great deal of difficulty learning accurate information that conflicts with those misconceptions. Existing knowledge structures also can facilitate understanding. When students complain about instructors' use of jargon in basic courses, it is because they lack prior knowledge. Once they have sufficient background to understand the context, they are able to decipher the meaning of the new terms.

Instructors should find out what prior knowledge students bring to the subject. Knowing what is taught in prerequisite courses, giving a brief pretest on terms and concepts, and asking students to provide some background information early in the instruction can help instructors to become aware of what is or is not present in their students' knowledge bases.

Activating prior knowledge at the start of an instructional sequence is highly recommended. Explicit links between old and new learning can be forged by asking students to recall previous experiences or information or by drawing connections between current content and the previous class period or assignment. Students with different levels of prior knowledge may need more or less help in making connections between ideas. Some situations may call for a common class experience, such as a field trip or common reading, to provide a basis for later work.

Encoding and Organization

Encoding lies at the very heart of what we mean by learning. When things are learned, they are incorporated into the existing organization of the learner's memory, creating encoding. If something is not encoded so that it can be retrieved later, meaningful learning has not occurred.

Encoding is at work all around us. For example, information presented in some sort of structured format (say, three main ideas, ten basic principles, the "three Rs") is easier to recall. Additionally, information tends to be recalled as it was structured. For example, lists are recalled according to item type (all the fruits, all the vegetables together); recalling one item from a category often stimulates the recall of other items from that same category. Also, learners will impose a familiar structure on information if none is provided; in a history class, students tend to organize the content chronologically unless the instructor strongly emphasizes some other structure.

Most instructors already understand the need for outlining during lectures. Making the outline explicit only strengthens its power to aid learning, so instructors are encouraged to put outlines on the board—or to emphasize them through the use of *verbal* cues. Furthermore, if it is important for students to understand connections between ideas, such as contrasts between time periods, it is better to structure the lecture as a comparison alternating between the two main categories rather than as a chronology of events.

In contrast, discussion poses a greater challenge for organization. Lectures are fairly linear in nature; discussions are more branching. Therefore, the kind of linear-outline notes that increase the learning potential of a lecture are almost impossible for discussions. More appropriate would be a note-taking system that mimics the branching nature of the discussion, like concept mapping. Or instructors might initially identify three or four main categories of ideas that will form the basis for a discussion and make those categories the headings of columns on a sheet of paper. As ideas are raised during the discussion, they are jotted down under the most appropriate category heading. Later students can go back and summarize the discussion under each of the headings.

Active, Mindful Involvement with Feedback

Learning will not take place until the *learner* does something to process the new information. When the learner is actively involved, attention is focused on the task, and connections are being made with the learner's personal knowledge structure. Simultaneously, learners test understanding by using the new information and getting feedback on the accuracy of that use. This repeated and purposeful encoding, retrieval, and feedback gradually refines the learner's grasp of the content.

The push to involve learners more in instruction has been building recently (Bonwell and Eison, 1991). Innovative instructional methods such as collaborative learning, case studies, problem-based learning, and computer-based learning revolve around active student involvement. Moreover, active learning does not necessarily involve massive course redesign. It can be grafted onto any instructional template, including lecture.

Instructors who lecture can interject opportunities for students to think actively about the content. This may involve pausing to allow students to review or summarize what they have just heard, asking questions (rhetorical or real) with an accompanying pause for thinking or responding, having pairs of students discuss an idea briefly or work on an example before proceeding, and taking time at the beginning or end of the class to have students write briefly about their learning. The possibilities are endless and can be tailored by any instructor to the specific class, content, or students.

Feedback in these situations will be to the group rather than individuals and will depend on the ability of the students to compare their responses to the models presented. However, even when no individual feedback can be given, just being asked to react to the content can shape the way students approach it.

In those instructional methods where active learning is the norm, care should be taken to see that the activity is "mindful," that the students understand what they are doing and its relation to the overall course goals. If the goal is to teach process rather than specific content, the feedback should point toward that process. For example, credit should be given for setting up the problem correctly or for making a strong case even if the main point being made is not the one the instructor would have made. The success of such active learning strategies as cases and simulations depends on the debriefing portions of the method, in which the instructor highlights how the problems were approached and solved.

Metacognition and Self-Regulation of Learning

Metacognition refers to how people think about their cognitions (Garner, 1987), which is essential for self-regulation, that being defined as "the degree that (students) are metacognitively, motivationally, and behaviorally active participants in their own learning" (Zimmerman, 1989, p. 4). The ability to build self-regulatory skills is an important instructional goal. This "metaknowledge" helps students become aware of the learning strategies necessary in different contexts and teaches them *when* and *how* to use those strategies.

There are three important implications of these ideas for instruction. First, at the beginning of a learning experience, when students need the most help, instructors support the development of metacognitions when they help students apply positive self-appraisals and suggest forms of self-management. The instructor may demonstrate the metacognitive activities by thinking aloud while working through a difficult example, modeling what the students might do. Second, the responsibility for such processing can be shifted gradually to the students by requiring them to suggest strategies for problem solutions and having them describe their thought processes to a peer. Finally, students should be given explicit instruction in metacognitive skills. Weinstein, Meyer, and Hagen (1991) refer to "metacurriculum," which involves teaching the skills necessary for assuming responsibility for learning. As Wang and Peverly (1986) argued, if good students are to be defined as motivated, active, planful, and resourceful, then they should be taught those skills.

Teaching students how to learn course content helps them evaluate their efforts and strategies as they acquire new knowledge and form new beliefs about themselves as learners. Asking students to reflect on their thinking is a central component in many methods, among them cooperative learning, explicit instruction, and other forms of interactive teaching (Jones and Idol, 1990). Assignments such as journals, reading logs, thought cards, and self-critiques can be used to encourage self-reflection.

Conclusion

There has been much progress in understanding how learning occurs and how to use that information to modify instruction. Instructors who are aware of these learning principles can begin to understand what is happening as students grapple with the content, and they can modify their instruction accordingly. No longer tied to a specific methodology, they will be more flexible in responding to student needs and more comfortable in coping with all the possible problems that arise in everyday teaching.

Our goal has been to discuss the effectiveness of instructional methods and then to link these research findings with what we know about learning. It is our hope that this will change the way instructors think about their task. Rather than asking, What is the best instructional method for this content? they will wonder, Given what I know about learning, what should be included in my instruction, regardless of the particular instructional method I am using?

References

Albright, M., & Graf, D. (1992). New directions for teaching and learning: No. 51. *Teaching in the information age: The role of educational technology* (pp. 8–15). San Francisco: Jossey-Bass.

Ames, C. (1992). Classrooms: Goals, structures, and student motivation. *Journal of Educational Psychology, 84*, 261–271.

Anderson, T. H., & Armbruster, B. B. (1986). *The value of taking notes during lectures* (Technical Report No. 374). Urbana: Center for the Study of Reading, University of Illinois.

Bereiter, C. (1990). Aspects of an educational learning theory. *Review of Educational Research, 60*(4), 603–624.

Bloom, B. (1984). The 2 sigma problem: The search for methods of group instruction as effective as one-to-one tutoring. *Educational Researcher, 13*(6), 4–16.

Bonwell, C., & Eison, J. (1991). *Active learning: creating excitement in the classroom*. Washington, DC: Association for the Study of Higher Education, ERIC Clearinghouse on Higher Education. (ASHE-ERIC Higher Education Reports)

Brown, J. S., Collins, A., & Duguid, P. (1989). Situated cognition and the culture of learning. *Educational Researcher, 18*(1), 32–47.

Browning, M. E., & Lehman, J. D. (1988). Identification of student misconceptions in genetics: Problem solving via computer program. *Journal of Research in Science Teaching, 25*(9), 747–761.

Burger, D. L. (1992, October). *The importance of living in the case*. Paper presented at the American Association of Colleges of Teacher Education, San Antonio.

Carlsen, W. S. (1991). Questioning in classrooms: A sociolinguistic perspective. *Review of Educational Research, 61*(2), 157–178.

Carrier, C. A. (1983). Note-taking research: Implications for the classroom. *Journal of Instructional Development, 6*(3), 19–26.

Christensen, C. R. (1981). *Teaching by the case method*. Boston, MA: Harvard Business School.

Dorn, D. S. (1989). Simulation games: One more tool on the pedagogical shelf. *Teaching Sociology, 17*(1), 1–18.

Dubin, R., & Taveggia, T. C. (1968). *The teaching-learning paradox*. Eugene, OR: Center for the Advanced Study of Educational Administration.

Dubois, N. F. (1986, August). *Review of the research on note-taking from lecture: Some new directions to investigate*. Paper presented at the Annual Convention of the American Psychological Association, Washington, DC.

Eccles, J. (1983). Expectancies, values, and achievement behaviors. In J. T. Spence (Ed.), *Achievement and achievement motives: Psychological and sociological approaches* (pp. 75–146). San Francisco: W. H. Freeman.

Ellner, C. L., & Barnes, C. P. (1983). *Studies of college teaching*. Lexington, MA: D. C. Health.

Feldman, K. (1989). The association between student ratings of specific instructional dimensions and student achievement: Refining and extending the synthesis of data from multisection validity studies. *Research in Higher Education, 30*(6), 583–645.

Gall, M., & Gall, J. (1976). The discussion method. In N. L. Gage (Ed.), *The psychology of teaching methods*. Chicago: University of Chicago Press.

Garner, R. (1987). *Metacognition and reading comprehension*. Norwood, NJ: Ablex.

Gray, S. H. (1987). The effect of sequence control on computer-assisted lecturing. *Journal of Computer-Based Learning, 14*(2), 54–56.

Guskey, T. R., & Pigott, T. D. (1988). Research on group-based mastery learning programs: A meta-analysis. *Journal of Educational Research, 81*(4), 197–216.

Hasselbring, T. (1984). *Research on the effectiveness of computer-based instruction: A review* (Technical Report No. 84.1.3). Nashville: Learning Technology Center, George Peabody School for Teachers.

Henk, W., & Stahl, N. A. (1985). A meta-analysis of the effect of note-taking on learning from lecture. *National Reading Conference Yearbook, 34*, 70–75.

Herrmann, T. F., & Leppmann, P. K. (1981, August). *PSI: Personalized for whom?* Paper Presented at the Annual Convention of the American Psychological Association, Los Angeles.

Hidi, S. (1990). Interest and its contribution as a mental resource for learning. *Review of Educational Research, 60*(4), 549–571.

Hiltz, S. R. (1986). The "virtual classroom": Using computer-mediated communication for university teaching. *Journal of Communication, 36*(2), 95–104.

Iran-Nejad, A., & Ortony, A. (1982). *Cognition: A functional view*. Cambridge, MA: Bolt, Beranek, and Newman Inc.

Jones, B. F., & Idol, L. (1990). *Dimensions of thinking and cognitive instruction*. Hillsdale, NJ: Erlbaum.

Kahn, A. S., & Brookshire, R. G. (1991). Using a computer bulletin board in a social psychology course. *Teaching of Psychology, 18*(4), 245–249.

Kallison, J. M. (1986). Effects of lesson organization on achievement. *American Educational Research Journal, 23*(2), 337–347.

Kiewra, K. A. (1984). Acquiring effective note-taking skills: An alternative to professional note taking. *Journal of Reading, 27*(4), 299–302.

Kiewra, K. A. (1985). Examination of encoding and external storage functions of note taking for factual and higher order performance. *College Student Journal, 19*(4), 394–397.

Kiewra, K. A. (1987). Note taking and review: The research and its implications. *Instructional Science, 16*(3), 233–249.

Kiewra, K. A., DuBois, N. F., Christian, D., & McShane, A. (1988). Providing study notes: Comparison of three types of notes for review. *Journal of Educational Psychology, 80*(4), 595–597.

Kiewra, K. A., DuBois, N. F., Christian, D., McShane, A., Meyerhoffer, M., & Roskelley, D. (1991). Note-taking functions and techniques. *Journal of Educational Psychology, 83*(2), 240–245.

King, A. (1989). Effects of self-questioning training on college students' comprehension of lectures. *Contemporary Educational Psychology, 14*(4), 366–381.

King, A. (1991). Strategy for enhancing peer interaction and learning during teacher-training sessions. *Teacher Educational Quarterly, 18*(1), 15–28.

King, A. (1992). Comparison of self-questioning, summarizing, and note-taking review as strategies for learning from lectures. *American Educational Research Journal, 29*(2), 303–323.

Kleinfeld, J. (1992, April). *Can cases carry pedagogical content knowledge? Yes, but we've got signs of "Matthew effect."* Paper presented at the American Educational Research Association Meeting, San Francisco.

Knight, L., & McKelvie, S. J. (1986). Effects of attendance, note taking, and review on memory for a lecture: Encoding vs. external storage functions of notes. *Canadian Journal of Behavioral Science, 18*(1), 52–61.

Kozma, R. B. (1991). Learning with media. *Review of Educational Research, 61*(2), 179–211.

Kulik, C.L.C., & Kulik, J. A. (1991). Effectiveness of computer-based instruction: An updated analysis. *Computers in Human Behavior, 7*(1–2), 75–94.

Kulik, C.L.C., Kulik, J. A., & Bangert-Drowns, R. (1990). Effectiveness of mastery learning programs: A meta-analysis. *Review of Educational Research, 60*(2), 265–299.

Kulik, J. A., Kulik, C.L.C., & Cohen, P. (1979). A meta-analysis of outcome studies of Keller's personalized system of instruction. *American Psychologist, 34,* 307–318.

Kulik, J. A., Kulik, C.L.C., & Cohen, P. A. (1980). Effectiveness of computer-based college teaching: A meta-analysis of findings. *Review of Educational Research, 50*(4), 525–544.

Lamwers, L. L., and Jazwinski, C. H. (1989). A comparison of three strategies to reduce student procrastination in PSI. *Teaching of Psychology, 16*(1), 8–12.

Lee, S., & Lee, Y. (1991). Effects of learner-control vs. program-control strategies on computer-aided learning of chemistry problems: For acquisition or review? *Journal of Educational Psychology, 83*(4), 491–198.

Leppmann, P. K., & Herrmann, T. F. (1981, August). *What are the critical elements?* Paper presented at the Annual Meeting of the American Psychological Association, Los Angeles.

Litchfield, B. C., Driscoll, M. P., & Dempsey, J. V. (1990). Presentation sequence and example difficulty: Their effect on concept and rule learning in computer-based instruction. *Journal of Computer-Based Instruction, 17*(1), 35–40.

Lowman, J. (1990). Failure of laboratory evaluation of CAI to generalize to classroom settings: The super-shrink interview simulation. *Behavior Research Methods, Instruments, and Computers, 22*(5), 429–432.

Marsh, H. (1987). Students' evaluations of university teaching: Research find-ings, methodological issues, and directions for future research. *International Journal of Educational Research, 11*(3), 253–388.

Marsh, H., & Ware, J. E., Jr. (1982). Effects of expressiveness, content coverage, and incentive on multidimensional student rating scales: New inter-pretations of the Dr. Fox effect. *Journal of Educational Psychology, 74*(1), 126–134.

Masoner, M. (1988). *An audit of the case study method.* New York: Praeger.

McKeachie, W. J. (1990). Research on college teaching: The historical back-ground. *Journal of Educational Psychology, 82*(2), 189–200.

McKeachie, W. J., Pintrich, P. R., Lin, Y., & Smith, D.A.F. (1987). *Teaching and learning in the college classroom: A review of the research literature.* Ann Arbor: NCRIPTAL, The University of Michigan.

Meier, R. S., & Feldhusen, J. F. (1979). Another look at Dr. Fox: Effect of stated purpose for evaluation, lecturer expressiveness, and density of lecture content on student ratings. *Journal of Educational Psychology, 71*(3), 339–345.

Olmstead, J. (1974). *Small-group instruction: Theory and practice.* Alexandria, VA: Human Resources Research Organization.

Osterman, D. (1984). Designing an alternative teaching approach (feedback lec-ture) through the use of guided decision making. In *Instructional Devel-opment: The State of The Art, II.* (ERIC Document Reproduction Service ED No. 298903)

Osterman, D., and others. (1985). *The Feedback Lecture.* (Idea Paper No. 13). Manhattan, KS: Center for Faculty Evaluation and Development in Higher Education, Kansas State University.

Paris, S. G., and Turner, J. (1990, April). *Keys for effective classroom instruction for strategic reading.* Paper presented at the annual meeting of the Amer-ican Research Association, Boston.

Pascarella, E., & Terenzini, P. (1991). *How college affects students.* San Francisco: Jossey Bass.

Perry, R. (1985). Instructor expressiveness: Implications for improving teaching. In J. G. Donald & M. Sullivan (Eds.), New directions for teaching and learning: No. 23. *Using research to improve teaching* (pp. 35–49). San Francisco: Jossey-Bass.

Pierfy, D. A. (1977). Comparative simulation game research: Stumbling blocks and stepping stones. *Simulation and Games, 8*(2), 255–268.

Redfield, D. L., & Rousseau, E. W. (1987). A meta-analysis of experimental research and teacher-questioning behavior. *Review of Educational Research, 80*(5), 290–295.

Reed, J. L., & Schallert, D. L. (1989, December). *Discourse involvement: An inves-tigation of a cognitive motivational construct.* Paper presented at the National Reading Conference, Austin, TX.

Rickards, J. P., & McCormick, C. B. (1988). Effects of interspersed conceptual prequestions on note taking in listening comprehension. *Journal of Educational Psychology, 80*(4), 592–594.

Roberts, M. S., & Semb, G. B. (1989). Student selection of deadline conditions in a personalized psychology course. *Teaching of Psychology, 16*(3), 128–130.

Roblyer, M. D. (1988). Effectiveness of microcomputers in education: A review of the research from 1980 to 1987. *Technological Horizons in Education, 16*(2), 85–89.

Ruhl, K. L., Hughes, C. A., & Gajar, A. H. (1990). Efficacy of the pause procedure for enhancing learning-disabled and non-disabled college students' long- and short-term recall of facts represented through lecture. *Learning Disability Quarterly, 13*(1), 55–56.

Sadker, M., & Sadker, D. (1992). Ensuring equitable participation in college classes. In L. Border & N. Chism (Eds.), New directions for teaching and learning: No. 49. *Teaching for diversity* (pp. 89–103). San Francisco: Jossey-Bass.

Samson, G. E., Strykowski, B., Weinstein, T., & Wahlberg, H. J. (1987). The effects of teacher-questioning levels on student achievement. *Journal of Educational Research, 51*(2), 237–245.

Sawyer, T. A. (1988). The effects of computerized and conventional study guides on achievement in college students. *Journal of Computer-Based Instruction, 15*(3), 80–82.

Seidner, C. (1976). Teaching with simulations and games. In N. L. Gage (Ed.), *The psychology of teaching methods.* Chicago: University of Chicago Press.

Shrager, L., & Mayer, R. E. (1989). Note taking fosters generative learning strategies in novices. *Journal of Educational Psychology, 81*(2), 263–264.

Shuell, T. (1990). Phases of meaningful learning. *Review of Educational Research, 60*(4), 549–571.

Smith, P. E. (1986, January). *Instructional simulation: Research, theory, and a case study.* Paper presented at the Annual Convention of The Association for Educational Communications and Technology, Las Vegas.

Smith, P. E. (1987). Simulating the classroom with media and computers: Past efforts, future possibilities. *Simulation and Games, 18*(3), 395–413.

Stewart, R. A. (1989). Interaction effects of teacher enthusiasm and student note taking on recall and recognition of lecture content. *Communication Research Reports, 6*(2), 84–89.

Stokes, M. T., Halcomb, C. G., & Slovacek, C. P. (1988). Delaying user responses to computer-mediated test items enhances test performance. *Journal of Computer-Based Instruction, 15*(3), 99–103.

Tobin, K. (1987). The role of wait time in higher cognitive-level learning. *Review of Educational Research, 57*(1), 69–95.

Tudor, R. M., & Bostow, D. E. (1991). Computer programmed instruction: The relation of required interaction to practical application. *Journal of Applied Behavior Analysis, 24*(2), 361–368.

Van-Damme, J., and Masui, C. (1980, April). *Locus of control and other student characteristics in interaction with the personalized system of instruction vs. lectures.* Paper presented at the Annual Meeting of the American Educational Research Association, Boston.

Van Patten, J., Chao, C. I., & Reigeluth, C. M. (1986). A review of strategies for sequencing and synthesizing instruction. *Review for Educational Research, 56*(4), 437–471.

Wang, M. C., & Peverly, S. T. (1986). The self-instructive process in classroom learning contexts. *Contemporary Educational Psychology, 11*, 370–404.

Weinstein, C. E., Meyer, D. K., & Hagen, A. S. (1991, April). *Work smart . . . not hard: The effects of combining instruction in using strategies, goal using, and executive control on attributions and academic performance.* Paper presented at the annual meeting of the American Educational Research Association, Chicago.

Wesp, R. (1986). Reducing procrastination through required course involvement. *Teaching of Psychology, 13*(3), 128–130.

Winne, P. (1979). Experiments relating teachers' use of higher cognitive questions to student achievement. *Review of Educational Research, 49*(1), 13–49.

Wolfe, J. (1985). The teaching effectiveness of games in collegiate business courses: A 1973–1983 update. *Simulation and Games, 16*(3), 251–288.

Yu, H. K., & Berliner, D. C. (April, 1981). *Encoding and retrieval of information from lecture.* Paper presented at the Annual Meeting of the American Educational Research Association, Los Angeles.

Zimmerman, B. J. (1989). Models of self-regulated learning and academic achievement. In B. J. Zimmerman & D. H. Schunk (Eds.), *Self-regulated learning and academic achievement: Theory, research, and practice.* New York: Springer-Verlag.

Part Three

Laying the Groundwork for Good Teaching

The view from the classroom tends to be myopic. Generalizations about students derive from those enrolled in the instructor's own courses or in a particular departmental program or major. Notions of how to teach spring from the culture of a discipline, are distilled in the crucible of the classroom, but are rarely infused with ideas and information from outside. For many faculty the world of higher education begins and ends with their institution and their discipline. What happens there are the events of all higher education.

Bear with this modestly overstated description in the interest of making clear that the faculty perspective on higher education is rarely broad-based and well informed. Obviously exceptions exist, but the rule is close to this description. Such criticism is not mean-spirited. Faculty are not hired as higher education experts. The focus of their work rarely includes the machinations of their profession in its organizational context.

However, there are issues in the broad arena of higher education that demand the attention and involvement of every faculty member, more now than previously. To be uninformed always bears a price, but today the potential costs are higher than they once were.

Theme of Part Three

Part Three aims to identify and describe some of the key issues that make up the current context of higher education. The goal is not to identify all important and relevant issues; there are too many. Rather, the purpose is to demonstrate the kind of issues affecting higher education and how these particular issues influence the conduct of teaching and learning at a particular institution, within a given department, and in the classroom of an individual faculty member.

It is still possible to teach as the proverbial ostrich, but issues like the ones explored and explained in this section affect the whole higher education creature. Even though it may bury its most important part, it is still vulnerable and stands a good chance of being overwhelmed despite trying to remain hidden.

The Theme in Variations: Chapter Summaries

More national attention is being focused on undergraduate teaching and learning than ever before. Such prestigious national organizations as the National Science Foundation have started funding education initiatives. National conferences, better attended than ever before, address faculty roles and rewards, issues of collaboration and community, service learning, diversity, and multiculturalism, to name a few. The attention highlights diverse topics, but the focus is on one prominent issue: the need to improve undergraduate teaching and learning.

Whether one sees the move to improve as springing from notions of remediation and deficiency (college teachers are not as effective as they should be), or one sees it in the context of changing student demography (these students are more difficult to teach), the question of the teacher's pedagogical knowledge base—

what it is that instructors should know and be able to do—is real and relevant.

Sarah Dinham, in the first chapter of Part Three, does something a bit courageous. She attempts to identify what a teacher should know in order to teach. This is a kind of teaching credo or manifesto, but without any political colorations. Teaching should result in student learning. From that premise, she proposes that teachers need foundational knowledge in four areas: knowledge of students as learners, knowledge about teaching, knowledge of the discipline, and knowledge of self as teacher.

Not only is Chapter Twelve an articulate description of the domains of teacher responsibility that are relevant to improvement efforts but it is written from the framework of the novice teacher. As the long-predicted wave of retirements (often happening via early-retirement incentives) begins to occur and as the smaller-than-expected army of replacements moves in to fill the ranks (usually at the instructor or part-time level), the integrity of the educational enterprise will be better guaranteed if the domains of pedagogical knowledge are clearly specified both in the individual faculty member's mind and at the department and institutional levels.

This chapter is placed in Part Three (dealing with context) because of its power as a framework-setting piece. It is time for departmental and institutional communities to join together in specific and constructive dialogues to explore what teachers should know and be able to do in the context of their work with students.

Equally relevant in the departmental and institutional communities are issues related to faculty vitality. Yes, individual teachers bear responsibility for on-the-job performance, but they do that within the context of a profession that has long ignored the potential, and sometimes the reality, of faculty burnout. Moreover, some institutional and departmental policies and practices contribute to the problem. Faculty teaching loads, courses, and schedules are often fixed, varying little from year to year. Class size at many places is on the rise. Faculty committed to teaching may do so at institutions where efforts expended on research garner more salary, respect, and reputation. With continuing uncertainties in the job market, many faculty who might be refreshed and reenergized by a move stay put, not willing to sacrifice the security of tenure and predictability.

The higher-education community, as it focuses on improvement issues, needs new and creative thinking about faculty vitality. Chapter Thirteen, by Charles Walker and Jennifer Quinn, offers a place to begin. Building on general theories of motivation, they propose four prerequisites for continued faculty vitality: (1) that faculty perceive themselves as competent, (2) that they be in fact autonomous, (3) that they manage their own goals, and (4) that their work occur in an environment compatible with their needs. This chapter breaks new ground. It challenges some prevalent assumptions, and it proposes alternatives made concrete with a variety of practical suggestions.

More and more, faculty who are less than vital, who are often not very productive, and who usually hold tenure have become the concern (if not responsibility) of the department and the institution. With pressure to be accountable and responsive to those constituencies they serve, faculty colleagues are increasingly being asked (in some cases required) to become involved in one another's professional lives. It is no longer enough to know how to keep oneself from professional dysfunction; faculty must now know how, when, and with what alternatives they might intervene in the instructional life of colleagues. Walker and Quinn help us think about this problem in new and potentially useful ways.

No issue to date has more polarized the academic community than efforts to diversify the faculty and open the curriculum to multicultural perspectives. Faculty know about this topic; they voice their opinions. Yet despite all the rhetoric, much of it emotional and combative, little has changed on the higher education landscape.

Old ways die hard in the academy. We might change more quickly if we saw our institutions in the cultural context put forth by William Tierney and Estela Bensimon in Chapter Fourteen. "An organization's culture . . . is reflected in what is done, how it is done, and who is involved in doing it." They say that culture concerns both decisions, actions, and communication both on an instrumental and symbolic level.

Tierney and Bensimon assume that institutions are committed to the multicultural agenda and are moving toward its goals. To realize progress, they challenge those in institutions to investigate issues of personnel, their mission as it is articulated and realized, issues of organizational structure, and the curriculum as it is manifest formally in course content and informally in institutional activities and events. For those in the academic community ready and willing to take action, the chapter proposes many steps that would make our institutions more diverse and inclusive.

An institution will not be made multicultural when one or even several faculty members, when one or even several departments decide to support and implement the required changes. It takes institutional commitment and the involvement of a majority of members of the faculty. Part of the individual faculty understanding that needs to occur in this arena is a clear understanding of what the changes mean, particularly in terms of implementation. This chapter creates that clear vision.

Finally, we note the cacophony being raised by those outside the academy. Higher education is not currently enjoying a time of lush funding and reverent respect. It is much more a time of constituencies all but beating down the door and demanding more accountability for our actions.

At most institutions, faculty are hiding in the top rooms of the ivory tower, desperately hoping those schooled in public relations will quiet the unhappy crowd. They pretend not to notice, but the crowd outside is not easily placated.

A good part of what the crowd demands relates to accountability, to assessment, and to the need to demonstrate and document that experiences in college do in fact make a difference.

Against the backdrop of these outside pressures, Trudy Banta proposes constructive means of better taking stock of what our programs in higher education do in fact accomplish. The focus here is not on what an individual faculty member may accomplish in the classroom, nor the very effective collection of classroom assessment techniques that can be used to describe their accomplishments, but an effort to direct our attention to programs, majors, and other curricular packages that separately and jointly form a student's learning experiences in college. Although the impetus for assessment may derive from outside pressure, the emphasis here is on better understanding the impact of our programs for our own sake, because it is our responsibility to know, because we care, and because knowing makes our efforts at improvement more focused and effective.

Like other chapters in Part Three, Banta's Chapter Fifteen with its many examples and illustrations begs to be discussed in a departmental or institutional context. What is proposed here can (possibly will, if the academic community hides out much longer) be done unto us. But the potential benefits of doing it ourselves are clearly and persuasively argued in this chapter.

Advancing the Thesis

As with the previous two parts, Part Three helps to answer the question of how scholarship can lead to improved practice. It shows the rich diversity of issues, the varied methodologies that can be used to describe and explain them, and the complexity of what it is that higher education must confront. These are issues to which simple solutions do not apply.

How does Part Three move forward the cause of scholarship as an orientation to improvement? It makes the case for reflection and for the infusion of ideas and information into the practice of teaching and learning in higher education. It does so by putting what transpires in the confines of the classroom with individual students into the larger, dynamic milieu of higher education. Faculty may well innovate based on what this book proposes about students, learning, and teaching. But the impact of those changes will not reach beyond the confines of the courses and classroom if faculty fail to see themselves and their work as part of a larger enterprise dedicated to goals that are organizational, societal, even global. The realities of higher education will not be answered with weak voices and faint hearts. They require an engaged, involved, and committed faculty community doing battle on the front lines.

Chapter Twelve

What College Teachers Need to Know

Sarah M. Dinham
University of Arizona

What do teachers need to know? "Everything!" gasps the novice college teacher. While it's true that teaching is complex, we need not know everything. Yet as teachers, we must be able to integrate the many things we do know into a coherent whole that will bring about student learning. Fortunately, most of the things we need to know about teaching and learning can themselves be learned.

But what are teachers to know? What is the knowledge base for teaching? Is it enough to know the field? Is it developing a repertoire of strategies to use with finesse and confidence? Is it more than talent? Shulman (1987) points out that school teachers' knowledge includes not only knowledge of the content to be taught but also the ability "to reason soundly about our teaching as well as to act skillfully" (p. 325).

What exactly are teachers to reason soundly about? While there are many definitions of teaching, we begin with the presumption that the purpose of teaching is to bring about student learning. From this perspective, then, teaching is arranging an environment in which student learning can flourish. This chapter examines several domains of college teachers' knowledge, implying how teacher knowledge influences the flourishing of student learning. It considers, in turn, knowledge of students and of teaching, knowledge of the discipline and of discipline-specific teaching, knowledge of the context in which teaching occurs, and knowledge of oneself as a teacher.

Knowledge of Students as Learners

Successful teaching focuses first on the learners. The early chapters of this book give helpful insight into the students whose learning teachers want to foster, and other chapters address knowledge of students as well. What else should new teachers understand about students?

Perhaps most importantly, today's college students are probably not very much like what today's college teachers once were as students. They may be younger, but then again today they may not be younger than their teacher. In either case, theirs has been a different life trajectory from their teacher's. For example, the typical college student today is somewhat older than the stereotype, may be employed, will spend longer than four years in college, is probably interested in a profession, and might change majors several times. These interests and life trajectories surely influence their responses to a course. The students may be interested in our field, but perhaps not. If they are not, they may not become excited about the field through the same ideas that drew their teacher; other strategies for enticing students into the subject may be necessary. Students may be well prepared for the course, or perhaps not. Teachers need to remember, however, what Stark and colleagues found: while many teachers in many kinds of colleges believed their students were inadequately prepared, it was impossible to know whether the "unpreparedness" actually resulted from student inadequacies or from unmet (or unrealistic) teacher expectations (1990a).

Knowledge of students as learners and concern about their learning directly influences teaching success. Boice found that teachers who had "decided to see things from the perspective of students and to like students" were happier as teachers, and their teaching was rated better (1992, p. 80). Understanding students as learners grows with experience through thoughtful student contact, with coaching of mentors, from reading about students, with insight into oneself. Most importantly, it begins with discerning appreciation of students as learners.

New teachers can benefit by understanding how students approach learning. For example, consider the model of intellectual development based on the work of Perry (1981) and others (Belenky and others, 1986), nicely summarized by Kurfiss (1988). Many college students expect a course—and the teacher as the "expert"—to provide them with "information," or "the truth," which they will "learn" and then demonstrate on a paper or examination. These students, not understanding intellectual complexity, may frustrate teachers with demands for the concrete ("How do I know if this is important?") when teachers are aiming for the abstract ("Here's an example of how historians work"). Other students are frustrated to realize that in this discipline in particular, or in education in general, many views are expressed, many avenues pursued, many interpretations made. They may retreat into despair at the untidiness of knowledge or reject intellectual rigor and deem all interpretations equally valid. They can foil the teacher struggling to build a searchin~ intellectual climate in a course. However, with guidance and understanding, students will mature through these phases to understand the criteria by which the multiplicity of arguments may be assessed, "knowledge" defined, and merit determined. They can come to understand how knowledge is context-bound and often value-laden; they can take responsibility for their own knowing and thinking. Ultimately, mature learners incorporate the complexity of a field into their own thinking, arriving at an intellectual commitment toward interpretations they trust and therefore believe they can embrace. Recognizing when students are stuck in this process and bringing them along the path is an important task of teaching. Thus teachers need to understand their students' intellectual evolution in order to foster their learning.

Knowledge About Teaching

Chapters in Part Two of this book offer considerable wisdom about strategies and procedures of teaching. Much of this wisdom rests on a teacher's knowledge of teaching.

What do college teachers need to know about teaching? Centuries of thought and decades of research have yielded innumerable maxims, lists, advice, debate, and prescriptions for effective college teaching. Several years ago, Chickering and Gamson led an ambitious effort to synthesize the accumulated wisdom about pedagogy into a set of principles for undergraduate education (1987, 1991). Their work led to seven principles of effective undergraduate education. What do teachers need to know about pedagogy? These seven principles provide a useful start.

First, students learn from *contact with teachers*. Boice (1992) poignantly describes how the simple act of arriving five minutes early for class and talking with students sets a tone for the class. Although a new teacher may at first feel reluctant about informal conversation with students, the mere act of showing interest—or better yet, checking on students' thinking and progress—can let students know their learning is important. Accessibility outside class and other informal but intellectually stimulating contact with faculty has also been shown to influence students more than we might realize. Office hours, ten minutes for questions after class, study sessions, seminars, even cheery recognition in the hall all matter to students.

Students learn from *real* teacher contact in class, of course. They gain more from a lecture punctuated by pauses for clarification, reorganization, checking understanding, or commentary than they do from the best-organized unbroken monologue. They learn better when they understand what is important, how new ideas relate to their existing understanding, and how to transfer new understanding to other applications. They learn best, too, when they understand how well they are learning and how to improve their learning (Svinicki, 1991).

Second, students not only learn from contact with teachers but also from *collaboration with other students*. Teachers encourage collaborative learning by arranging the opportunities for students to have contact with one another: study groups, peer teaching, student-directed class segments. Matthews's Chapter Five offers a thoughtful and useful discussion of collaborative learning, and Billson and Tiberius (1991) present both the theoretical and the practical aspects of social arrangements for learning.

Thirdly, students learn more from *active learning* than passive learning. When we think back to our own education, we often most vividly remember a project, a study group, a class simulation, a set of problems. Sometimes "activity" originates with the teacher; sometimes students generate it themselves. Students can even learn actively during a lecture if we plan the lecture to include advance study outlines, mock quiz questions, pauses, demonstrations, opportunities for synthesis, and "one-minute papers" (Cross, 1991).

Because not all students learn best from linear, narrative language, active learning for others can mean their creating a conceptual "map" of the subject matter being discussed, or an algorithm or other depiction of the course content. Suggestions for teachers interested in involving students more actively can be found in many sources, among the best being Bonwell and Eison's (1991) *Active Learning*. Those authors suggest how teachers can move securely from teacher-centered to student-centered teaching without passing through chaos. They also give many practical examples, realistically address the institutional obstacles to more active learning, and suggest what teachers can do about them.

Fourth, student learning benefits from *prompt and constructive feedback*. Students not only learn more but respond more favorably to the course when assignments are planned to help them understand how well they are progressing, when examinations and papers are promptly returned with opportunities to learn from the results, when individual student contact with teachers provides early assistance, and when teachers provide students with specific, positive, and substantive responses to their thinking and work.

Fifth, students benefit when they devote *focused and sustained attention* to the substance of the course content; this attention is called "time on task," implying simply that both in-class and out-of-class time should focus on the subject matter. The academic work of college learning—the weekly problem assignment, in-class exercise, term-paper assignment—is designed carefully so it will bring students into contact with the subject matter in ways that will make the course content accessible. While it is easy to plan academic work to fit our own purposes (such as providing defensible evidence for grading), it is better to plan work that will demonstrably benefit students. Moreover, because much of college students' academic work takes place beyond our control, we must be especially sure that the time they spend on these tasks will further their learning.

Sixth, *clear communication of high expectations* contributes to student learning. Clear communication means that students understand what teachers have in mind. The only way a teacher can be sure about this is to check frequently, either by talking with students about the expectations themselves, or by early, frequent, and constructive review of student work, or preferably both. High expectations foster learning when they are both attainable and challenging. High expectations that are uninspiring and incomprehensible not only obstruct student thinking but by wasting their time give students messages about the course that no otherwise-well-intentioned teacher can erase.

Lastly, effective teachers also acknowledge and act on their students' *diverse talents and ways of learning*. They select course materials and design their teaching to accommodate the students' preparation and comprehension. They offer a variety of instructional approaches. When students don't understand, their repertoire includes other ways to explain, depict, or illustrate. The vast and challenging diversity of student backgrounds and talents implied in Upcraft's second chapter in this book, and in Tierney and Bensimon's later chapter, illustrate this principle.

Knowledge of the Discipline

College teachers teach subject matter: organic chemistry, art history, cultural anthropology, accounting. The field not only represents an academic specialization, it also provides the lens through which the academic views life itself. The discipline thus influences teaching not only in selection of course content but in the teacher's very thinking.

Donald (1987, 1990) has confirmed that teachers in varied disciplines differ substantially in the ways they conceive of the nature of the concepts of their fields, the fields' logical structures, their organizing principles for truth criteria, and their methods of inquiry. A teacher therefore must know not only the obvious—the field's substantive content—but also how the field frames the substantive content. Teachers do, as Stark and others (1990a, p. 162) explain, "draw heavily upon their background and expertise to make planning decisions, using their academic field as a foundation for content selection, arrangement, and conceptual integration." This being so, teachers must not only know the substance of the discipline but also its shape and character, its logic and epistemology.

A disciplinary body of knowledge can be divided in several ways. Grossman, Wilson, and Shulman (1989) quote Dewey's (1983) observation: "Every study or subject thus has two aspects: one for the scientist as a scientist; the other for the teacher as teacher. These two aspects are in no sense opposed or conflicting. But neither are they immediately identical" (pp. 285–286). Grossman, Wilson, and Shulman (1989) suggest three aspects of teachers' knowledge of their field. First, teachers must be knowledgeable about the content. When beginning teachers do not know (or do not think they adequately know) the field's content, they often lecture impersonally, avoid eye contact, discourage discussion, misdiagnose students' thinking, and avoid some topics.

Second, teachers need to understand a discipline's substantive structures, "the explanatory frameworks or paradigms that are used both to guide inquiry in the field and to make sense of data" (p. 29).

Third, teacher knowledge must include the field's syntactic knowledge, understanding of "the ways in which new knowledge is brought into the field" (p. 29). Without this deeper understanding, teachers can parrot information about the course content, but in the end they will be unable to help students understand and assimilate the field's complexities.

As teachers, we seldom separate knowledge from beliefs about our discipline and teaching it. We may believe, for example, that cultural anthropology or Asian history provides the key to understanding the human experience. Our beliefs may be supportable as claims on knowledge, or they may not. It is important for teachers to recognize beliefs as beliefs, and to examine them as rigorously as we examine our disciplinary knowledge itself.

To teach effectively, then, teachers draw upon not only the substance of the field (a set of equations, an author's typical themes, a school of painters) but also its paradigmatic bases, its syntactic structures, and their own beliefs—all of which deserve thoughtful attention. Teachers need to reflect upon the diverse ways their own discipline can be viewed, how their own professional preparation has brought about their knowledge of the subject matter, how they themselves view the field, what they believe about education in the field, and how these beliefs influence their teaching.

Discipline-Specific Teaching Knowledge

A further form of teaching knowledge lies at the intersection of content and pedagogy. Effective college teachers concern themselves in a scholarly manner not only with the discipline's content but also with how that subject matter is most effectively taught. How can a teacher transform the course content to make it ready for effective instruction (Shulman, 1987, p. 326)?

How should a teacher design and manage that instruction? A teacher's understanding about teaching a *particular* subject matter has been termed "pedagogical content knowledge" (Shulman, 1987, p. 327). This term refers to such questions as these. How is this particular subject matter best connected to students' minds? Should course content be arranged according to the field's conceptual relationships in the real world? Should it be arranged according to how students will use it in social or career settings, or how the field's major concepts and relationships are theoretically organized, or to how students learn (Stark and others, 1990b)? "What analogies, metaphors, examples, demonstrations, simulations, and the like can help to build a bridge between the teacher's comprehension and that desired for the students?" (Shulman, 1987, p. 328). When should a teacher select one approach for teaching about a topic, and when is another approach better? Does cooperative learning benefit students studying this topic, or are simulations better? How can the material to be learned be adapted to these students' past experience? "What student conceptions, misconceptions, expectations, motives, difficulties, or strategies might influence the ways in which they approach, interpret, understand, or misunderstand the material?" (Shulman, 1987, p. 329).

An introductory college algebra teacher needs to understand, for example, students' typical conceptions of algebra and how prior mathematics experience influences these conceptions, the many strategies students use to solve different kinds of problems, the varied ways texts represent problems to students and how students respond to each, the kinds of difficulties students face when confronting new concepts, how students will falter and succeed when problems are presented in differing forms, and how students' understanding of college algebra can be shaped to help them in later courses. This knowledge will be different when the mathematics teacher moves into a calculus course.

A government professor may teach political economics in one way because she knows how the subject matter is best transformed for student understanding, but she may design a course on the political process entirely differently.

A psychology statistics teacher needs to know that beginners will stumble when they encounter the concept of "standard deviation" and must know how to represent that important topic to overcome the barriers and smooth the way for its later appearance in more elaborate forms.

Learning how to be an effective teacher of subject matter X does not guarantee effective teaching of Y. Having been an effective teacher of art history does not guarantee success in the beginning watercolor studio, even for an accomplished watercolorist. Indeed, having been an effective teacher of medieval art history does not guarantee success in teaching twentieth-century art history (although it will certainly help). There is no guarantee, not only because a teacher might be more expert in one than the other, but (more importantly) because there are differences in the most effective ways to represent medieval versus twentieth-century art history and to transform one or the other into student understanding.

How do college teachers gain this discipline-specific knowledge about effectively teaching a specific field? Beyond the two prerequisites—knowledge of the content to be taught, and knowledge of pedagogy itself—college teaching experience provides many lessons. A teacher knowledgeable about students, student preconceptions and difficulties with the subject, alternative learning strategies, and alternative means of representing the subject matter will approach subject matter thoughtfully and flexibly.

To supplement sheer experience, college teachers can learn the discipline's specific teaching knowledge by careful research. Teachers can learn particularly well from others, most likely colleagues in their own field. Many talented and experienced college teachers have learned through years of practice how their discipline is most effectively translated into students' learning. Newer teachers can co-teach, or they can systematically observe and interview experienced teachers to find alternative ways to represent the subject matter and to discover students' sources of difficulty with it. Teachers can look at a variety of texts to see how the subject can be organized, how difficult concepts can be represented, and how specific illustrations can help students grasp the field's complex ideas.

Gaining this essential knowledge is a significant intellectual process, rather than a talent. Being adept at intellectual inquiry, college teachers can be as inquiring and analytic about this new knowledge as about their research and creative work. Content-specific teaching knowledge can be learned.

Knowledge of the Context

Teachers teach and students learn course material not in a vacuum but in a context: the context of the department or program, of teaching colleagues, of resources.

Few courses exist independently of a program context. Teachers therefore acknowledge that context, and they plan their teaching within it. Stark and others (1990b) found that teachers' course planning was most influenced by the goals of a program or department, the general responsibility of the program to the institution's goals, and the requirements of courses that students would take later. What teachers need to know, then, is how to plan a course to fit into a larger curriculum so that students can move with confidence from one course to the next. (Occasionally, a teacher will plan a course to contrast with the program's usual purposes or viewpoint, so that students will be exposed to an alternative paradigm or interpretation. To manage this kind of course successfully, the teacher must understand the program context even more thoroughly.) Knowing the program context for teaching requires detective work, for we do not always know the details of our students' prior work in other courses or the nature of the courses they will take later. Yet knowledge of these two is essential for effective course planning. Administrators such as department heads are responsible for helping new faculty understand and work within these contexts.

Teaching in the context of a program also means teaching in a collegial context. Because a program or department is a collection of individuals, those individual colleagues influence our teaching in important but indirect ways. Sometimes an entire faculty's teaching habits—perhaps expressed as "delivering the content" rather than stimulating students' learning—can narrowly define what is expected from teachers and discourage change (Grimmett and MacKinnon, 1992, p. 390). The program's grading patterns are important too, particularly for new faculty. The department's instructional habits may be traditional or visionary; in either case new faculty members need to know how their own teaching fits with department patterns. Again, the institution bears some responsibility in seeing that new faculty understand these contexts. Boice (1992), who found obstacles to collegiality formidable for new faculty, emphasized that early involvement with colleagues concerning teaching paid off for beginners, even though talking about teaching is rare.

Teachers need to know the practical contextual constraints, too. Austin and Sorcinelli (1992) emphasize how important it is for junior faculty members to understand institutional expectations and resources. What kind of assistance can a teacher expect from the department office? Are there constraints on use of photocopiers for class handouts? If so, is there a campus copy center where handouts can be distributed? How are book orders managed? How does the library reserve reading room support courses? When are next year's courses scheduled and rooms assigned? Teachers must know the pedestrian as well as the esoteric, the concrete as well as the abstract.

Knowledge of Oneself as a Teacher

While "know thyself" is good advice for anyone, college teachers truly must know themselves because they confront themselves at every turn. "Shall I spend the rest of the afternoon developing more class handouts, or doing a literature search at the library?" "How should I answer that student's question?" "Is it OK to avoid interruptions by working at home one or two mornings a week?" "How can I negotiate with my department chair?" "Do I automatically assume that students are trying to evade work?" "Why do I feel like an outsider?" "I'm so uncomfortable with discussions in my freshman class!"

The first term, the first year, and even the first few years of college teaching, while exciting and rewarding, also bring isolation, insecurity, and unaccountable "busyness" (Boice, 1992). New teachers need to work consciously to find collegial support, intellectual stimulation, and professional friendships, to realize that this will take time, and to count this as productive, important time. Some campuses support these efforts, but most, alas, do not. Even if the campus doesn't help in this search, new teachers must privately acknowledge that the search is central to well-being as a teacher. Time and energy devoted to collegiality are time and energy well spent.

Time management challenges the college teacher as never before. While new teachers typically see their time problem as being not enough time (Sorcinelli, 1992), in fact the issue of time is much more complex. Course preparation can consume all of life, but that temptation should be resisted. Boice (1992) found that new teachers "who persisted in trying to come up with better and more error-free lectures made little progress in finding comfort, student acceptance, or time for other activities. Those who moderated and balanced time spent on teaching preparation fared far better as teachers" (p. 80).

Teaching style develops over time, and it can differ from one subject matter to another. Finding one's best style of teaching requires experimentation and reflection ("Well, I can see that lecturing and *then* expecting discussion didn't work!"). Sometimes new teachers feel fragmented because they find they teach inconsistently; one day the students actively pursue simulated problems, and the next the teacher must lecture. It may be small consolation, but all good teachers experiment and reflect on the results, and they refine their teaching style accordingly. Most important, effective teachers monitor their own teaching: experimenting, reflecting, using feedback, changing.

Teaching style is but an extension of personal style itself. Because one has never been anyone else but oneself, it's often difficult to imagine other styles of working, of learning, of thinking. Yet in order to understand students and to communicate with them, one must first understand oneself. For example, many academics are energized by working in solitude, reading late into the night, or sitting hunched over the word processor for hours; yet the majority of adults learn better in interactive, social settings. Many academics are verbal, linear, precise, logical; while some students are like them, others are visual, graphic, artistic, intuitive, kinesthetic. The teacher who learns one way finds it hard to imagine how students could learn in other ways, and in trying to be helpful ("This is how I learned it") he or she can easily give advice exactly contrary to a student's needs.

Knowing oneself as a teacher can seem an insurmountable task. Chapter Ten in this book offers helpful advice on seeing oneself through information from students and peers. Understanding oneself requires diverse sources of information. Information from students can come from small feedback groups, end-of-class one-minute student comments, or formal evaluation programs. Information from peers can come from observation by local colleagues, consultations outside class, and through asking colleagues at other colleges to review teaching materials.

Beyond the help of friends, colleagues, and professional teaching specialists, one of the best sources for understanding oneself as a teacher is a good mentor. Unfortunately, because few campuses can point to sound, established, widely used teaching mentor programs (Boice, 1992), teachers might have to arrange good mentoring themselves. A good teaching mentor agrees to spend time with the new teacher, to share experience and encouragement, to observe and be observed, question and be questioned. A good teaching mentorship is planned: it includes scheduled elements as well as unscheduled encounters, joint experimentation as well as emulation (Schön, 1987), periods of active involvement as well as other periods of distance. A teaching mentor helps expand one's vision of oneself.

Those Who Can, Do; Those Who Understand, Teach

The head for this section shows how Shulman (1986, p. 14) twists George Bernard Shaw's aphorism, calling on teachers to "understand." What does a new teacher need to understand? The content of the discipline, surely—including not only its facts, concepts, and organizing principles but also its explanatory frameworks and syntactic structures. Also, a teacher must have the specialized understanding about learning the discipline that is specific to the field, that is, the particular context for teaching. Insight about today's students in general and in particular about students as learners is important, as is wisdom about ourselves and how our talents, styles, fears, and beliefs influence our teaching.

Understanding these complexities sends us on our way as teachers.

References

Austin, A. E., & Sorcinelli, M. D. (1992). Summary and further reflections. In M. D. Sorcinelli & A. E. Austin (Eds.), New directions for teaching and learning: No. 50. *Developing new and junior faculty* (pp. 97–99). San Francisco: Jossey-Bass.

Belenky, M. F., Clinchy, B. M., Goldberger, N. R., & Tarule, J. M. (1986). *Women's ways of knowing: The development of self, voice, and mind.* New York: Basic Books.

Billson, J. M. & Tiberius, R. G. (1991). Effective social arrangements for teaching and learning. In R. J. Menges & M. D. Svinicki (Eds.), New directions for teaching and learning: No. 45. *College teaching: From theory to practice* (pp. 87–109). San Francisco: Jossey-Bass.

Boice, R. (1992). *The new faculty member.* San Francisco: Jossey-Bass.

Bonwell, C. C., & Eison, J. A. (1991). *Active learning: Creating excitement in the classroom.* Washington, DC: George Washington University, School of Education and Human Development. (ASHE-ERIC Higher Education Report No. 1)

Chickering, A. W., & Gamson, Z. F. (1987). Seven principles of good practice in undergraduate education. *AAHE Bulletin, 39*(7), 3–7.

Chickering, A. W., & Gamson, Z. F. (Eds.). (1991). New directions for teaching and learning: No. 47. *Applying the seven principles for good practice in undergraduate education.* San Francisco: Jossey-Bass.

Cross, K. P. (1991). How to find out whether students are learning what you are teaching. In J. D. Nyquist, R. D. Abbott, D. H. Wulff, & J. Sprague (Eds.), *Preparing the professoriate of tomorrow to teach* (pp. 232–242). Dubuque, IA: Kendall/Hunt.

Dewey, J. (1983). The child and the curriculum. In J. A. Boydston (Ed.), *John Dewey: The middle works, 1899–1924: Vol. 2. 1902–1903* (pp. 273–291). Carbondale, IL: Southern Illinois University Press.

Donald, J. G. (1987). Learning schemata: Methods of representing cognitive, content, and curriculum structures in higher education. *Instructional Science, 16,* 187–211.

Donald, J. G. (1990). University professors' views of knowledge and validation processes. *Journal of Educational Psychology, 82,* 242–249.

Grimmett, P. P., & MacKinnon, A. M. (1992). Craft knowledge and the education of teachers. In G. Grant (Ed.), *Review of Research in Education* (Vol. 18, pp. 385–458). Washington, DC: American Educational Research Association.

Grossman, P. L., Wilson, S. M., & Shulman, L. S. (1989). Teachers of substance: Subject matter knowledge for teaching. In M. C. Reynolds (Ed.), *Knowledge base for the beginning teacher* (pp. 23–34). New York: Pergamon.

Kurfiss, J. G. (1988). *Critical thinking: Theory, research, practice, and possibilities*. Washington, D.C.: George Washington University, School of Education and Human Development. (ASHE-ERIC Higher Education Report No. 2)

Perry, W. G. (1981). Cognitive and ethical growth: The making of meaning. In A. W. Chickering (Ed.), *The modern American college* (pp. 76–116). San Francisco: Jossey-Bass.

Schön, D. A. (1987). *Educating the reflective practitioner*. San Francisco: Jossey-Bass.

Shulman, L. S. (1986). Those who understand: Knowledge growth in teaching. *Educational Researcher, 15*, 4–14.

Shulman, L. S. (1987). Knowledge and teaching: Foundations of the new reform. *Harvard Educational Review, 57*, 313–337.

Sorcinelli, M. D. (1992). New and junior faculty stress: Research and responses. In M. D. Sorcinelli & A. E. Austin (Eds.), New directions for teaching and learning: No. 50. *Developing new and junior faculty* (pp. 27–37). San Francisco: Jossey-Bass.

Stark, J. S., Lowther, M. A., Bentley, R. J., & Martens, G. G. (1990a). Disciplinary differences in course planning. *The Review of Higher Education, 13*(2), 141–165.

Stark, J. S., Lowther, M. A., Bentley, R. J., Ryan, M. P., Martens, G. G., Genthon, M. L., Wren, P. A., & Shaw, K. M. (1990b). *Planning introductory college courses: Influences on faculty*. Ann Arbor: University of Michigan National Center for Research to Improve Postsecondary Teaching and Learning.

Svinicki, M. D. (1991). Practical implications of cognitive theories. In R. J. Menges & M. D. Svinicki (Eds.), New directions for teaching and learning: No. 45. *College teaching: From theory to practice* (pp. 27–37). San Francisco: Jossey-Bass.

Chapter Thirteen

Fostering Instructional Vitality and Motivation

Charles J. Walker, St. Bonaventure University
Jennifer Woods Quinn, Northwestern University

Some college teachers simply do not age. Their work, if anything, becomes more vibrant and youthful as they mature. How do they sustain their vitality throughout a long career in teaching? What keeps them motivated? These questions have intrigued researchers for nearly a century and are particularly relevant to higher education today. In this chapter, we will offer new viewpoints and new answers to these questions by drawing on current research and theory on human motivation.

Early research on instructor motivation focused on the satisfactions and dissatisfactions of individual instructors. The findings of this research have been amazingly consistent over a forty-year period. College faculty, whether from the 1950s or the 1980s, said that they like to work with capable young people, enjoy intellectual challenges and lifelong learning, and appreciate the autonomy and independence granted to college professors. In contrast, they said that they dislike meaningless distractions, doing too much work (service, research, and teaching), not being recognized for their teaching, and not receiving the resources they need to do their work effectively (Bess, 1977; Blackburn and others, 1986; Eble and McKeachie, 1985; Eckert and Stecklein, 1957).

The dissatisfactions reported by college professors are considerable and would, on the surface, appear to erode their motivation to teach. However, instructors from a variety of disciplines and institutions have reported that they would choose teaching again if they were given the chance (Mooney, 1989). But why would they choose to do something that is often frustrating and rarely recognized or rewarded? An answer frequently given by faculty and researchers alike is that teaching is its own reward; teachers do not need external incentives to teach. The pursuit of excellence in teaching, they believe, is guided by internal standards and fueled by intrinsic motivation. While this answer may be partially true, more insight and alternative explanations can be gained by considering other views of human motivation.

In this chapter, we present at least four alternative views of human motivation. Some are not surprising and reinforce what we already know, while others are provocative and stimulate us to reconsider the common assumptions we have about the vitality of college instructors. A review of the recent literature on human motivation leads us to conclude that instructors will be most vital when they (1) are competent, (2) have sufficient autonomy, (3) set and assess challenging goals, and (4) receive fair and equitable rewards for excellent teaching. We examine each of these alternative views on instructional vitality.

Competence and Motivation

Six major theories of motivation are unanimous about the role that competence plays in human performance. According to theories of self-efficacy (Bandura, 1982), self-worth (Harter, 1986), and self-determination (Deci and Ryan, 1985), without basic skills and competencies the vitality of an instructor will surely decline. Many other theories of motivation assume that the human performer is at least minimally competent, or they view competence as an intervening condition for the achievement of success (goal setting, Locke and Latham, 1990a; sense of coherence, Antonovsky, 1987; optimal experience, Csikszentmihalyi, 1990). The implication of this literature is unequivocal: for instructors to stay motivated, they must be proficient at what they do.

However, this seemingly simple idea has complex overlays. What do we mean by competence? How can competence be assessed, developed, and maintained? The theories that stress competence also offer helpful ways to define it. For example, to define competencies it logically follows from goal-setting theory (by Locke and Latham, 1990a) that one must begin by examining the goals of individuals and then infer from these goals what competencies are required to achieve them. Similarly, Mihaly Csikszentmihalyi, the author of optimal-experience theory (Csikszentmihalyi and Csikszentmihalyi, 1988; Csikszentmihalyi, 1990), suggests observing the daily activities of instructors and then listing the competencies that are required to do these activities effectively.

Like goal-setting theory, optimal experience theory predicts that the greatest improvements in intrinsic motivation will occur when there is harmony between the competencies of an individual and the challenges of his or her task environment. Specifically, this theory advises eliminating goals that are beyond the competencies of faculty or encouraging faculty to improve their competencies so that they can meet the challenges of teaching. According to optimal-experience theory, a kind of euphoria is experienced by instructors when the challenges they face are gracefully dispatched by their competence.

Although it would be quite easy to construct a long list of competencies for college teaching, we restrict ourselves to a short list of three core areas of competence. Based on survey data we have collected (Quinn, 1993) and other research on faculty goals and aspirations (Bayer, 1973; Angelo and Cross, 1993; Stark and Morstain, 1978), it appears that college instructors require knowledge and skills in *scholarship, pedagogy,* and *human development and interpersonal relations*. This last area might be called "generativity," a term borrowed from the psychological literature (Kotre, 1984). Let us now describe and discuss each of these three areas of competency.

Scholarship

All of the leading theories of motivation predict that the professional self-worth of instructors will be enhanced when they believe that they are experts in their disciplines. Instructors should feel more confident about themselves and more motivated to teach when they thoroughly know what they are teaching. Although it is frequently assumed that instructors "know their stuff," for several reasons this may not be so. Most doctoral programs provide specific advanced training in research; however, this type of training may be too advanced or irrelevant for the teaching of some courses. The professional research interests of some instructors may not prepare them for teaching and may even distract them from learning the substantive knowledge they must have to teach undergraduate courses. Over time, the content of disciplines changes, and this new content may not be learned by instructors. Because instructors may not have the opportunity to rehearse their knowledge, they may forget what they have learned. Finally, like other people, instructors may misunderstand what they had to learn on their own.

There are several possible ways to help faculty keep abreast in their disciplines. Scholarship *for* teaching, not scholarship *of* teaching, has to be supported and maintained (Boyer, 1990; Rice, 1991). It is stressful for faculty to teach unfamiliar subjects, and they should be given the resources they need to learn the content of the courses they must teach. For example, at Carleton College new faculty teach only five courses instead of the six otherwise required, to give them time to learn and prepare what they must teach. Experienced faculty at Trinity College are granted comparable time to prepare new courses. Just as there are norms to keep abreast of one's discipline for the purpose of doing research, so should there be norms for acquiring new knowledge expressly for teaching.

Institutions can promote scholarship for teaching in ways other than giving release time to faculty. For example, San Jose State

University has recently implemented a teacher-scholars mentor program. In this program, selected teacher-scholars make themselves available to colleagues for class visitations, consultations, and workshops. This program strives to increase the competencies of faculty in both what and how content is taught.

To promote scholarship for teaching, professional societies and national organizations are increasingly providing seminars and conferences for upgrading the skills and knowledge of college teachers. Instructors themselves could support this effort by organizing regional seminars on timely, important topics and, in response to suggestions from colleagues, bringing experts to campus to help broaden the scholarship of specific groups of faculty. However, unlike traditional colloquia, such seminars could try to answer two questions: what is new and important, and what are some effective ways to teach this new material? Helping instructors answer these questions would reinforce the natural intimacy between disciplinary knowledge and pedagogy (Shulman, 1987). But more importantly, doing this would deliver on the promise of invigorating faculty in an area too easily overlooked: scholarship *for* teaching.

Pedagogy

While it may be obvious that teachers must know what they are teaching and that scholastic competence supports the vitality of instructors, just as consequential is their ability to communicate what they know to students. Theory suggests that ineffectiveness in the classroom will eventually tire even instructors who are masters of their disciplines. The more that instructors know about teaching and learning and about classroom management and leadership, the more persistent they will be in their teaching.

Many instructors are curious about the craft of teaching and committed to improving their competence as teachers, particularly when their institutions are also committed to teaching (Blackburn and others, 1991). A majority of new faculty in liberal arts colleges, and virtually all new faculty in community colleges, are more interested in teaching than in research (Grey, Froh, and Diamond, 1992). Over one-third of the fifty-four award-winning teachers surveyed by Quinn (1993) at five research universities said that a vital source of satisfaction for them is their effectiveness as instructors.

On the other hand, three-fourths of these same faculty said that a continuous source of dissatisfaction was the problems they faced daily in teaching, such as evaluating student work, dealing with student misconduct and dishonesty, managing large classes, and stimulating interest in apathetic students. Apparently there is an important need here that is not being met. Helping instructors acquire the skills and knowledge to promote learning on the one hand and, on the other, to deal with the problems of teaching should not only improve the effectiveness of these instructors, it should also enhance their motivation to teach.

Generativity

According to Erikson (1950), during the later stages of human development individuals become increasingly concerned with the welfare of future generations. For these mature individuals, caring for the young becomes as important as caring for the self. Kotre (1984, p. 10) has defined generativity as "a desire to invest one's substance in forms of life and work that will outlive the self." There are four kinds of generativity: (1) the bearing of children, (2) the raising of children, (3) the teaching of skills to an apprentice, and (4) the passing of symbolic systems to the next generation. The last two types are called, respectively, *technical* and *cultural* generativity. Teaching skills such as how to read and write or sing are examples of technical generativity. Passing on the artistic, religious, or ideological importance of these skills is what is meant by cultural generativity.

Evidence indicates that a substantial number of college teachers attempt to fulfill their cultural and technical generativity needs through their teaching. A shift of focus from the self to others has been observed by investigators of teaching styles and faculty roles (Baldwin and Blackburn, 1981; Lawrence and Blackburn, 1985). As some faculty mature, their interest in teaching increases, and through their teaching they attempt to have an enduring influence on the lives of their students. A third of the instructors we surveyed report their most fulfilling teaching experience as when past students have told them through letters, cards, and visits how much they have changed their lives. When these instructors are asked to elaborate on these experiences, it is clear that their teaching goals go beyond merely sharing knowledge with students; these faculty see themselves as developers of people. They like to be connected with all of their students, and with some of their students it is important for them to establish long-term professional relationships.

The profession of teaching appears to attract individuals who are more generative than those in other occupations (McAdams and de St. Aubin, 1992). How can we help instructors pursue generativity? The training of faculty, the design of their work, and the definition of their role could be changed to develop and support generativity.

In the training of faculty, we suggest including more emphasis on interpersonal skills and other social skills. Teaching is an intensely social activity, and establishing rapport with students requires social skills and knowledge that many faculty may not possess. Faculty may also benefit from knowing more about human development so that they can appreciate the role they are playing in the development of others (Bess, 1977).

If generativity is to be taken seriously as a source of motivation for college teaching, then many teaching situations should be reassessed and changed. For example, generativity may be especially difficult to achieve in large classes or in required survey courses and any other courses that do not support close teacher-student relations. In contrast, small classes and courses that allow teachers and students to pursue mutual interests are more likely to encourage the kind of relationships wherein generative needs can be fulfilled. Secondly, faculty should also be encouraged to increase their contact with students by changing the style of their teaching and the kind of work they assign to students. Where possible, faculty should try to teach sequences of courses that attract the same students; in some cases doing this may require the broadening of faculty expertise across discipline boundaries. A third way to support generativity would be to enlarge and redefine the role of instructors to include career advisement and meaningful participation in student life and extracurricular activities. Finally, who the "student" is may change significantly over time for some faculty. Highly generative faculty may view their younger colleagues as students and consequently may welcome the opportunity to help their junior colleagues through mentor programs or other programs that legitimately allow them to share their wisdom.

Because of their generativity, most college teachers need to be wanted. However, not all students may be prepared for, nor desire to engage in, the kind of student-teacher relationships that teachers expect. For example, disrespect from students and plagiarism or other forms of student dishonesty should be particularly painful to instructors with high generativity needs. Therefore, changes have to occur in the socialization, training, and orientation of students to prepare them for their encounters with some of the most caring individuals they will ever meet: college teachers. They must be made ready for a potentially life-long partnership in learning.

Autonomy and Motivation

When college faculty are asked what attracted them to the profession, many will say the autonomy and independence granted to professors (Bess, 1977; Blackburn and others, 1986). When asked about what is the most satisfying aspect of being a college teacher, a majority of faculty cite the independence and freedom they have (Eble and McKeachie, 1985). However, recent theory and research on human performance compel us to entertain a rival hypothesis: college instructors may not in fact have as much autonomy as they need to stay vital throughout a long career in teaching (Deci and Ryan, 1990; Hackman and Oldham, 1980).

A surprising amount of the work of college teachers does not reinforce their autonomy. For example, many college teachers are assigned to courses, inherit texts and syllabi, have little say about how many students take "their" classes or who these students are, and have even less to say about where and when their classes are taught. The location, condition, and architecture of a classroom can impose severe constraints on the performance of its occupants. Likewise, damaged or antiquated audiovisual equipment can limit the effectiveness of instructors. Lenient policies concerning course enrollment, add-drop, and withdrawal can make it impossible for instructors to know who is in their course and consequently force them to make unwanted changes in their teaching. In addition, many instructors do not believe they can do what they wish in teaching, research, and service. All of this amounts to a work environment that Deci and Ryan (1990) would say does not nurture autonomy and ultimately is exhausting.

In fact, some new faculty in our surveys reported symptoms of stress that were more indicative of insufficient control than merely low levels of autonomy (Karasek and Theorell, 1990). While it may be true that most college faculty have more autonomy than workers in many other professions, theories of motivation suggest that for college teachers to be productive and creative throughout a twenty-to-thirty-year career, they need more autonomy and control than is currently granted to them (Deci, 1992).

Senior faculty in some research institutions apparently have the freedom and autonomy they need to do research, but the same cannot be said of most teaching faculty (Bieber, Lawrence, and Blackburn, 1992). In the main of college teaching today, the self-determined autonomous professor is unusual. Theories of self-determination, creativity, and work design all point to one conclusion: in the future, if we want instructors who are more creative and motivated, we must grant sufficient autonomy to those who teach.

College teaching is not a solitary activity. It is a social activity done in the context of a human organization, in some cases an enormously complex organization. In this kind of social situation, is it possible to grant sufficient autonomy to instructors? Goal-setting theory may offer at least a partial answer to this question. This theory suggests that the autonomy of all stakeholders in the classroom can be promoted through *mutual* goal setting. We next discuss mutual goal setting and other implications of the theory of Locke and Latham (1990a).

Goal Management and Motivation

According to the extensive research that supports goal-setting theory (Locke and Latham, 1990a), human motivation is enhanced when people have challenging, yet feasible, goals. Their goals should be specific enough to be operational and may be set by themselves or assigned by legitimate authorities. Whether goals are set or assigned, persistence and high achievement are seen only when people pursue difficult goals *and* receive feedback on goal performance. Goals alone or feedback alone do not enhance performance.

Locke and Latham have found that for people to achieve high levels of performance, they have to be competent and possess high self-efficacy. However, without supportive leadership, people will not consistently achieve high performance. To help people achieve high performance, the theory suggests that leaders must reward successful performance and do it in a manner that is fair and equitable. Extrinsic rewards *and* intrinsic rewards are needed to sustain the motivation of people (Cameron and Pierce, 1994).

Goal Setting

Goal-setting theory (Locke and Latham, 1990b) predicts that instructors will be more persistent when they have challenging goals to achieve. According to the theory, no goals, vague goals, easy goals, impossible goals, or too many goals will not inspire high performance. For example, a calculus instructor with the specific goal of having over 50 percent of her high-risk students achieve greater than the 80th percentile on a nationally standardized test will be more motivated than an instructor whose goal is to do a good job of teaching calculus.

Research on the goals of college teachers has revealed findings that are consistent with goal-setting theory. Using the Teaching Goals Inventory (TGI), Angelo and Cross (1993) found that many instructors are only dimly aware of their goals; when they are asked to articulate their goals, they describe goal structures that are difficult to manage. Examples of goals from the TGI are teaching students higher-order thinking skills (such as analytical skills), helping students improve basic academic skills (perhaps writing skills), or assisting students in their learning of discipline-specific knowledge (say, the history of a discipline).

The most common problems revealed by the TGI were instructors who had too many "essential goals," or instructors who had vague, unfeasible goals. Angelo and Cross (1993) observed considerable dissatisfaction among instructors with no goals or among instructors with unmanageable goals. On the other hand, they observed less dissatisfaction and more satisfaction with teaching among instructors with a manageable number of goals and goals that were moderately difficult, but feasible. These results not only support goal-setting theory but have exciting implications for methods to improve the motivation of college teachers.

Mutual Goal Setting

College teaching pursues the goals of many parties: instructors, students, disciplines, institutions, accrediting agencies, and state and federal governments, to name a few. Achieving the goals of one or two of the parties at the expense of the others will surely invite conflict and dissatisfaction. For example, instructors will feel compromised if they help achieve the goals of students at the expense of their own goals and the goals of their disciplines; likewise, they will not be happy if they achieve the goals of their disciplines in spite of the goals of their students and themselves.

The goals of instructors, students, and disciplines have to be mutually set and collaboratively pursued. If this is done, not only will students and instructors achieve more, but they will be more motivated. Moreover, according to theories of group cohesiveness (Shaw, 1981) and principles of job design (Hackman and Oldham, 1980), instructors and students will be more likely to share the perception that the teaching-learning experience is meaningful and important. These outcomes can be easily achieved if two steps are taken: first, academic departments have to articulate their curriculum and course goals; and second, with departmental goals in mind, in each course instructors and students have to define their own goals and agree on ways to achieve them.

Sometimes the goals of departments may not be well articulated, and sometimes the goals of students may be hard to discern. If it is not feasible for instructors to consider the goals of students and a department, and if they are left to manage only their own goals, doing such things as setting goals for a course, units, and lectures should improve their teaching performance and at the same time bolster their motivation.

In practice, goal setting may be difficult to do. Fortunately, methods for doing it have been explored by practitioners in a variety of task environments, both academic and nonacademic (Locke and Latham, 1984). Several ways to establish course goals and set class objectives have been proposed by Cross and Angelo (1988). In a more recent publication, these researchers have suggested procedures for coordinating goal setting in departments with goal setting in classrooms (Angelo and Cross, 1993).

Performance Feedback

Goal setting alone will not necessarily improve performance or increase the motivation of an instructor. Frequent performance feedback is also needed to obtain optimal results. Neither end-of-the-semester evaluations nor even midsemester evaluations are sufficient. The theory predicts that the highest performance and most motivation will be seen with goal-achievement feedback that is specific, unambiguous, and continuous. Research in higher education supports this prediction. Walker (1991a) found increases in student learning and increases in instructor motivation when teaching-performance feedback was received weekly and sometimes daily throughout a semester. Larkin (1987) found that instructors who monitor their students continuously while lecturing were more effective teachers than those who devoted less attention to student feedback.

Good teachers may be more effective, in part, because they obtain and interpret student feedback better than average teachers do. The initial results of a recent study on exceptional teachers at research universities appear to support this conclusion. Quinn (1993) found that award-winning teachers are good at generating, interpreting, and using student feedback. When asked what makes teaching most satisfying for them, nearly 95 percent of their replies concerned performance feedback; 82 percent of their replies were about feedback from students, while only 13 percent were about self-reflective, self-administered feedback. Roughly a third of these exceptional instructors cited immediate, specific student feedback as a source of their teaching satisfaction (several instructors reported seeing flashes of insight appear in the faces of their students during a lecture). However, a majority cited a more delayed type of feedback as the cause of their satisfaction with teaching (receiving letters from appreciative alumni).

Interpreting Performance Feedback

Not only did these exceptional teachers receive feedback, but they attended to it and interpreted it in a way that enhanced their motivation. Interestingly, these teachers gave evidence that they have the cognitive style of optimists (Seligman, 1991). Specifically, they viewed positive feedback as enduring, pervasive, and caused by their teaching skills. On the other hand, they viewed negative feedback as enduring, less pervasive, and not caused by them or their teaching. Like the optimists that Scheier, Weintraub, and Carver (1986) have studied, award-winning teachers attributed negative events to changeable, external causes such as student effort or study skills. Other researchers have found this type of cognitive style to be associated with better learning, stronger personal development, and much more persistence in the face of negative feedback (Bandura, 1982; Dweck, 1991). Investigators of teaching effectiveness report similar observations. Persistence, enthusiasm, and liveliness are traits that consistently distinguish effective teachers from average teachers (Dunkin and Precians, 1991; Murray, Rushton, and Paunonen, 1990; Walker, Rohan, and Scott, 1993). One reason why effective teachers are so persistent is because they view student feedback, particularly negative feedback, with optimism and hope.

The results of this research on performance feedback make us conclude that two conditions are necessary for the maintenance of instructional vitality: first, instructors have to adopt teaching methods that allow them to receive performance feedback, and second, instructors have to learn to interpret performance feedback in a way that supports their self-worth but inclines them to continually improve themselves. These two conditions can be achieved by (1) training instructors to get more feedback, either through teaching them to "read" immediate classroom feedback or by training them to do classroom assessment, and (2) helping them acquire the cognitive habits of optimists. Advice and procedures for teaching instructors how to use classroom assessment is readily available (Angelo, 1990; Angelo and Cross, 1993; Menges, 1990; Rando and Lenze, 1994; Walker, 1991b), and methods to modify the cognitive habits of people have been extensively researched and need only to be adapted for college teachers (Beck, 1976; Ellis, 1987; Seligman, 1991; Scheier, Weintraub, and Carver, 1986). New methods and procedures for managing feedback are available to help us improve instructor motivation. What is most needed now are practitioners who are willing to adapt these promising new technologies to the profession of teaching.

Rewards and Recognition

Some practitioners and researchers believe that intrinsic rewards are all that is needed to keep instructors vital. Locke and Latham (1990b) argue that while intrinsic rewards may affect the motivation to perform well, valuable extrinsic rewards affirm high performance and increase the commitment of people to perform well in the future.

Rewarding Individual Instructors

Instructors might teach excellently, get confirming feedback, and attribute success to their teaching ability, but goal-setting theory predicts that they will not persevere without meaningful external rewards and recognition. Instructors strongly agree with this. Surveys have consistently found that college teachers desire more rewards and recognition than they or their profession receives. A frequent suggestion is that teachers should be given the same status and recognition as researchers (Finkelstein, 1984; Grey, Froh, and Diamond, 1992).

Equity of awards and recognition is also an important concern among teaching faculty. Seventy-seven percent of the faculty surveyed by Quinn (1993) perceived their awards to be equitable; nonetheless, these award winners made several suggestions for improving the administration of such programs. The most common suggestion was that the award criteria and the nomination and selection process need to be communicated. When the process is not open and the criteria are vague, faculty believe that winners are chosen not by merit but by popularity and political lobbying.

These results suggest that if excellent teaching is rewarded, it should be rewarded in a fair and equitable way. Meaningless awards, mismanaged recognition programs, and unfair merit pay or no merit pay can only deepen the feelings of inequity already felt by many college instructors. According to Locke and Latham (1990b), in organizations with high performance norms, inequitable rewards are like discordant notes: playing them louder and more often just adds to the suffering of the listener, while not playing them at all creates an unsettling silence. Meaningful, valuable rewards equitably applied to exemplary teaching, according to their theory, will not only enhance the future performance of an individual instructor but will legitimize a norm of teaching excellence among all instructors.

Rewarding Groups and Teams

Who or what group receives rewards is an issue as important as equity in higher education. Should teams as well as individuals be rewarded? The literature on organizational behavior suggests that some forms of work are best done by teams, and there are theories in psychology that predict that some individuals perform best when they work with others (Hackman, 1991).

The idea that instructors prefer to teach in isolation is certainly another myth about professors. Evidence suggests that precisely the opposite is true (MacGregor, 1991; Turner and Boice, 1987). One of the reasons that instructors are so eager to become involved with community learning, team teaching, and interdisciplinary teaching is because they get the opportunity to work with others and escape isolation.

However, groups can present problems not found with individuals (Austin, 1992). Problems emerge when the naïve management strategy of treating teams as individuals is practiced or when teams are expected to do work designed for individuals. Reward and recognition systems designed for individuals, for example, will actually undermine group cohesiveness when these reward systems are applied to work teams (Douglas, 1983; Hackman, 1991). Doing this presents workers with an impossible dilemma: people are asked to work as a team, yet they compete as individuals for scarce rewards. A partial solution to this problem is achieved when entire groups—teams or whole departments—are recognized and rewarded as well as outstanding individuals.

Certainly there is a need for more teamwork in higher education; moreover, if we want college teachers to be more vital, it is imperative that the satisfaction of their social needs not compete with the satisfaction of their achievement needs. Both the individual and the group should be rewarded, but not one at the expense of the other.

Summary and Conclusion

To enhance the motivation of college teachers, we recommend that faculty and others consider both traditional and nontraditional views of human motivation. The notion that college teaching is an activity primarily motivated by intrinsic rewards needs to be reexamined. Recent theories of motivation suggest several additional ways to enhance the vitality of instructors. These are (1) helping instructors increase their competencies to be a scholar, a teacher, and a developer of others, (2) granting them sufficient autonomy, and (3) helping them to set and assess challenging goals. However, in addition to these largely internal sources of motivation, we suggest that institutions support instructors by implementing meaningful and equitable external reward and recognition programs.

For faculty who want to improve their motivation to teach and for those who would like to assist them, we propose several steps that can be taken. First, regarding competency, instructors need support and training (1) to be competent in the subject matter they teach, (2) in the way they communicate that subject matter to students, and (3) for the relationships they form with students as they teach.

Second, despite high levels of autonomy in the college teaching profession, theory suggests that motivation might increase if instructors had more control over the type, size, and structure of the courses they teach. Instructors also need more control over their career development through a more flexible tenure-and-promotion process. Third, the motivation of instructors could be increased by training them to set and achieve clear, challenging, and feasible goals. The achievement of such goals should be monitored, and continuous feedback should be given to instructors as they work. Some instructors may need cognitive training to help them interpret this feedback in positive ways.

We argued that the beneficial effects of any changes in teaching will eventually weaken if instructors are not rewarded and recognized for excellent work. Current rewards for instructors are not meaningful and are biased in favor of scholarship. Instructors strongly desire recognition for the activity in which they spend the most time: teaching. The proverbial pat on the back for a job well done is probably encouraging, but instructors need tangible rewards such as merit pay, promotion, and tenure to affirm their good work and to sustain their motivation to teach.

Few of the changes we recommend can be quickly or easily realized. However, new technologies have been developed, or can be developed, to assist change. Theory and research on human motivation can help us conceive and plan change, change that has the promise of giving new life to teaching and increased vitality to those who practice it.

References

Angelo, T. A. (1990). Classroom assessment: Improving learning quality where it matters most. In M. D. Svinicki (Ed.), New directions for teaching and learning: No. 42. *The changing face of college teaching* (pp. 71–82). San Francisco: Jossey-Bass.

Angelo, T. A. (1991). Ten easy pieces: Assessing higher learning in four dimensions. In T. A. Angelo (Ed.), New directions for teaching and learning:

No. 46. *Classroom research: Early lessons from success* (pp. 17–31). San Francisco: Jossey-Bass.

Angelo, T. A., & Cross, K. P. (1993). *Classroom assessment techniques: A handbook for college teachers* (2nd ed.). San Francisco: Jossey-Bass.

Antonovsky, A. (1987). *Unraveling the mystery of health.* San Francisco: Jossey-Bass.

Austin, A. E. (1992). *Faculty collaboration: Enhancing the quality of scholarship and teaching.* An address given to the 12th Annual Lilly Conference on College Teaching, Miami University, Oxford, OH.

Baldwin, R. G., & Blackburn, R. T. (1981). The academic career as a developmental process: Implications for higher education. *Journal of Higher Education, 52,* 26.

Bandura, A. (1982). Self-efficacy mechanisms in human agency. *American Psychologist, 37,* 122–147.

Bayer, A. E. (1973). *Teaching faculty in academe: 1972–1973* (ACE Research Reports, 8[2]). Washington, DC: American Council on Education.

Beck, A. T. (1976). *Cognitive therapy and emotional disorders.* New York: International Universities Press.

Bess, J. L. (1973). Integrating student and faculty life cycles. *Review of Educational Research, 43,* 377–403.

Bess, J. L. (1977). The motivation to teach. *Journal of Educational Research, 48,* 243–258.

Bieber, J. P., Lawrence, J. H., & Blackburn, R. T. (1992). Through the years: Faculty and their changing institution. *Change, 24*(4), 28–36.

Blackburn, R. T., Lawrence, J. H., Bieber, J. P., & Trautvetter, L. (1991). Faculty at work: Focus on teaching. *Research in Higher Education, 32,* 363–382.

Blackburn, R. T., Lawrence, J. H., Ross, S., Okoloko, V. P., Bieber, J. P., Meiland, R., & Street, T. (1986). *Faculty as a key resource: A review of the research literature.* Ann Arbor: National Center for Postsecondary Teaching and Learning, University of Michigan.

Boyer, E. P. (1990). *Scholarship reconsidered: Priorities of the professoriate.* Princeton: Carnegie Foundation for the Advancement of Teaching.

Cameron, J., & Pierce, D. (1994). Reinforcement, reward, and intrinsic motivation: A meta-analysis. *Review of Educational Research, 64,* 363–423.

Cross, K. D., and Angelo, T. A. (1988). *Classroom assessment techniques: A handbook for faculty.* Ann Arbor: National Center for Research to Improve Postsecondary Teaching and Learning, University of Michigan.

Csikszentmihalyi, M. (1990). *Flow: The psychology of optimal experiences.* New York: Harper & Row.

Csikszentmihalyi, M., & Csikszentmihalyi, I. (1988). *Optimal experience: Psychological studies of flow in consciousness.* Cambridge: Cambridge University Press.

Deci, E. L. (1992). On the nature and functions of motivation theories. *Psychological Science, 3*(3), 167–171.

Deci, E. L., & Ryan, R. M. (1985). Intrinsic motivation and self-determination in human behavior. New York: Plenum Press.

Deci, E. L., & Ryan, R. M. (1990). A motivational approach to self: Integration in personality. In R. Dienstbier (Ed.), *Nebraska Symposium on Motivation* (Vol. 38, pp. 237–288). Lincoln, NE: University of Nebraska Press.

Douglas, T. (1983). *Groups: Understanding people gathered together.* New York: Tavistock.

Dunkin, M. J., & Precians, R. P. (1991). *Orientations to teaching of award-winning university teachers.* Sydney, Australia: The Centre for Teaching and Learning, The University of Sydney.

Dweck, C. S. (1991). Self-theories and goals: Their role in motivation, personality, and development. In R. Dienstbier (Ed.), *Nebraska Symposium on Motivation* (Vol. 38, pp. 199–235). Lincoln, NE: University of Nebraska Press.

Eble, K. E., & McKeachie, W. J. (1985). *Improving undergraduate education through faculty development.* San Francisco: Jossey-Bass.

Eckert, R. E., & Stecklein, J. E. (1957). *Job motivations and satisfactions of college teachers: A study of faculty members in Minnesota colleges* (Cooperative Research Report No. 7). Washington, DC: U.S. Department of Health, Education, and Welfare.

Ellis. A. (1987). The impossibility of achieving consistently good mental health. *American Psychologist, 42,* 364–376.

Erikson, E. H. (1950). *Childhood and society.* New York: Norton.

Finkelstein, M. J. (1984). *The American academic profession: A synthesis of social scientific inquiry since World War II.* Columbus, OH: Ohio State University Press.

Grey, P. J., Froh, R. C., & Diamond, R. M. (1992). *A national study of research universities on the balance between research and undergraduate teaching.* Syracuse, NY: Center for Instructional Development, Syracuse University.

Hackman, J. R. (1991). Group influences on individuals in organizations. In M. D. Dunnette & L. M. Hough (Ed.), *Handbook of industrial and organizational psychology* (2nd ed., Vol. 3, pp. 199–267). Palo Alto, CA: Consulting Psychologist Press.

Hackman, J. R., & Oldham, G. R. (1980). *Work redesign.* Reading, MA: Addison-Wesley.

Harter, S. (1986). Processes underlying the construction, maintenance, and enhancement of the self-concept. In J. Suls & A. Greenwald, *Perspectives on the psychology of self* (Vol. 3, pp. 178–201). New York: Erlbaum.

Herzberg, F. I., Mauser, B., & Snyderman, B. B. (1959). *The motivation to work.* New York: Wiley.

Karasek, R., & Theorell, T. (1990). *Healthy work: Job stress, productivity, and the reconstruction of working life.* New York: Basic Books.

Kotre, J. (1984). *Outliving the self: Generativity and the interpretation of lives.* Baltimore: Johns Hopkins University Press.

Lawrence, J. H., & Blackburn, R. T. (1985). Faculty careers: Maturation, demographic, and historical effects. *Research in Higher Education, 22,* 135–154.

Larkin, J. E. (1987). Are good teachers perceived as high self-monitors? *Personality and Social Psychology Bulletin, 13,* 64–72.

Locke, E. A., & Latham, G. P. (1984). *Goal setting: A motivational technique that works.* Englewood Cliffs, NJ: Prentice Hall.

Locke, E. A., & Latham, G. P. (1990a). *A theory of goal setting and task performance.* Englewood Cliffs, NJ: Prentice Hall.

Locke, E. A., & Latham, G. P. (1990b). Work motivation: The high-performance cycle. In U. Kleinbeck, H. Quast, H. Thierry, & H. Hacker (Eds.), *Work motivation.* Hillsdale, NJ: Erlbaum.

MacGregor, J. (1991). What differences do learning communities make? *Washington Center News, 6*(1), 4–9.

McAdams, D. P., & de St. Aubin, W. (1992). A theory of generativity and its assessment through self-report, behavioral acts, and narrative themes in autobiography. *Journal of Personality and Social Psychology, 62,* 1003–1016.

Menges, R. J. (1990). Using evaluative information to improve instruction. In P. Sheldin (Ed.), *Providing administrative leadership to improve college teaching.* San Francisco: Jossey-Bass.

Mooney, C. J. (1989). Professors are upbeat about profession but uneasy about students, standards. *Chronicle of Higher Education, 36*(10), pp. Al, A18–A21.

Murray, H. G., Rushton, J. P., & Paunonen, S. V. (1990). Teacher personality traits and student instructional ratings in six types of university courses. *Journal of Educational Psychology, 82,* 250–261.

Quinn, J. W. (1993). University teaching award winners: Their perceptions of award programs, reading habits, satisfactions, and dissatisfactions. *Report of the Focus on Teaching Project and the National Center on Postsecondary Teaching, Learning, and Assessment.* Pennsylvania State University.

Rando, W. C., & Lenze, L. F. (1994). *Learning from students: Early-term student feedback in higher education.* University Park, PA: National Center on Postsecondary Teaching, Learning, and Assessment, Pennsylvania State University.

Rice, R. E. (1991). Rethinking what it means to be a scholar. *Teaching excellence: Toward the best in the academy*. Stillwater, OK: New Forums Press.

Scheier, M. F., Weintraub, J. K., & Carver, C. S. (1986). Coping with stress: Divergent strategies of optimists and pessimists. *Journal of Personality and Social Psychology, 51*, 1257–1264.

Seligman, M.E.P. (1991). *Learned optimism*. New York: Alfred A. Knopf.

Shaw, M. E. (1981). *Group dynamics: The social psychology of small-group behavior* (3rd ed.). New York: McGraw-Hill.

Shulman, L. (1987). Knowledge and teaching. *Harvard Educational Review, 57*, 1–22.

Stark, J., & Morstain, B. R. (1978). Educational orientations of faculty in liberal arts colleges: An analysis of disciplinary differences. *Journal of Higher Education, 49*, 420–437.

Turner, J. L., & Boice, R. (1987). Starting at the beginning: Concerns and needs of new faculty. *To Improve the Academy, 6*, 41–55.

Walker, C. J. (1991a). Classroom research in psychology: Assessment techniques to enhance teaching and learning. In T. A. Angelo (Ed.), New directions in teaching and learning: No. 46. *Classroom research: Early lessons from success* (pp. 67–78). San Francisco: Jossey-Bass.

Walker, C. J. (1991b). Classroom assessment for literacy: Searching for course content worth teaching and learning. *Educational Forum, 2*, 105–116.

Walker, C. J., Rohan, K., & Scott, F. (1993). *Instructor optimism and syllabus content: Associations with teaching effectiveness*. Report presented at the American Psychological Society National Convention, Chicago.

Chapter Fourteen

Supporting Diversity Through Campus Culture

William G. Tierney, Estela Mara Bensimon
University of Southern California

Our understanding of higher education is often based on knowledge derived from the experiences of traditional stakeholders. The experience of students of color is understood in relation to their white counterparts; the productivity of women faculty is compared to that of men faculty; and the effectiveness of returning adult students often is understood in terms of a traditional-aged clientele. Our assumption is that an organizational worldview that is monocultural has a teaching and learning environment that is neither effective for those of us who are "different" nor helpful for those of us who have to live and work in an increasingly multicultural world.

Hence in this chapter, we offer a cultural approach to improving the climate for diversity in postsecondary institutions. Our work is informed by critical and feminist theories (see Tierney, 1991, and Lather, 1991, for examples). Our goals are twofold. First, we outline a framework for how those of us in academic institutions might conceptualize, and thus act, in a multicultural world. Second, we offer academic leaders strategies for improving the climate on their campuses. Accordingly, the chapter divides into two parts. We first define what we mean by multiculturalism in academe, and we offer a schema for administrators and faculty to consider. We then discuss a series of strategies institutional leaders might ask themselves and others to use in order to develop a dialogue about creating a multicultural campus.

Defining Multiculturalism

A new president arrives on campus and discovers that a senior vice president has told the director of Native American studies that the university will not increase funding for the program because "Indians don't count. We need blacks."

The women's basketball coach is quoted as saying that there are not more black coaches because "they don't have the organizational skills necessary to coach."

A gay student's dorm room is firebombed in the middle of the night, and no one investigates the crime.

After mispronouncing the name of an Asian faculty member in his college, the dean jokes that "she does laundry too."

Each of these examples is harmful not only to an individual or group; the incidents also create a potentially explosive climate on campus and promote a monocultural atmosphere of misunderstanding. Too often, we belatedly react to incidents such as these because we have not developed a comprehensive strategy for building diversity on our campuses. We think of individual acts and how best to deal with them rather than develop an overarching scaffolding that sustains an ongoing change in the culture of the organization.

For example, a Stanford doctor gave up her tenured position because she could no longer tolerate the sexist behavior of the individual who was promoted to chair her department. The institution's response was to treat this as an individual case; the university administration prescribed training in sexual harassment for the accused doctor. Although we do not question that such training is helpful to an individual, our point here is that a more appropriate strategy might have been to also question how the organization's structures, norms, and values fostered and reinforced such behavior.

We define multiculturalism as a complex set of relationships that are framed around issues relating to race, gender, class, and sexual orientation and are related to concerns over power. One of the struggles in multicultural organizations is to understand the commonalities and differences that underrepresented groups face and to find out how we might create alliances for change. As bell hooks has noted, to segregate problems that diverse constituencies face "feeds the erroneous notion that racism and sexism are two radically different forms of oppression, that one can be eradicated while the other remains intact" (1990, p. 66). Thus, the argument advanced here is that we respect the differences that diverse groups have, and at the same time we work to develop institutions whose central organizing concept is the creation of multicultural excellence.

We are suggesting that to improve the climate for teaching and learning with regard to multiculturalism demands an understanding of the organization's culture. By looking at the culture of the organization, we are able to investigate institutional processes and goals. In this light, a college president will fail if she merely reacts to a senior vice president or dean who makes a derogatory comment. An athletic director or dean of students will similarly fall short by simply responding to an individual act or comment. Instead, we must develop in ourselves and our colleagues an appreciation for the power of diversity and the necessity of building multiculturalism into the fabric of our institutions.

A Cultural Framework

"An organization's culture," write Chaffee and Tierney, "is reflected in what is done, how it is done, and who is involved in doing it. It concerns decision, actions, and communication both on an instrumental and a symbolic level" (1988, p. 7). Thus if we are going to come to terms with our institution's culture, we might look at the daily activities that take place across campus as well as the major events and ceremonies that are institutional hallmarks. We also investigate the degree to which the institutional actors agree about particular acts and decisions and to what extent there are disagreements and conflicts. If we utilize these definitions of culture, what will we find if we investigate the cultures of our institutions with regard to multiculturalism? We answer the question by way of a four-step analysis: people, mission, structure, curriculum/co-curriculum.

People. Basic facts are well known. Ethnic faculty form less than 12 percent of the professoriate (Tierney and Bensimon, 1995); women account for less than 28 percent full-time faculty (Mooney, 1990). Women or people of color make up less than 15 percent of senior administrative positions in postsecondary institutions (Leatherman, 1991). Students of color remain underrepresented in four-year institutions, particularly in the sciences and engineering (Quality Education, 1990). With regard to gay, lesbian, and bisexual people, we find that they are essentially invisible for fear that they will lose their jobs if they reveal their sexual orientation. If a central component of an organization's culture is the people who populate it, then it stands to reason that the academy needs to develop dramatically different strategies that are more inclusive; otherwise, we will remain an organization that is homogenous.

Most institutional participants, however, offer rationales about why their particular institution is unsuccessful at recruiting and retaining diverse faculties, administrators, and students. "We are isolated," some say. "They would prefer to be in communities where there are others like themselves," others add. "The good ones go to the better schools," continue still others. "There just aren't enough in the pipeline," concludes yet another.

We want to be clear here. Each of these rationales is in part correct. For example, isolation may well be a barrier to attracting a particular cadre of people. And there are not enough people of color in graduate school. However, an institution that views diversity as a central component of its organization's culture will not accept such rationales. Patrick Hill is helpful in defining an institution that wants to diversify its constituencies: "Such a college would make it the *highest priority* to recruit women, minorities, persons of color, and persons from other cultures to their faculties and student bodies as soon as possible. As a temporary measure, a measure of significant inadequacy, such colleges would undertake a massive retraining of their faculties (mis)educated in one discipline and one culture" (1991, p. 44).

Mission. The mission of an institution refers to the overarching vision and purpose to which the organization subscribes. In general, a commitment to diversity is absent from institutional mission statements. As Chesler and Crowfoot note, "The emphasis on preserving and passing on the traditions of Western (Eurocentric and Anglo-Christian) civilization reflects higher education's origins in service by and for privileged white males" (1989, p. 20). What might an institution have as a mission statement that honors diversity?

The point here is not simply to have a mission statement that speaks against injustice but rather to advocate for the centrality of multiculturalism in an institutional definition of education and excellence. Such statements are critical symbols about the beliefs of the institution. That is, organizational goals help define meaning and purpose, and they also underscore what needs to be emphasized.

Yet as we approach the twenty-first century, we all have become suspicious of the empty platitudes of mission statements that merely speak about "the educated citizen," or a "multicultural world," or "respect for diversity." We are not suggesting that a president simply rewrite the mission statement. Rather, we argue that missions and goals need to be explicitly tied to institutional strategic plans and objectives. In this light, we have much to learn from religious or distinctive institutions such as Evergreen State College or Reed College about how their mission affects the daily work of the institution's participants. When we have visited such institutions, we have found that virtually all of the citizens of the institution buy into the notion of the mission, and they try to enact that vision in the processes and goals of their jobs. Simply stated, an institutional culture that values multiculturalism will have as its mission statement a clear directive that makes it impossible for the organization's actors, programs, and departments to overlook such a goal in its activities.

Structure. Organizational structure refers to the full complement of decision-making procedures that the institutional participants use to achieve their mission and goals. The structure of the institution reflects not only the manner in which activities get decided but also organizational power and authority. When we look at an organization's structure with regard to multiculturalism, we discover three points.

First, as noted with the first topic raised, we are able to see how many people of color are incorporated into the decision-making structure of the institution.

Second, we uncover how many individuals have specific tasks related to diversity and multiculturalism. We investigate diversity-related positions to determine if they merely reflect an appendage to the institution or if they are fundamental mission-related changes in the organization's direction. Clearly, an institution that has one individual who is a diversity coordinator in student services is not as concerned with diversity as an institution that has a vice provost and an array of different individuals whose task it is to enhance diversity. A corollary to this point is to see how high diversity-related positions are within the organization's structure.

Third, and most importantly, we uncover how each individual in the institution perceives his or her task in terms of diversity. That is, rather than cordon off issues of multiculturalism as if they are the sole responsibility of a select few, an institution that honors diversity will make multiculturalism a central task of all individuals. From this perspective, we find an institutional culture where it is necessary for individuals to be involved with one another in diversity-related issues if they are to accomplish their jobs.

Curriculum/Co-Curriculum. Given the spate of news reports in the last few years, one might suspect that every institution in the

United States has been overtaken by diversity-driven curricula (Kimball, 1991). Although modest changes have occurred, in general no sweeping alterations have taken place. We offer four specific concerns that need to be addressed by academic leaders as they change the teaching and learning environment.

First, the vast majority of individuals who teach diversity-related courses are those who are considered "diverse." Any number of issues arise here. We already have commented on the small number of faculty of color and women faculty. When one group of faculty are expected to teach in a new curricular area that is interdisciplinary, we find that the more mainstream group of faculty often feel as if those courses are unimportant and unnecessary. Consequently, faculty who teach diversity-related courses do not receive adequate support vis-à-vis the promotion and tenure system for teaching such courses, and we see that multicultural classes have been placed in a ghetto where other faculty dare not tread.

A second related concern pertains to how the institution might actively encourage all of its faculty to develop multicultural courses and to infuse their current courses with diversity-related material. As Hill points out, "Marginalization ends and conversations of respect begin when the curriculum is reconceived to be unimplementable without the central participation of the currently excluded and marginalized" (1991, p. 45). Thus rather than simply having a course or two that pertain to one or another diversity-related group, we are suggesting that institutional commitment is shown when teaching and learning is geared toward the exploration of one another's differences.

Third, we often seem to overlook the crucial relationship of curriculum to pedagogy. That is, faculty and administrators usually think of multiculturalism and diversity as content-related issues that affect courses in the humanities and social sciences but have little to do with the sciences or professional schools.

However, a multicultural approach to the organization takes into account those individuals who populate our institutions and classrooms. Thus, faculty in all disciplines need to develop strategies for teaching in a multicultural classroom. We need to come to terms with how we can be more sensitive in conveying material to the diverse populations that make up our classrooms. In doing so, we will be more effective in teaching our curricular content, whether it be math, English, or mechanical engineering.

The implications of our third point in terms of the relationship of curriculum to pedagogy also relate to our final point. A commitment to multiculturalism suggests dramatically different approaches to the way we conceptualize knowledge (Rosaldo, 1989). If we accept that there is more than one culturally specific way to interpret the world, then the manner in which we define knowledge and the way we think about teaching and learning need to be reconfigured. The authority of the teacher is lessened, and the worth of the student becomes central. Rather than accept that there is one coherent answer to a specific topic, we find that there may be multiple interpretations. In effect, the curriculum and the classroom become more dialogical and inclusive.

An institution that is multicultural in its people, mission, structure, and curriculum will undoubtedly also honor multiculturalism in its out-of-class activities. What might a multicultural campus look like with regard to such experiences?

Surely, we will find the citizens of the community engaged in multiple dialogues about the meanings and direction of their community, but no one's legitimacy will be brought into question. Ambiguity and conflict, rather than clarity and consensus, will be encountered. Tolerance and a desire to understand those who are different from ourselves will be a central goal. College administrators and faculty will encourage diverse viewpoints. Most importantly, co-curricular activities will not be seen simply as learning experiences for students; rather, all of the institution's participants will capitalize on such activities as a way to overcome their own biases and preconceived notions as well as to demonstrate to the community at large the importance of this particular topic. The point here is simple: how can we suggest that students need to be committed to diversity while those of us who create the courses and policies do not demonstrate a similar commitment?

Strategies to Create a Multicultural Campus

The creation of a multicultural campus requires that institutional leaders be willing to shed conventional notions of leadership that valorize the maintenance of a conflict-free campus. In the multicultural campus, administration is neither a matter of "negotiating" concessions of special-interest groups clamoring for equal treatment, or, as some would have it, "a piece of the pie." Nor is administrative concern with diversity expressed only at those times when there is a racial- or sexual-harassment incident. In a multicultural campus the task of senior administrators is to discern and to act responsively from an understanding of differences among "a plurality of voices vying for the right to reality—to be accepted as legitimate expressions of the true and good" (Gergen, 1991, p. 7).

The dominant image that people typically have of the college or university is of a cohesive whole, with all persons aspiring to common goals. We rarely acknowledge that the word "student" does not represent a unified collegiate experience, that "community" can refer to life within a group that holds itself apart from the whole, and that "knowledge" may lie outside the center, at times in opposition to what is viewed as legitimate. Even though there is a tendency to assume that the campus environment is experienced in similar ways, studies of institutional climates suggest that this is not the case. For example, an analysis of the institutional climate at Stanford University revealed that faculty of color are considerably less optimistic than white faculty about the university's commitment to equality.

An article in *The New York Times* with the headline "Separate Ethnic Worlds Grow on Campus" makes us aware that our campuses, contrary to idealized images, are not integrated cultures;

instead, they are sites of differentiation and fragmentation. Accordingly: "Sergio Perez lives in an off-campus apartment with other Chicano students at the UC-Berkeley. A senior, he is majoring in Chicano studies, and participating in bilingual commencement exercises reserved for Chicano and Latino students" (DePalma, 1991, p. 1).

In a campus context such as this, the task of leadership is to come to know the differences in identity and experience that Sergio Perez and his community proclaim and to foster an environment where those differences can be expressed and where they can thrive (Bensimon and Neumann, 1993). The ascendancy of "communities of difference" (Tierney, 1993)—such as those of the Chicano and Latino community at UC-Berkeley—highlights the fact that administrators need to consider approaches to administration that are discerning of, and responsive to, the multicultural context of their institutions.

In the previous section, we discussed a cultural view of colleges and universities. We pointed out that the culturally minded administrator who actively engages in the creation of a multicultural campus focuses attention on people, mission, structure, and curriculum/co-curriculum. In this section we discuss the specific organizational strategies needed to create a multicultural campus.

Before moving on to these strategies, we point out that to create multicultural campuses, senior administrators need to envision a campus that is not organized according to patriarchal, white, heterosexual norms. Administrators need to articulate this vision of the campus to deans, department chairs, faculty, staff, and students. The strategies we discuss reflect the means by which senior administrators might shape a vision of a multicultural campus. These strategies are not presented prescriptively. Rather, consistent with the cultural framework of organizational change, we describe how language, communication, power, and policies affect the creation of a multicultural campus. Our intent is to provoke administrators to engage in actions that advance multicultural goals.

People

We consider here how administrators might diversify their faculties and the strategies used to create a multicultural framework.

Diversity.   To diversify the composition of faculty, administrators, and students, institutions need to develop recruitment and retention strategies that acknowledge differences based on gender, race, and sexual orientation. This requires conscious efforts to establish institutional climates that incorporate norms of difference. Even though the pledge to affirmative-action goals has become routinized in colleges and universities, there remain countless ways in which people are denied access or remain as "outsiders within" (Collins, 1986), even after having gained access. The recent decision by Carolyn Heilbrun to resign her professorship at Columbia University because of perceived sexism among her colleagues illustrates how gender, race, sexual orientation, or scholarly interests that fall outside traditional forms often make persons feel isolated from their immediate academic community.

Administrators need to assume more responsibility for the daily struggles that women, people of color, and lesbian and gay persons wage in the face of institutional norms that fail to acknowledge their identities. To this end, we recommend the following strategies.

Search for Inconsistencies.   Administrative leaders need to become more conscious of the ways in which taken-for-granted norms, structures, and policies are in contradiction with initiatives to combat discrimination. We recognize that policies intended to create climates of inclusiveness are important and necessary. Yet on many campuses, administrators are oblivious to institutional actions that disavow policies intended to be supportive of diversity. Inconsistencies related to discrimination based on sexual orientation are perhaps the most blatant (McNaron, 1991). Most campuses that have adopted clauses forbidding discrimination on the basis of sexual orientation violate their own policies by (1) allowing ROTC to remain on their campuses despite its discriminatory admissions and retention policies, and (2) denying benefits to same-gender couples that are available to heterosexual married couples.

Administrators need to be aware of inconsistencies in how different groups experience an institution's environment. The results of a Stanford University survey revealed that while the majority of white faculty agreed that the university administration is "genuinely committed to promoting multiracial understanding and cooperation" (Stanford University, 1989, p. 24), only a minority of the faculty of color showed similar agreement.

Develop Awareness of Privilege. The creation of a multicultural campus requires recognition of "white" privilege. An incident at a campus we visited a few months ago provides a good illustration. The Black Student Union invited Dr. Leonard Jeffries, the former chair of the Black Studies Department of CUNY's City College, to give a speech at a special dinner in celebration of Black History Month. Dr. Jeffries is viewed as a controversial figure; his speeches have been denounced for their anti-Semitic tone, and on several occasions he has made anti-gay remarks. Jewish faculty and administrators protested Dr. Jeffries's presence on campus, and on the days following his appearance the Faculty Senate and the college's Planning Committee put aside their regular agenda to discuss the "Jeffries" issue. At these meetings white faculty and administrators accused the Black Student Union of having violated the institution's goals of antiracism by, as one professor put it, "inviting an undesirable guest into our home." What is most instructive about this incident is that the faculty and administration, in their anger, failed to see how their control over institutional structures (the planning committee and the faculty senate) gave them access to formal forums and enabled them to express their outrage.

Although no one denies the right of the faculty and administration to voice their views against someone whom they perceive as threatening, this incident exposes the barriers to dialogue when there is blindness to white privilege. None of the aggrieved faculty and administration seemed aware that for students, faculty, and staff of color, racism is part of their daily life. Symbols of racism are embedded in institutional practices, making them less apparent than the presence of Dr. Jeffries as an invited speaker. Consequently, the imperative for administrative leaders is to cultivate an institutional culture that invites reflection on the manifestations of white privilege. Moreover, incidents such as the one at the campus we visited are not uncommon. Yet administrators tend (as did the ones at this campus) to treat them as isolated and miss out on the opportunity for encouraging difficult dialogues. Once they are over and things have quieted down, it is back to business as usual. We think this is a mistake. Administrators need to see incidents such as these as "teachable moments" and plan ways in which activities designed to promote dialogue and education about the issues related to the incident can be incorporated into the ongoing work of the institution. The faculty need to address the issue in their classrooms and among themselves at departmental meetings; the president needs to address it as part of senior cabinet meetings; trustees need to make it part of their agenda.

Value Multiple Forms of Diversity.   There is a misconception that multiculturalism will be achieved simply by recruiting more people of color into the ranks of the administration and faculty. However, one of the obstacles to achieving the aims of multiculturalism is the tendency, even when hiring a person of color, to look for individuals whose values, scholarship, experience, and other characteristics mirror those of the majority. For example, an all-male department that commits to hiring a professor of color is often more likely to look for a woman whose scholarly interests and methods are similar to those of the men, rather than for a feminist scholar whose work might challenge tradition. Without clear definitions of the meaning of diversity, monocultural values and norms will remain in place despite affirmative action efforts.

The message to those who represent the Other is to fit into the organization, play by the rules, and not make an issue of their race or gender or sexual orientation (Katz, 1988). Such institutions are fearful of differences, and although they have made strides to "colorize" their faculties, administrative bodies, and student bodies, they have not paid such close attention to exchanging monocultural for multicultural values.

Mission

To move monocultural institutions toward multiculturalism demands organizationwide change. It is not enough to conduct special workshops or to establish ad hoc offices dedicated to advancing the diversity agenda. Multiculturalism cannot be achieved through isolated policies that take place outside day-to-day organizational decision making.

A cultural perspective of organizational change directs administrators to the need for changing norms, values, and beliefs. Katz points out that "there is a great deal of discomfort stemming from the fact that people have a clear sense that they no longer want racism, sexism, or other forms of oppression within the organization, but few clear models or visions of what they would be like if they were operating as a multicultural system" (1988, p. 29).

A necessary step toward the creation of a multicultural campus is the development of a mission statement that directly speaks to the requisite values for the establishment of an institutional climate that is supportive of diversity. Because there are so many misconceptions about the meaning of multiculturalism, it is important to distinguish between mission statements that are reflective of an assimilationist philosophy (for example, training a nonwhite working force to function effectively in the corporate world) and those that reflect a concern with social justice and respect for differences.

The mission statement for a multicultural institution should: (1) make visible individual and institutional forms of racism, sexism, and heterosexism; (2) forbid discrimination of any kind; (3) establish guidelines for the recruitment and retention of individuals who are diverse on the basis of gender, race, ethnicity, and sexual orientation; (4) delineate curricular goals that expose students to diverse forms of knowledge based on scholarship that arises out of the experiences of women and men, white and of color, heterosexual and homosexual, privileged and oppressed; (5) educate students to work on behalf of social justice and the creation of a democratic society; and (6) create reward structures that recognize individual and group efforts to promote multicultural values.

Mission statements that reflect a concern with multiculturalism are varied. For example, one campus developed a human relations statement that committed everyone in the institution to abide by the following pledge: "I will neither exercise nor tolerate discrimination based on race, ethnic origin, gender, disability, age, religion, or sexual orientation. I will not support individuals, organizations, and departments who practice discrimination . . . I challenge myself and others to recognize the diversity of our community and to incorporate our multi-faceted population in our decision-making processes." On another campus, the new president rewrote the mission to be more reflective of the institution's multiracial character, to read:

The College is committed to enabling students, particularly those who have traditionally been excluded from higher education, to realize their intellectual and personal goals. Programs of study are rooted in the liberal arts and assist students in obtaining the skills, knowledge, and values they need *to become empowered, active individuals engaged in renewing themselves, their relationships, their work places, and their communities* (emphasis added). . . . We believe students must gain a greater understanding of and appreciation for other cultures and for the unique racial and cultural diversity of the United States.

Although statements such as these are of great significance insofar as they symbolize institutional commitment to multiculturalism, their power lies in the extent to which they can be a force for altering an institution's "design for living." The effectiveness of mission statements ultimately lies in their ability to bring about the transformation of individuals who have been acculturated in a monocultural environment so they will see the need to change established structures. While most institutions of higher education view themselves as sites of liberalism and tolerance, attempts at "institutionalizing" mission statements through specific initiatives that threaten established patterns of power and decision making are very likely to engender conflict and resistance.

Conflict over mission change is inevitable. We do not view such conflict as negative because the changes we propose make it imperative that campus constituents engage in difficult dialogues about values, the nature of knowledge, and power. The task of administration is to create or, as we indicated above, take advantage of spaces for such dialogues.

The task of administration is also to be aware that efforts toward multiculturalism are often thwarted by fears about a breakdown in "community." In part, there is a tendency toward dichotomous thinking where "difference" is perceived to be in opposition to the ideals of a harmonious academic community. On this point, Johnella Butler and Betty Schmitz observe, "Talking about difference in this country upsets people because they believe in the 'melting pot' and don't see the connection between difference and sameness, diversity and unity. They force characteristics into polar opposites instead of onto continua" (1992, p. 40).

Thus on many campuses, the conflict arising from efforts to create multicultural institutions has been met with what Martha Crunkleton (1991) describes as "the flight to community." She says, "With the conflicts comes an understandable desire to talk about community, in part because of the hope that community, were it to occur, would make these conflicts disappear." But, she points out, "Such a flight to that kind of understanding of community is premature. We need to experience our conflicts and understand them before we can have community, and we need to realize that community will not function as a warm blanket, should we ever have it on our campuses" (1991, p. 8). The role of administrators in the difficult dialogues about multiculturalism is to confront romanticized notions of community and encourage its redefinition as "communities of difference" (Tierney, 1993).

The role of administrators is to uphold the principles of the multicultural mission. On one campus, the newly appointed president enlivened the multicultural mission by replacing the previously all-white and male team with a highly diverse group of senior administrators. He also communicated the seriousness of the mission by mounting a vigorous recruitment effort for faculty of color and refused to make faculty appointments to individuals who emerged from searches that had not included persons from underrepresented groups. The president's insistence on affirmative action was met with resentment from old-time professors who until then, despite supporting affirmative action, had never taken action to fulfill its intent. The president's decision to make affirmative action work, even as it may be perceived as administrative intrusion into faculty decision making, has resulted in the "colorization" and "genderization" of a faculty body that had no African Americans and was predominantly male. On this campus, where students of color account for 60 percent of the student body, the recruitment of faculty of color was particularly urgent in order to make the teaching and learning environment more responsive to the needs of the rapidly changing student population. At a minimum, the diversification of the faculty provides students with role models. It also increases the likelihood of a more multicultural curriculum.

Structure

What kinds of structures need to be developed and maintained for a multicultural campus? What strategies might be implemented? These are the kinds of questions we focus on in this section.

Planning. Most campuses today are engaged in some type of strategic planning. The creation of a multicultural campus should be an integral component of the planning process. All units should be directed to discuss the ways in which they will implement the multicultural goals specified in the institutional mission. Thus the task of administering an institution that adopts a human-relations statement (as in the example earlier in this section) is to direct all academic units to delineate multiple strategies to translate the spirit of the human-relations statement into specific actions.

Establishing methods of monitoring progress toward the achievement of multicultural goals is also an important strategy for change. For example, one institution has as one of its four universitywide strategic goals "To build a supportive environment for both women and men in the university's classrooms and research centers and in our communities that reflects our nation's diverse racial and ethnic populations and the multifaceted histories, experiences, and knowledge of all humankind."

The institution directs all units to report annually on the strategies used to accomplish five issues related to this goal:

- Strategies to develop curricula, research, and service agendas that reflect diversity, promote human understanding, and prepare students to participate in the global community
- Strategies to initiate and/or encourage efforts to actively change behaviors toward women and minorities
- Strategies to be responsive to changing state, regional, national, and international demographics
- Strategies to encourage more women and minorities to pursue graduate and professional education
- Strategies to recruit and retain diverse students, faculty, and staff within the community

The progress each academic unit is making on this goal and on related issues is monitored by a special group convened by the provost. The group is charged with reviewing the plans submitted by the units with the guidance of three assessment questions: (1) did the unit's plan include a clear statement of commitment to diversity? (2) did the unit make an assessment of the present diversity climate? and (3) is there evidence of the unit's financial commitment to diversity? A monitoring process is useful in that it provides an assessment of institutional progress.

Sharing Power.   A planning and monitoring process such as the one put into effect by this university will not work unless structures that concentrate decision-making power on white males are dismantled. A planning and monitoring process, regardless of its comprehensiveness, will have a limited effect in the creation of a multicultural campus if the power structure that oversees such a process is predominantly male and white. The absence of diverse individuals among the upper echelons of the administrative hierarchy suggests the absence of a substantive moral commitment to the goals of multicultural education. It is not uncommon for administrators to engage vigorously in the "symbolic management" of diversity, yet leave intact the traditional structures that disempower women, people of color, and gay and lesbian persons.

Absence of diversity in the upper administrative echelon works against the creation of a multicultural campus because decision makers will have a shared view of reality and be less likely to reflect on campus events from multiple perspectives. At the simplest level, within the circles of power there have to be individuals who can and are willing to "take the role" of those whose realities tend to be imperceptible to individuals who have internalized dominant norms. Accordingly, the creation of a multicultural campus requires leaders to welcome differences (in composition and thinking) within their decision-making administrative groups. Administrative groups need to include individuals who will argue for the concerns of women, people of color, and lesbian and gay persons without feeling stigmatized or dismissed as pursuing a "one-person agenda." Undoubtedly, much of the responsibility for creating a climate of openness and support for multicultural goals within the higher ranks of the administration falls upon the president.

Establishing a Structure for Communication. The creation of a multicultural campus requires formal structures to link administrative leaders to multiple communities. At a minimum, universities need to (1) establish commissions on women's equity, race equity, and lesbian, gay, and bisexual equity that report directly to the president, and (2) establish offices staffed by professionals dedicated to addressing the educational, professional, and personal concerns of these groups.

Curriculum and Co-Curriculum

Arguably, the most important task we can focus on in creating a multicultural campus is the development of curricular and co-curricular activities that honor diversity.

Curricular Integration. The creation of a multicultural campus requires the transformation of curriculum so as to be more reflective of the traditions, histories, philosophies, and methodologies of diverse groups. It requires a curriculum and co-curriculum that enable students to encounter difference. Unfortunately, the majority of institutions of higher education address multicultural curricular change in an ad hoc and conventional manner to avoid disturbing the status quo.

According to a recent issue of *Change*, more than one-third of all colleges and universities have adopted a multicultural general education requirement (Levine and Cureton, 1992). The preferred route to "curricular multiculturalism" appears to be "diversity" curricular policies. Such policies make it a requirement for students to enroll in courses that concentrate on "differences" such as race, gender, class, sexual orientation, ethnicity, and so on. At the University of Minnesota, for example, the "U.S. Cultural Pluralism

Requirement" directs undergraduates to complete two courses with a primary focus on African Americans, American Indians, Asian Americans, and/or Chicanos (Zita, 1988). While the University of Minnesota's requirement focuses on four racial/ethnic groups that have been traditionally oppressed, most universities that have passed "diversity" requirements have tended to deal with the conflict that such changes have unleashed by compromising on the definition of diversity. The result is that many diversity requirements deal with "differences" as if they were technical, exchangeable, and depoliticized categories, stripping them of their transformative potential. Legislated approaches to multicultural education do not construe the realities of diversity in more empowering terms—as the "insurrection of subjugated knowledges" (West, 1991), or as the "teaching of conflicts" (Graff, 1992), or as a "politics of difference" (Giroux, 1992). Differences are marginalized by virtue of being defined in reference to the "national common culture."

A multicultural campus requires a curriculum and co-curriculum that make it impossible to learn about women without confronting sexism, race without confronting racism, sexual orientation without confronting heterosexism, ethnicity without confronting ethnocentrism, and social class without confronting classism (Pratt, 1992). What this suggests is that as colleges and universities consider multicultural curricular change, it is imperative to first engage in co-curricular dialogues about the meanings ascribed to "diversity" and to "multiculturalism" as well as its educational purposes. Bensimon (1992) has suggested that questions need to be raised about the nature of a multicultural curriculum, questions such as: is the purpose of multiculturalism to create harmonious encounters with difference? Is it to create a pedagogy of empowerment? Is it to advance the ideal of an unoppressive society and the affirmation of a politics of difference? Without such dialogues it becomes less possible to develop a curriculum that advances the goals of a multicultural campus.

We recommend the following strategies.

Faculty Development Activities. Organize seminars and institutes to help faculty revise and create courses to include gender, race, and sexual orientation. These activities provide opportunities for interdisciplinary collaboration in the pursuit of multicultural goals. Through these educative activities, faculty learn that multiculturalism is not simply a matter of adding women or people of color to preexisting course syllabi. At a minimum, we view these activities as exposing faculty to the epistemology and pedagogy of curricular integration so that they are able to:

- Understand the process of curricular integration
- Identify bias in the traditional curriculum (to examine ways in which gender, race, and sexual orientation are embedded in the language of instruction and traditional texts)
- Explore the thinking and scholarship grounded in feminism, African American thought, lesbian and gay studies, Latino studies, and so forth
- Examine empowering pedagogies such as feminist, critical, and nonracist teaching practices
- Develop intercultural communication and create classroom contexts for collaborative learning

Academic Units. In most institutions, departments and/or colleges have curriculum committees made up of faculty, students, and administrators who make decisions on new-course approvals and programs. On many campuses, the work of these committees tends to be administrative and routinized; the committees are primarily reactive and rarely take the initiative for reform. Indeed, most of the leadership for curriculum projects on the integration of gender, race, ethnicity, and sexual orientation in the curriculum has emerged from women's studies and ethnic studies. However, curriculum committees have enormous potential from which to develop ongoing curricular integration efforts. Such committees can initiate college- and departmentwide dialogues around two basic questions:

- In what ways do our curriculum and instructional materials integrate or exclude the experiences of women, people of color, and lesbian and gay persons?
- In what ways do our curriculum and instructional materials address issues of racism, sexism, ethnocentrism, and homophobia?

We envision that the initiation and maintenance of these dialogues could socialize faculty members of curriculum committees to assume a more active role as change agents.

Academic Administrators and Curricular Change. Senior academic administrators need to be more "consciously responsible" for critically assessing the impact of organizational structures, policies, and new mandates vis-à-vis women, students of color, and lesbian and gay students. As with others, administrators might benefit from workshops and seminars if the intent is to create a critical mass of top academic administrators who understand the purposes of curricular integration and how it might improve the teaching and learning environment for all undergraduates. A clear advantage of such "consciousness raising" sessions is that they increase the awareness of academic decision makers for the need to reward faculty involvement in multicultural curricular change formally by making it part of the evaluation criteria in promotion and tenure reviews.

Conclusion

Racism, sexism, and heterosexism tend not to be expressed in overt acts of bigotry. Instead, they are embedded in organizational structures, norms of evaluation, networks of communication, language, forms of power, and definitions of legitimacy that shape institutional practices. A college or university usually is not overtly anti-gay, yet its policies exclude the partners of lesbian and gay employees from enjoying the same benefits extended to their colleagues' spouses. An administrative cabinet is not overtly sexist; however, there is a tendency among the senior officers to listen to those whose voices are representative of the norm (say, white males) while ignoring the women in the group.

We have suggested cultural strategies informed by critical and feminist theories to overcome obstacles to creating a multicultural organization. We have purposely defined multiculturalism broadly so that we might find commonalities across differences while maintaining the unique strengths of differences. As noted by the black lesbian feminist Audre Lorde (1985), unity does not have to mean similarity. Indeed, as we confront the multitude of challenges that await academe in the twenty-first century, how can we not call upon these unique strengths to solve some of our most intractable problems?

References

Bensimon, E. M. (1992, April). The normalization of diversity: Multicultural curricular change at an urban university. Paper presented at the annual meeting of the American Educational Research Association, San Francisco.

Bensimon, E. M., & Neumann, A. (1993). *Redesigning collegiate leadership: Teams and teamwork in higher education.* Baltimore, MD: Johns Hopkins University Press.

Butler, J., & Schmitz, B. (1992). Ethnic studies, women's studies, and multiculturalism. *Change, 24*(1), 36–41.

Chaffee, E. E., & Tierney, W. G. (1988). *Collegiate culture and leadership strategies.* New York: Macmillan (American Council on Education).

Chesler, M. A., & Crowfoot, J. (1989). *Racism in higher education I: An organizational analysis.* Ann Arbor: Center for Research on Social Organization, University of Michigan.

Collins, P. H. (1986). Learning from the outsider within. *Social Problems, 33*(6), 14–32.

Crunkleton, M. A. (1991). The flight to community: Pluralism, democracy, and higher education. *Liberal Education*, *77*(1), 8–11.

DePalma, A. (1991, April 16). Separate ethnic worlds grow on campus. *The New York Times*, p. 1.

Gergen, K. J. (1991). *The saturated self: Dilemmas of identity in contemporary life*. New York: Basic Books.

Giroux, H. (1992). *Border crossings: Cultural workers and the politics of education*. New York: Routledge.

Graff, G. (1992). Teach the conflicts. In D. J. Gless & B. H. Smith (Eds.), *The politics of liberal education* (pp. 57–73). Durham, NC: Duke University Press.

Hill, P. (1991). Multiculturalism: The crucial philosophical and organizational issues. *Change*, *23*(4), 38–47.

hooks, b. (1990). *Yearning: Race, gender, and cultural politics*. Boston: South End Press.

Katz, J. H. (1988). *Facing the challenge of diversity and multiculturalism*. Ann Arbor: Center for Research on Social Organization, Working Paper Series, University of Michigan.

Kimball, R. (1991, January). Tenured radicals: A postscript. *The New Criterion*, 4–13.

Lather, P. (1991). *Getting smart: Feminist research and pedagogy within the postmodern*. New York: Routledge, Chapman, and Hall.

Leatherman, C. (1991, November 6). Colleges hire more female presidents, but questions linger about their clout. *The Chronicle of Higher Education*, pp. A19–A21.

Levine, A., & Cureton, J. (1992). The quiet revolution: Eleven facts about multiculturalism and the curriculum. *Change*, *24*(1), 24–29.

Lorde, A. (1985). *I am your sister: Black women organizing across sexualities*. Latham, NY: Kitchen Table, Women of Color Press.

McNaron, T. (1991). Making life more livable for gays and lesbians on campus: Sightings from the field. *Educational Record*, *72*(1), 19–22.

Mooney, C. J. (1990, February 7). New U.S. survey assembles a statistical portrait of the American professoriate. *The Chronicle of Higher Education*, pp. A15–A18.

Pratt, M. L. (1992). Humanities for the future: Reflections on the western culture debate at Stanford. In D. J. Gless & B. H. Smith (Eds.), *The politics of liberal education* (pp. 13–31). Durham, NC: Duke University Press.

Quality Education for Minorities Project. (1990). *Education that works: An action plan for the education of minorities*. Cambridge, MA: Massachusetts Institute of Technology.

Rosaldo, R. (1989). *Culture and truth: The remaking of social analysis*. Boston: Beacon Press.

Stanford University. (1989). *Building a multiracial, multicultural university community: Final report of the university committee on minority issues.*

The Chronicle of Higher Education Almanac. (1991, August 28). The nation: Faculty and staff. *The Chronicle of Higher Education Almanac*, pp. 29–34.

Tierney, W. G. (Ed). (1991). *Culture and ideology in higher education: Advancing a critical agenda.* New York: Praeger.

Tierney, W. G. (1993). *Building communities of difference: Higher education in the 21st century.* Granby, MA: Bergin & Garvey.

Tierney, W. G., & Bensimon, E. (1995). Promotion and tenure: Socialization and community in academe. New York: SUNY.

West, C. (1991). The dilemma of the black intellectual. In b. hooks & C. West (Eds.), *Breaking bread: Insurgent black intellectual life.* Boston: South End Press.

Zita, J. (1988). From orthodoxy to pluralism: A postsecondary curricular reform. *Journal of Education, 170*(2), 58–76.

Chapter Fifteen

Using Assessment
to Improve Instruction

Trudy W. Banta
Indiana University-Purdue University, Indianapolis

Interest in workforce competitiveness has focused attention on higher education as a resource in the preparation of future employees. Moreover, growing interest on the part of consumers in the quality of goods and services and the scarcity of financial resources for public services are producing intense interest in accountability by enterprises such as higher education. Thus most states, all six regional higher education accrediting associations, and all disciplinary accrediting associations that are approved by the U.S. Department of Education now have policies that encourage or require colleges and universities to assess their effectiveness. A recent American Council on Education *Campus Trends* survey reveals that as a consequence, nine of ten colleges and universities in this country are either planning or are in the process of implementing a program of student-outcomes assessment (El-Khawas, 1992).

These external pressures have produced predictable campus responses: large groups of students are being tested with standardized exams in an effort to furnish evidence that participants in higher education are attaining college-level learning standards, and samples of enrolled students and graduates are being surveyed to assess their levels of satisfaction with campus programs and services. Some of this activity has a perfunctory air, as faculty and administrators do just what is needed to satisfy external requirements, giving little thought to capitalizing on the results of assessment. In fact, a follow-up survey (Johnson and others, 1992) indicated that no more than one-third of the respondents who said they were planning or implementing outcomes assessment initiatives actually had a comprehensive program in place. Most were, in fact, doing a few unconnected projects in order to meet mandates.

None of this is really surprising, given the propensity of academics to find ways around external initiatives for which there is little internal support. The encouraging fact is that where thoughtful faculty and administrators have taken the process of assessment seriously and made a concerted effort to use the findings, evidence of real improvements in the design of curricula, instruction, and academic services continues to grow.

Distinguishing Features of Outcomes Assessment

Individual student assessment has been a fixture in higher education since the beginning. Professors have tested students to ascertain what they have learned and to give them formative feedback. Throughout the world, external examiners and members of licensing boards assess students' learning at the end of their academic programs for the purpose of certifying a minimally acceptable level of competence in their discipline. More recently, resulting from efforts to increase access, colleges and universities have initiated entry-level basic-skills testing for individual students. The results of this kind of assessment are currently used to advise, place, and counsel individual students.

The use of assessment in evaluating program effectiveness has a much briefer history in higher education. Alverno College and Northeast Missouri State University were pioneers in application of student assessment in the early 1970s (Ewell, 1984). In 1979, Tennessee became the first state to require its public institutions to assess student outcomes (Banta, 1988). Within five years, outcomes-assessment policies for state institutions were put into effect in New Jersey and Virginia, and a flood of states followed suit by the end of the 1980s.

Hanson (1988) and others began to argue that the theories of measurement that support individualized testing were not applicable when used to assess *groups* of students. Assessment theories and methods were needed that would enable faculty to (1) use the results of basic-skills testing to plan courses and curricula for first- and second-year college students, (2) use "rising junior" examinations to determine the effectiveness of general education programs, (3) use comprehensive exams for graduating students to assess the effectiveness of the curriculum in the major, and (4) survey enrolled students and graduates in attempts to use levels of satisfaction to direct improvements in educational programs and related student services.

This second use of assessment, as a tool in evaluating and stimulating improvements in program effectiveness, is the focus of this chapter. Hereafter, the term *assessment* will be used as shorthand for "measurement of outcomes of the student experience in higher education for the purpose of improving the programs and services which constitute that experience." Assessment thus conceptualized may be used to demonstrate accountability in institution-initiated or state-operated peer review and to obtain regional or disciplinary accreditation. The most important purpose from an institutional perspective, however, is to use outcomes assessment to suggest internal program improvements that will promote student learning.

The definition of assessment used herein is much broader than the stereotypical concept of assessment via standardized, paper-and-pencil achievement tests. It encompasses also measures of performance, perceptions, attitudes, and opinions. Its methods include essays, portfolios, surveys, interviews, and observations of behavior in naturalistic settings.

Due to the insufficiency of current instruments in furnishing reliable and valid data, no single assessment technique can provide all of the information needed to evaluate a program. The need for triangulation, or the use of multiple assessment methods, is strongly indicated. The involvement of faculty and others who are expected to use the data from assessment is essential. Those who are ultimately responsible for using the information must set the course for its collection and review the findings.

Assessment as Faculty Development

While assessment in response to a mandate can be perfunctory, it can also be a powerful force for innovation, renewal, and long-term improvement. The principal thesis of this chapter is that when faculty become fully involved in assessment, they create and become active participants in their own program of professional growth and development. Products of this effort can include stronger curricula, more effective classroom instruction, increased student-faculty interaction, and enhanced student motivation. This theme is developed here within the context of four steps in the assessment process: (1) setting objectives for student learning, (2) ensuring that these objectives are taught within the curriculum, (3) assessing student learning, and (4) using findings to improve instruction.

Step One: Setting Objectives

In establishing objectives for student learning in an academic program, constituent groups such as enrolled students, other faculty who also teach the students, student services personnel, graduates of the program, and employers of graduates, as well as faculty responsible for the academic program, should be involved. Dialogue with representatives of these groups offers faculty an opportunity to acquire new perspectives on their approaches to curriculum and instruction.

After a general discussion about goals and objectives, faculty must ask, What should students know and be able to do when they finish the set of experiences we have planned for them? Answers to this question should produce assessable goals and objectives.

However, without courses in curriculum development or pedagogy, many faculty have not thought of goals and objectives in terms of behaviors students are expected to exhibit.

At the University of Tennessee, Knoxville, faculty were introduced to Bloom's Taxonomy of Educational Objectives (Bloom, 1956) and asked to write objectives that promote student development in all levels of the cognitive domain, from knowledge and comprehension, through application and analysis, to synthesis and evaluation. Learning how to write assessable objectives prepares faculty not only for outcomes assessment at the end of a program of study but also for assessment in their individual courses.

Step Two: Ensuring That Objectives Are Taught

Faculty next need to ask, What experiences within the curriculum promote student attainment of the knowledge and skills we think are important? Before outcomes assessment began to call attention to the need for this step, many curricula omitted it entirely. Programs of study were designed as series of course titles and brief descriptions. Once courses were approved for inclusion in the curriculum, no ongoing monitoring occurred to ensure that students were being exposed to the knowledge and skills specified for that course in the overall curriculum design.

An illustrative professional-development experience occurred at Samford University in Birmingham, Alabama, when the faculty charged with developing a new general education program were asked to create a content-by-skills matrix. They wrote the generic skills they wanted students to develop along the left margin of the matrix and then created columns by listing across the top the new interdisciplinary courses they hoped to develop. Then they were asked to check which of the generic competencies they thought should be covered in each of the interdisciplinary courses. The dialogue that occurred during this exercise helped the faculty agree on some fundamental issues and concepts that students should experience in each of the new core courses. This led faculty to suggest that every course instructor be evaluated periodically through review of the course syllabus, inspection of course examinations, and even peer observations, to ensure that the core concepts continue to be taught even as the instructor continuously updates and improves the content.

Step Three: Assessing Student Learning

After constituent groups have been consulted, assessable goals and objectives have been developed, and a process is in place for ensuring that the goals and objectives are being taught, the next question can be tackled: How do we know that students are attaining the knowledge and skills we think are essential? Once again, in formulating responses to these questions, faculty become engaged in valuable professional development experiences.

Often, faculty with no formal training in pedagogy discover in their discussion of assessment that they actually know very little about the finer points of developing tests and measures. They learn that in addition to tests of cognitive skills, which utilize the familiar media of the paper-and-pencil multiple-choice exam and the inevitable short essay, a portfolio or an observation of the application of knowledge in a realistic setting might be used. Cognitive measures also can be supplemented with surveys to assess students' perceptions of how well courses and programs are serving their intended purposes. Attitudes and values should be assessed if faculty are interested in promoting student development more broadly within their courses. And finally, faculty learn that student records showing rates of self-selected participation in certain courses and programs can yield additional information about program effectiveness.

If faculty elect to use a standardized test to assess student learning, they will need to match their curriculum carefully with what the test's developers, through their choices of items, specify that a curriculum should contain. The notion of whether a given course is covering what faculty colleagues believe it should cover often emerges in this discussion.

Assessing Student Achievement in General Education. Exploratory studies at the University of Tennessee (UT), Knoxville, between 1988 and 1992 encouraged faculty groups to scrutinize four commercially developed standardized exams as tools for assessing the effectiveness of the general education curriculum (Banta and Pike, 1989). Faculty rated the congruence between the content of each of these tests and the intended content of the UT Knoxville general education curriculum; then students who took the tests provided similar ratings. Next, the psychometric properties of these exams were investigated, and their sensitivity to educational experiences was assessed. These studies led the faculty who were involved to conclude that most of the standardized exams evaluating general education programs are flawed because (1) insufficient technical work has been done on the items in these instruments, (2) norms are not true national norms but rather are based on the scores accumulated by "user" institutions, and (3) by far the most important determinant of students' scores on these exams is their prior ability and knowledge. The UT Knoxville faculty developed an appreciation for locally conceived and constructed tests because they (1) involve faculty and students in the assessment process, (2) test what the faculty intends to teach, and (3) help faculty improve their skills in designing measurement instruments and assessment activities.

In 1988, faculty at the University of Connecticut began to discuss how to assess their general education program. They organized six interdisciplinary teams—foreign language, literature and the arts, Western and non-Western civilization, philosophy and ethics, social science, and science and technology—and developed a series of assessment activities for freshmen and seniors. The dialogue about the structure of the curriculum was the most important outcome of this foray into assessment (Watt and Rodrigues, 1993).

In New Jersey, faculty from across the state engaged in substantive discussions about general education under the auspices of the College Outcomes Evaluation Program of the State Department of Higher Education (Morante and Jemmott, 1993). Faculty designed the sophomore level General Intellectual Skills Assessment, which checked levels of competence in forty-eight skills in the natural sciences, social sciences, and humanities-fine arts. Scoring of sophomores' responses created an opportunity for faculty to develop skills in evaluating essay responses: two readers were asked to evaluate each response for evidence of skill development, and two additional readers assessed the response for writing competence.

At Kean College in New Jersey, a faculty group designed a course-embedded approach to the assessment of general education. A central committee specified program outcomes for students and the types of measures that would be appropriate to assess student achievement. Then the outcomes were assigned to courses within the general education curriculum, and the related measures were embedded in course exams. Instructors then evaluated students' responses in order to determine course grades, and the central committee reviewed responses across students and across classes for the purpose of assessing program effectiveness.

Faculty across the country are developing skills in portfolio assessment (Forrest, 1990). They recognize the value of studying over time collections of students' course assignments, research papers, materials from group projects, artistic productions, self-reflective essays, correspondence, and taped presentations. Faculty at Kean College and elsewhere have found the audio- or videocassette portfolio to be particularly useful in assessing student growth in oral presentation skills, musical performances, visual artistic productions, foreign language pronunciation, interaction skills, laboratory techniques, and psychomotor skills.

Faculty experience in developing outcome assessment measures has made clear the need to use multiple measures of students' growth and development. Students' own perceptions of their growth in certain skills have been shown by Pace (1986) and others to be reasonably dependable measures. Thus more and more faculty now ask students to describe the extent to which their education has helped them learn to communicate orally and in writing, apply mathematics skills, understand literature, prepare for employment, and get along with others.

Faculty immersed in assessment also learn not to shy away from identifying goals that are difficult to measure or for which assessment tools are not readily available. They become more willing to struggle with the measurement of growth in self-esteem, capacity for ethical decision making, openness to change, capacity for self-directed learning, respect for cultural diversity, and leadership skills (Erwin, 1991).

Assessing Student Achievement in the Major. Faculty interested in assessment in some major fields have turned first to the data available from licensing and certification exams such as those developed by professional associations in nursing, accounting, engineering, law, and medicine. Some disciplinary associations also have helped assessors by developing achievement tests that can be used in evaluating program effectiveness. The Educational Testing Service has used its advanced field tests in the Graduate Record Exam series as the bases for abbreviated exams that can be applied to program evaluation in fifteen disciplines. Nevertheless, most faculties have not found the use of standardized exams alone to assess learning in a major or program satisfactory for a variety of reasons. Standardized exams are available in only a fraction of the major fields that exist in higher education. Those that are available assess only a fraction of what is taught in a given academic program. If too much emphasis is placed on students' scores on a standardized test, the content may unduly influence what is taught. Most paper-and-pencil tests assess primarily lower-order intellectual skills and may well be standardized on norm groups that do not represent the students being tested on a given campus. These tests generally provide few, if any, subscores, thus making it difficult to determine where students' strengths and weaknesses lie. And even the best standardized test does not provide information about *why* students' scores may be low.

These concerns have led faculty in almost three-fourths of the institutions responding to a recent survey (El-Khawas, 1992) to begin to develop their own assessment instruments. As in the case of the development of general education measures, the result of faculty work on tests is significant professional development for the instructors. Some faculty wanted to use a certification test to assess student exit competence but found that information insufficient; they have developed supplements for standardized measures. At UT Knoxville, faculty responsible for the French major supplemented the National Teacher Exam Specialty Area Test in French with homemade tests of reading comprehension, writing, listening comprehension, and speaking in French. In the UT Knoxville department of theatre, the faculty supplemented a traditional objective exam that they had developed with a video-taped exercise in which students criticize an excerpt from a play in terms of the directing, acting, or set design, depending on the focus of their major.

Faculty at Central Missouri State University (CMSU) evaluate senior theatre majors using a comprehensive cumulative assessment program that begins with sophomore juries, continues in the junior year with critique by faculty of a one-act play directed by each student, and culminates in faculty evaluation of a ten-minute performance or a portfolio at the senior level (Assessment in CMSU's Theatre Department, 1989). Seniors in theatre at CMSU also take a written comprehensive exam that covers all their course work, and the faculty have designed a survey for their graduates in order to round out the series of measures they feel is needed to provide a comprehensive evaluation of their program.

Faculty in the occupational therapy program at Kean College review student evaluations of instruction and students' scores on the national certification exam. But more importantly, they have developed a multiple-assessor approach to evaluating their students' experience in field work. Occupational therapy majors evaluate their own performance using an instrument developed jointly by students, faculty, graduates, and employers. Then faculty supervisors and employers who supervise field work use the same instrument in their evaluation (Knight, Lumsden, and Gallaro, 1991).

Faculty involved in assessment have developed a number of creative approaches to assessing students' abilities to apply their classroom learning in practical settings. Examples include an in-basket exercise for a hospital dietician, an advertising campaign aimed at the sponsor of a new product, identification of an unknown substance in the laboratory, and a personnel problem for the manager of a radio station.

While faculty in the humanities seem to have a particularly difficult time in agreeing upon a body of *content* that every student should master as part of their experience in the major, religious studies faculty at UT Knoxville were able to agree on a set of *skills* for their majors. They believe their majors should develop the research skills of a scholar in their field and thus be able to define a topic and write a paper that satisfies a team of faculty evaluators. These faculty developed a team-taught seminar for seniors that serves as a culminating experience for their majors. The most important seminar activity involves the development of a comprehensive paper with step-by-step faculty critique. The concept of using external examiners as reviewers of student work also has been applied here, as it has been in a consortium project developed by the Association of American Colleges (Fong, 1988). The UT Knoxville religious studies faculty enlisted colleagues at other institutions to serve as readers of their seniors' papers in exchange for the agreement by UT Knoxville faculty to read papers written by seniors on the other campuses. These reviews of students' papers and other evidence of their performance in the seminar led to curriculum redesign and a greater emphasis on the development of writing skills.

Good opportunities for faculty to review their own curricular objectives and testing strategies have taken place with the development of "cooperative tests" by Anthony Golden at Austin Peay State University. Golden has collected from faculty in political science, psychology, social work, English literature, and other fields their objectives for student learning in the major and a related set of multiple-choice test items. Any department that has contributed questions to the pool may administer a set of core items yielding a score that can be compared with that achieved by students at peer institutions, as well as subsets of items in specialty areas of the discipline that are considered strengths of the student major at that institution.

Again, as in the case of assessment in general education, faculty who have become involved in the assessment of student learning in the major have seen the need to broaden the evaluation by adding measures of student development in noncognitive as well as cognitive areas.

Step 4: Using Findings to Improve Instruction

As previously illustrated, faculty involvement in assessment sparks conversation and developmental experiences that produce improvements in curricula, instruction, and ultimately in student learning. In addition, the findings resulting from the application of the assessment instruments and activities designed by faculty have produced other kinds of changes. Almost no research literature existed to document the effectiveness of these changes until publication of the author's 1993 book, *Making a Difference: Outcomes of a Decade of Assessment in Higher Education* (Banta, 1993). What follows is a brief overview of the findings stemming from this experience that are slowly but surely making their way into the literature.

Using Findings from Assessment in General Education. Perhaps the single most common finding in outcomes assessment studies has been that students' writing competence, even as they approach graduation from college, leaves much to be desired. Faculty have responded to this need in different ways. For instance, at Dyersburg (Tennessee) State Community College, students' responses to the Community College Student Experiences Questionnaire and feedback from employers documented the need to improve students' writing skills. Through professional development experiences, the college encouraged faculty to make more assignments requiring writing and to spend more time providing written feedback so that students would know how to improve their work. Dyersburg now has survey data that reveal an increase in employers' satisfaction with the writing skills of its graduates.

Dissatisfaction with writing skills led faculty of Lehman College of the City University of New York to develop explicit statements of student outcomes in writing and criteria for evaluating achievement of those outcomes. At UT Knoxville, a writing laboratory staffed by faculty from the department of English was expanded in response to a faculty senate policy specifying that students with writing deficiencies will be given an incomplete in the course and sent to the writing lab for remedial work. These students must reach a specified level of writing proficiency before the incomplete is removed. UT Knoxville also implemented a faculty development program in writing instruction.

At the State Technical Institute at Memphis, low scores on the Communicating subscale of the ACT College Outcome Measures Project (COMP) exam led faculty to establish a word processing lab to help students improve their communication skills. An evaluation of lab reports before and after this facility was established documents that writing skills are improving.

Ongoing research with learning styles inventories at Virginia Military Institute (VMI) revealed that the teaching of writing is often not sensitive to variations in student learning style. Consequently, VMI faculty are encouraged to use portfolios in the assessment of writing, since this medium can foster learning for students regardless of their learning style.

Student development of mathematics skills is a second area in which many institutions have found student deficiencies. At Northeast Missouri State University, the finding that sophomores and seniors seemed to know less about math than they did when they were freshmen prompted faculty to institute an institution-wide requirement that students take and pass college algebra.

At UT Knoxville, faculty consideration of the range of cognitive levels assessed by items on the ACT COMP exam resulted in selected faculty learning to write assessable objectives for students' performance at each cognitive level and in developing the means to test for those skills. Lower-than-anticipated scores on the Problem-Solving subscale were responsible for the appointment of a universitywide committee that, after a year of study, recommended emphasis on problem solving across the curriculum accompanied by appropriate faculty development experiences.

Using Findings from Assessment in the Major. Investigation of student records by faculty has raised questions about course placement that have prompted constructive changes. At Mt. Hood Community College in Oregon, failure rates in chemistry and math courses were unacceptably high. Higher cut scores on placement tests were instituted. At Western Michigan University, faculty found that students often failed courses to which they had been admitted without presenting evidence of the proper prerequisite experiences. Careful analysis of the prerequisite system was undertaken, and those experiences found to be appropriate are now being enforced more assiduously.

At UT Knoxville, faculty in the department of geography designed a test for senior majors covering four topics: physical geography, economic geography, cultural geography, and technique. Disappointing student performance on the economic geography section of the exam led faculty to introduce a new course in that area. Dismay at the overall level of scores caused the faculty to review students' course-selection patterns; they found that students were not taking courses in all the four areas that they considered part of the core of the major. Consequently, new core-course requirements were instituted.

Evidence from a number of colleges and universities indicates that faculty involvement in the process of *test development* has resulted in the following actions aimed at improvement: assessment instrument reviewers from other campuses have made suggestions that faculty have subsequently implemented; faculty are more agreed upon specific learning outcomes for students now than they were prior to assessment; these newly developed learning outcomes are used in planning curricula as well as in assessing students; faculty approaches in core courses taught by several individuals are more consistent; and upper- and lower-division courses in the disciplines are more effectively integrated.

After faculty have administered assessment instruments to students and reviewed their work, they have been motivated to develop more stringent curriculum requirements and to place more emphasis on knowledge application in internships, field work, and research projects. The student outcome objectives that have come from the process of assessment now provide more structure for courses; students are asked to write more; assignments require more problem solving and critical thinking; and classroom tests now require the use of more complex intellectual skills.

Using Findings from Measures of Opinion. If deficient writing skill is an almost universal finding of assessment activity, student dissatisfaction with the academic service of advising is a close second. At Winthrop University in South Carolina, at Austin Peay State University in Tennessee, and at UT Knoxville, enrolled students have given some of their lowest satisfaction ratings to career advising. At UT Knoxville, focus-group interviews uncovered the fact that although faculty thought career advising could be handled most appropriately by the Office of Career Services, leaving them to deal with academic advising, students wanted "one-stop shopping." As a consequence, Career Services is now more closely linked with academic advising through modifications in the training process for advisers. At Austin Peay, training for advisers has also been modified to include more career information. At Winthrop University, a faculty retreat focused on the need for career advising, Career Services was reorganized and expanded, and the Winthrop curriculum now includes an elective course called Career Exploration.

At Virginia Western Community College, alumni surveys suggested the need for better academic advising, and the college installed a new computerized academic advising system. When student surveys and focus groups revealed an incongruence between faculty and student perceptions of advising at Kean College, the student handbook was revised to include a broader definition of advising, and orientation sessions were held for students and faculty. Readministration of the student surveys reveals that students are more satisfied with advising, and so are faculty.

At the State Technical Institute at Memphis, students complained that faculty were not available outside class. More night office hours to accommodate working students were initiated, and the commitment of faculty to serve as staff for learning laboratories has been increased. Students now express greater satisfaction with the availability of faculty.

At Virginia Western Community College, graduates let it be known that they were experiencing difficulties in transferring to four-year institutions. This caused the college administration to undertake efforts to strengthen articulation agreements with appropriate four-year institutions.

Other outcomes of the assessment process that work to enhance the learning environment for students include increasing faculty awareness of the importance of student-faculty interaction and of the need to appropriately train and supervise graduate teaching assistants. Students at some institutions have let it be known that they were dissatisfied with the printed information available to them about curricula in general education and in their major. A number of departments have taken steps to remedy this situation by creating new descriptive materials about their offerings, and students have responded positively to the changes.

In summary, the process of assessment can help faculty develop skills that enable them to design stronger curricula and more effective methods of instruction. In addition, assessment findings provide direction for improving academic programs and related services for students. Assessment's potential for impact on the improvement of the environment for learning is extended when it is linked with broader processes such as program review, total quality management, and faculty scholarship and research.

Assessment and Program Review

In the early 1970s, peer review of doctoral programs was inaugurated at many U.S. research universities. By the early 1980s, many institutions had extended their review process to include undergraduate and master's degree programs. However, prior to 1985, most campus peer-review processes focused almost exclusively on input and process measures such as the quality of the faculty, the ability levels of incoming students, financial resources available to the department, structure of the curriculum, quality of classroom and laboratory facilities, and extensiveness of the library collection. As early as 1983, UT Knoxville incorporated the assessment of outcomes in its review process. The guidelines for self-study at the department level were expanded to include attention to such outcomes as student achievement in general education and the major field; student perceptions of their development toward faculty-specified objectives; opinions of program quality from students, alumni, employers, and others; rates of job placement; rates of placement in graduate and professional education; and external recognition of students and graduates (Richards and Minkel, 1986).

When conscientiously implemented and linked with administrative decision making at departmental, college, and central levels, the program review can be a very powerful assessment tool. At

UT Knoxville, the incorporation of student achievement data and survey responses of various constituent groups was recognized by internal and external reviewers alike as an important addition to the array of indicators of program quality and thus very helpful in the review process.

At UT Knoxville, the department of agricultural economics faculty learned from student surveys undertaken in connection with their program review that their majors were not happy with career advising, their internship experiences, or the quality of computer support in the department. The faculty responded by appointing a coordinator for internships, by expanding their contact with their own graduates to identify more placement opportunities for current students, and by introducing freshman and senior seminars with expanded opportunities for computer skill development.

Assessment data collected in connection with program reviews can help reviewers focus their questions during their visit and thus be more specific in making recommendations. Over a ten-year period of connecting outcomes assessment and program review at UT Knoxville, reviewers' recommendations have been implemented in ways that increase the sense of purpose about academic programs on the part of students as well as faculty. Faculty better focus their curricula and communicate more often with students. Linking program review with budgeting and a well-implemented follow-up process ensures that reviewers' recommendations are implemented.

Assessment and Total Quality Management

The philosophy of continuous improvement of processes and employee skills, total quality management (or TQM), relies heavily on the collection of data about processes. Much of the data of outcomes assessment can be applied to advantage within the TQM framework. The need for participatory leadership, setting assessable goals, ensuring that the goals are implemented, gathering data to serve as evidence of goal achievement, and using the results to improve the process are all TQM principles with a familiar ring to active participants in comprehensive assessment programs.

The application of TQM in the classroom is a powerful, but virtually untapped, source of direction for improvements in teaching and learning. Students and faculty can become collaborators in a continuous process of feeding useful information back to the instructor, much like the process proposed in the Menges and Rando chapter in this volume. While the application of TQM to teaching and learning is relatively new, and few academic units have tried it, schools of business at the University of Minnesota, Rochester Institute of Technology, and the University of Chicago do report successful experiences.

Assessment as a Topic of Faculty Scholarship and Research

Program evaluation can and should be a valued part of the conduct of every academic program. Using outcomes assessment as a component of comprehensive program evaluation, faculty within a discipline can contribute to the literature of that discipline by reporting evaluation findings and creative departmental responses to them. In addition, most disciplines pay attention to the process of instruction in the field—perhaps even supporting a journal devoted to pedagogy in the discipline—and assessment used to improve teaching and learning can be the topic of scholarly articles written for such journals.

If, in fact, good teaching and good scholarly writing go together, then the involvement of faculty in assessment-related research operates as a process to improve student learning. Moreover, the incorporation of assessment-related matters in the research agenda of faculty helps to ensure that faculty will take assessment seriously and utilize its results. The rewards and recognition that accompany involvement in research and scholarly activity are often perceived as being greater than those associated with teaching and the improvement thereof. Obviously, faculty must be motivated to take part in assessment, or they will not do it.

Contributions of Outcomes Assessment to Program Improvement

This chapter has provided concrete illustrations of the benefits of assessment beyond the classroom for improving curricula and classroom instruction, and therefore student learning. First, the process initiates a dialogue among faculty about learning. This fosters faculty collaboration and teamwork that result in more coherent curriculum design, attention to the details of implementation, and systematic evaluation.

Assessment also stimulates faculty and student collaboration in setting goals and gathering data about the effectiveness of implementation. Finally, involvement in assessment promotes faculty renewal and gives faculty new reasons to be interested in their work. At most colleges and universities, the history of substantial faculty involvement in outcomes assessment is recent. Thus documented instances of increases in student learning and affective development that may be attributed to program improvements undertaken in response to assessment findings are relatively rare.

Nevertheless, institution after institution report that assessment helps faculty establish a clear sense of mission and direction and a commitment to common goals. This provides a new perspective and sense of challenge that can revitalize the higher education enterprise. Faculty who are involved experience a sense of progress and accomplishment. Management is made more efficient through the improved quality of data available for use in decision making. Positive benefits of these developments for students include a better student-institution fit, an overall improvement in the student experience, and increased student retention.

References

Assessment in CMSU's theatre department. (1989). *Assessment Update, 1*(4), 11.

Banta, T. W. (Ed.). (1988). New directions for institutional research: No. 59. *Implementing outcomes assessment: Promise and perils.* San Francisco: Jossey-Bass.

Banta, T. W., & associates (1993). *Making a difference: Outcomes of a decade of assessment in higher education.* San Francisco: Jossey-Bass.

Banta, T. W., & Pike, G. R. (1989). Methods for comparing outcomes assessment instruments. *Research in Higher Education, 30*(5), 455–470.

Bloom, B. S. (Ed.). (1956). *Taxonomy of educational objectives: Handbook I. Cognitive domain.* New York: David McKay.

El-Khawas, E. (1992). *1992 campus trends* (Higher Education Panel Report No. 78). Washington, DC: American Council on Education.

Erwin, T. D. (1991). *Assessing student learning and development in college.* San Francisco: Jossey-Bass.

Ewell, P. T. (1984). *The self-regarding institution: Information for excellence.* Boulder, CO: National Center for Higher Education Management Systems.

Fong, B. (1988). Old wineskins: The AAC external examination project. *Liberal Education, 74*(3), 12–16.

Forrest, A. (1990). *Time will tell: Portfolio-assisted assessment of general education.* Washington, DC: American Association of Higher Education.

Hanson, G. (1988). Critical issues in the assessment of value added in education. In T. W. Banta (Ed.), New directions for institutional research: No. 59. *Implementing outcomes assessment: Promise and perils* (pp. 53–68). San Francisco: Jossey-Bass.

Johnson, R., Prus J., Andersen, C., & El-Khawas, E. (1992). *Assessing assessment: An in-depth status report on the higher education assessment movement in 1990* (Higher Education Panel Report No. 79). Washington, DC: American Council on Education.

Knight, M., Lumsden, D., & Gallaro, D. (1991). *Outcomes assessment at Kean College of New Jersey: Academic programs procedures and models.* New York: University Press of America.

Morante, E., & Jemmott, N. (1993). The impact of the College Outcomes Evaluation Program (COEP) on public higher education in New Jersey. In T. W. Banta & associates, *Making a difference: Outcomes of a decade of assessment in higher education.* San Francisco: Jossey-Bass.

Pace, C. R. (1986). *Measuring the quality of the college-student experience.* Los Angeles: Higher Education Research Institute, University of California, Los Angeles.

Richards, M., & Minkel, C. W. (1986). Assessing the quality of higher education through comprehensive program review. In T. W. Banta (Ed.), *Performance funding in higher education: A critical analysis of Tennessee's experience*. Boulder, CO: National Center for Higher Education Management Systems.

Watt, J., & Rodrigues, R. (1993). Faculty-developed approaches at large universities: University of Connecticut and Colorado State. In T. W. Banta & associates, *Making a difference: Outcomes of a decade of assessment in higher education*. San Francisco: Jossey-Bass.

Name Index

Subject Index

378–379; of reading assignments, 211–214; or redesign, 181–185, 198; sequencing, 195–196; student influence on, 138–139, 185, 366, 378–379; taxonomies, 193; teacher self-knowledge and, 309–310; Teaching Goals Inventory (TGI), 325

Course requirements, 72, 140, 164, 356–357

Course-learning scale, 134

Courses: components of, 95–97, 190–191; curriculum variables, 167, 356–359; evolution of, 180–181; hours dedicated to, 203–204; institutional variables in, 165–166, 321–322; introductory courses, 72, 305–306; multicultural, 343, 356–359; pedagogical variables, 166–167, 343–344; personalizing, 67–68; prerequisites for, 140, 164, 166, 169, 191, 197–198, 376; structured for student involvement, 67–68, 109–109, 207–208. *See also* Curriculum

Course-specific surveys, 136

Criteria: course content inclusion, 191–192; faculty recognition, 329, 330–331; student assessment, 113

Critiques, class. *See* Course assessment

Cross-disciplinary teaching, 118–119

Cultural generativity, 320–322

Culture, academic, 339–345, 359–360; and mission, 341–342; people, 340–341, 347–350; student transition to, 52–53. *See also* Multiculturalism in academe

Curriculum: assessment, 368–374; format variables, 167; multiculturalism of, 342–344, 356–359; writing across the, 224. *See also* Courses

Curriculum development, 181–185; assessment and, 139, 365–368, 374–379

Curve: grading on the, 165, 166; preparedness, 34

D

Debriefing, game, 268

Decision-making, institutional, 340, 342, 355–356, 379–380

Declines in disciplines, 158

Democracy and education, 120, 122

Demographics: racial/ethnic diversity, 22–23, 340, 354; of today's students, 21, 22–25

Departments, academic: assessment of student involvement in, 139–141; course development and, 183–184, 307–308; goal setting in, 245, 326; loss of majors, 158, 164–165; and new students, 68–69, 71–72

Developers, faculty, 97

Diagnostic testing, 140

Dialogical process of teaching, 155–156, 173–174, 344; case study, 162–172; philosophy of, 160–162

Dialogues: about multiculturalism, 348–349, 352–353, 357, 359; assessment-inspired, 369–374. *See also* Quotes from students

Difference, communities of, 345–346, 353, 356

Disabilities, students with, 24–25

Disciplines: assessment of majors in, 371–374; attrition within, 158, 164; bibliographies for specific, 111, 174; and course development, 184, 307–309, 326; faculty knowledge of, 303–304

Disconnected Discussion, Case of the, 234–235, 247, 249–253

Discrimination: learning about differences and, 357–359; sexual, 25, 338, 340, 347

Discussion, disconnected, 234–235, 247, 249–253

Discussion method, 242; and reading assignments, 213–214, 234–235, 247, 249–253; research findings on, 263–266, 268, 275, 279

Diseases, 28

Dissatisfactions: faculty, 315–316, 320, 325, 328; student, 241, 377–379. *See also* Dropping out

Divergers, 32

Diversity issues, campus, 19, 130, 357; cultural framework of, 339–345; faculty and staff, 38, 340, 343, 345, 347–350; strategies for facing, 345–359. *See also* Integration, multicultural; Multiculturalism in academe

Diversity of learning styles. *See* Learning styles